This practical cookery book, illustrated throughout in full colour, contains all you need to know to make the most of your freezer. It begins with an extensive section on freezing techniques including detailed step-by-step instructions for blanching and packaging. There are also invaluable charts on the storage life of foods, instructions on how and when to freeze and a glossary of freezing terms and techniques. The delicious dishes are arranged [illegible] the following general cha[illegible] Starters, Fish, Meat, Poul[illegible] Vegetables, Desserts, Ca[illegible]

THE FREEZER COOKBOOK

THE FREEZER COOKBOOK

Edited by
GILL EDDEN & WENDY JAMES

Home Economist
GILLY CUBITT

Orbis Publishing
London

Freezing consultant: Jeni Wright

First published 1981 in Great Britain by
Orbis Publishing Limited,
20–22 Bedfordbury,
London WC2

This book includes material published in *The Complete Cook*

ISBN 0-85613-353-1

Printed in Hong Kong

Cover photograph by Paul Williams, featuring Pâté de campagne, Beef ragoût and Liqueur fruit salad

Acknowledgments
Photographs were supplied by Editions Atlas, Editions Atlas/Cedus, Editions Atlas/Masson, Editions Atlas/Zadora, Danish Food Centre, Flour Advisory Board, Archivio IGDA, Lavinia Press Agency, Orbis GmbH, Tate and Lyle, Wales Tourist Board

Weights and measures: both imperial and metric measurements are given for each recipe in *The Freezer Cookbook*. It is advisable to follow just one set of figures as the imperial are not necessarily equivalent to the metric. All spoon measures are level unless otherwise stated and all fluid measurements are based on the imperial/metric standard measuring jug.

CONTENTS

YOU AND YOUR FREEZER

Food placed in a freezer in prime condition, frozen, stored and thawed correctly, should come out in the same condition, retaining all its original qualities and nutrients. With very few exceptions, this can be said of all foods – and no other method of preservation can claim such results

Owning a freezer for most of us is rather like owning a car – it's only when it breaks down that you wish you knew more about the workings. In fact, the running of a freezer is a little less complicated than a car, because correctly installed freezers from reputable manufacturers rarely go wrong.

To freeze food is to change it from being either liquid or pliable to solid, and by so doing to arrest (though not completely stop) the organic processes that would normally cause it to age, deteriorate and eventually rot. To do this, a freezer must have three basic components: an evaporator, compressor and condensor. These are connected by tubing, through which a refrigerant mixture circulates. It is this system of motor units and tubing which transfers the heat from the food inside the cabinet to the outside. The refrigerant passes first through the evaporator, where it is converted into a gas, then it goes into the compressor, at the same time drawing off heat from the food. The compressor forces the gas into the condensor, which in turn converts the gas back into a liquid and the cycle starts all over again. The condensor is the part that actually transfers the heat from the inside of the cabinet to the outside, and there are three different types. The most common is the skin-type condensor, which is between the inner and outer linings of the freezer and transfers the heat through the walls. The other less common types are fan assisted and static plate condensors.

During the freezing process the water between the tissues in food turns to ice crystals which occupy more space than water and, if too large, will damage the tissues, having an adverse effect on the texture of food when thawed. To keep the ice crystals as small as possible, the freezing process must be as quick as possible, which means the temperature must be lower than the normal one of 0F (−18C) required for keeping frozen foods frozen. This temperature, achieved by means of the fast or super fast freeze switch, depends on the overall loading capacity of the freezer and the amount of food to be frozen. It is this ability to freeze fresh food at lower than 0F (−18C) that distinguishes a freezer from a conservator. A conservator looks almost identical to a freezer, but it must never be confused with it, as it can only store food and can't freeze it.

Whether you choose a chest or an upright freezer will depend largely on where you intend to put it. A chest freezer is more economical to run and gives more storage space than an upright, but takes up a large amount of floor space. It is usually easier to fit an upright or combination fridge/freezer into a small kitchen.

Chest freezer
When you lift the lid of a full chest freezer, warm air bounces off the cold, and very little will enter the cabinet. The motor is therefore activated less frequently

Upright freezer
When you open the door of an upright warm air rushes in at the top, pushing the cold air out and raising the cabinet temperature. Close the door quickly

Star ratings
One large white and three small dark stars indicate that a freezer has the ability to freeze fresh food at a lower temperature than 0F (−18C) which is ideal only for storing. Freezing areas in fridges have ratings which correspond to symbols on frozen foods: 1 star indicates a temperature of 21F (−6C) and a storage time of 1 week; 2 stars, 10F (−12C), 1 month; 3 stars, 0F (−18C), 3 months

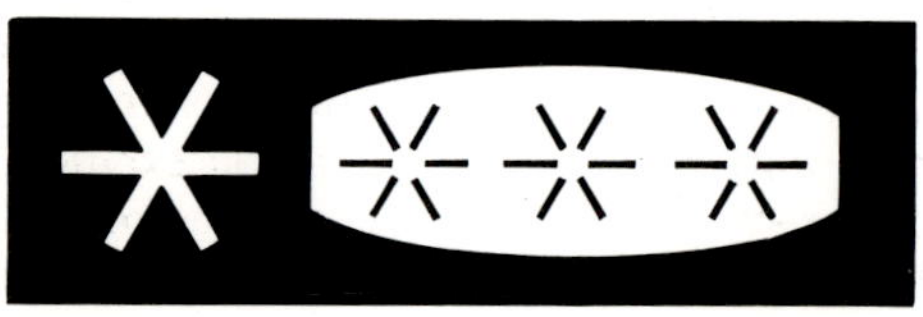

Freezing terms and techniques

Blanching

The scalding process by which enzyme action is halted in vegetables and some fruits. To blanch vegetables, place about 8oz (225g) vegetables in a blanching basket and immerse in about 7 pints (4 litres) boiling salted water. Bring back to the boil quickly, then calculate the blanching time from the moment the water reboils. Plunge basket and vegetables immediately into ice-cold water for the same length of time to prevent further cooking, then drain thoroughly before packing. The same blanching water can be reused 6 or 7 times. Blanching times are on pages 20 and 21.

Cooling

Before packaging for the freezer, food must be as cool as possible or moisture in the form of steam will be retained. This, and the warmth of the food, causes large ice crystals to form between the tissues of the food and thus damage them. The most efficient method of cooling cooked foods quickly is to stand pans and dishes in bowls of ice cubes or ice-cold water.

Covering

All food must be covered before freezing to protect it from freezer burn and prevent it from drying out. All containers should therefore have sealable lids or covers to prevent moisture escaping and air entering.

Dating

Before placing food in the freezer, it should be marked with the date of freezing or, more importantly, the date by which it should be eaten.

Defrosting

This is the removal of frost from the inside of the freezer cabinet. If the frost is allowed to build up indefinitely, the freezer's motor will have to work overtime in order to regulate the temperature. Some freezers have an automatic defrosting device, but most have to be defrosted manually, about once or twice a year if a chest freezer, three or four times if an upright. Check the build-up of frost from time to time; if it is more than ¼ inch (6mm) thick, it is time to defrost.

To defrost and clean a freezer:

(1) Choose a cold day if possible.

(2) Disconnect freezer from mains.

(3) Remove food and baskets/shelves from cabinet, then pack food quickly in insulated bags or wrap in newpaper or rugs. Keep in a cool place. If convenient, some food can go in the fridge or its freezing compartment.

(4) Line the bottom of the freezer with thick newspapers, then place a bowl of hot water inside the freezer and close the lid or door. Wait until the ice begins to loosen then scrape off gently with a plastic (not metal) spatula. Remove the ice from the paper as you work. Once all the ice is removed, wash the inside of the freezer with a solution of 2 teasp (2×5ml) bicarbonate of soda to 1 pint (560ml) water. Wipe dry. Close lid or door, reconnect electricity and fast freeze for 30 minutes before replacing food. Keep on fast freeze for 4–6 hours or until temperature registers OF (−18C).

(5) An alternative and quicker method is to simply sprinkle neat bicarbonate of soda on the ice inside the cabinet. This breaks down the ice; bowls of hot water are unnecessary.

Dry sugar pack

A method of packing soft juicy fruits. It is commonly used for berries, but can also be used for other whole, sliced and crushed fruit. Mix fruit and sugar gently together until fruit is evenly coated, then pack in a rigid container, or pack fruit and sugar in equal layers directly into container. Usually 4–6oz (125–175g) sugar is sufficient for every 1lb (450g) fruit. Leave ¾in (2cm) headspace before sealing.

Fast freezing

The lowering of the temperature inside the freezer in order to freeze down fresh or cooked foods as quickly as possible. Switching to "fast freeze" over-rides the thermostat, causing the motor to run continuously and lower the temperature inside the cabinet.

Freezer burn

Freezer burn is a form of dehydration due to inadequate wrapping; it appears as greyish-white or brown patches on the surface of food. Meat and poultry are particularly susceptible. Although unsightly, it is not harmful. Bad patches of freezer burn can be cut off after thawing.

Headspace

The space between the surface of food and the lid of a rigid container. It is essential to leave headspace with all foods packed in liquid, as this expands during freezing and will force off the container lid if packed to the brim.

Interleaving

A method of separating pieces, portions and slices of food so that they freeze individually. Place sheets of freezer tissue, cling film or foil between each chop, steak, etc, then freeze together in one container or package. Individual portions can then be taken out and the package resealed without disturbing other portions.

Open freezing

A method of freezing food uncovered on trays to (1) keep individual pieces separate and (2) keep delicate, decorative and soft-textured foods intact. Line trays/baking sheets with foil or greaseproof, then spread out food on top so pieces are not touching. Freeze until solid, then remove from tray and pack in bags. Cakes with decorations of cream or icing are best packed in rigid containers after open freezing. Remove from container before thawing.

Overwrapping

Overwrapping protects against possible puncturing of fragile wrappings such as foil or cling film. Use a polythene bag sealed with a wire tie.

Preforming

A way of packaging food for the freezer into usable quantities and/or uniform shapes and sizes. A preformer is any kind of straight-sided rigid container that is lined with a polythene bag (or boil-in-bag). Fill bag with food, freeze until solid, then remove bag from preformer, seal and return to freezer. If you use a casserole as a preformer, you can unwrap the food and return it to the same casserole for reheating.

Refreezing

As a general rule, once food has thawed it should not be refrozen. Raw meat, poultry, fish, fruit and vegetables can be refrozen only if they are cooked first before returning to the freezer. Thawed food should be cooked as quickly as possible, and not kept for longer than one would normally expect to keep any fresh food before eating/cooking. Cooked made-up dishes that have thawed should be reheated and cooled before refreezing. Dairy products, and foods containing them (eg pastries and cakes containing cream), should not be refrozen.

Sealing

To make packages airtight and prevent dehydration, correct sealing is essential. Rigid containers with suction lids present no problem, nor do clip-on and screw-top lids. Foil that is moulded around solid food needs no further sealing. Food in polythene bags must have air excluded before sealing, and this can be done in several ways: suck out air with a clean drinking straw, use a mechanical pump (see page 11), or squeeze out air with the hands, working from bottom to top. Once air is excluded from bag, seal with wire closures or ties, freezer tape or dry heat sealing.

Freezing equipment

So that you can be sure that the food comes out of the freezer in the same good condition as it went in, you need strong wrappings and containers which seal well and keep the cold air out

The role of equipment in freezing is to smooth the path in the preparation sense, and to protect foods during storage.

Bags can be moulded round food and so take up no extra space in the freezer. All air must be excluded before sealing and freezing. Ordinary plastic bags will do but they puncture more easily than those designed for freezing.

Heavy-gauge polythene bags (called poly-bags) come in different sizes, usually with a bottom gusset. Wire closures and ties are included, and some bags have their own labels for you to write on. Some have ridged tops which you press to seal.

Boil-in-bags are made of a special polythene that can go straight from the freezer into boiling water. Useful for foods needing reheating.

Foil-lined freezer bags have a stiff paper coating. Not always recommended for liquids, but can take liquidy foods such as sauces, thick soups. They shouldn't be used for acid foods, and are not re-usable.

Containers are rigid shapes with lids and can be any of your own cooking pots (though while in the freezer they are out of kitchen action), empty ice cream cartons or any of a vast range available.

Polythene and plastic rigid containers have self-sealing lids to make them airtight. Re-usable, they can be stacked or packed in or out of a freezer to make the most economical use of space.

Foil containers (dishes, pudding basins, pie plates) are good for foods which are cooked and can be reheated straight from the freezer. Lids are usually cardboard which should be removed before cooking and replaced with foil if covering is needed. To prevent leaks from these containers, always overwrap.

Waxed cartons are not made for anything hot but they stack well and can be bought in many sizes. Useful for stocks, soups, fruit juices, purées.

Glassware is not always freezerproof and some can shatter at a low temperature. Test it first by placing it inside a thick polythene bag (so if it does break the pieces won't disperse). Never freeze bottles of wine or milk.

Microwave cookware has been especially developed for foods which can go straight from the freezer, and in some cases on to the table for serving. Made in polypropylene, or cardboard coated in polyester film, or TPX – an engineering plastic which resists extremes of temperature – some can be used in conventional ovens too.

Wrappings are vitally important to prevent air entering and moisture escaping from foods in the freezer. Inadequately wrapped foods will also cross flavour each other.

Aluminium foil comes in a variety of grades for strength. It's very versatile in that it can be moulded to any shape and all air can be excluded. Awkwardly shaped foods, especially any with bones, are best wrapped in foil. As lighter foil, usually

called kitchen foil, is prone to tearing and puncturing, use it in double thickness or choose a stronger one, generally called freezer foil. Foil can also be shaped to make containers (see preformers).

Cling film should really be the heavy-duty freezerproof type. It moulds itself round food and is self sealing because it clings to itself. It is also ideal for interleaving and for wrapping individual portions which, can be taken out one at a time (eg, slices of gâteau), though the whole package should be overwrapped in foil or placed in a rigid container so it won't be damaged in the freezer.

Interleaving sheets are made from a kind of waxed tissue which is paper thin and is used to divide food into separate portions before being overwrapped for storage in the freezer. Cling film, foil or greaseproof can also be used for interleaving.

Preformers are home-made containers which eliminate the problem of trying to cook an awkwardly frozen shape which won't fit any saucepans or pots. Good preformers are empty cardboard sugar cartons which can be lined with a plastic bag to make a brick shape. When making stews, pots can be lined with foil which after freezing can be lifted out, overwrapped and labelled.

A freezer pump is used to exclude all air from soft packages before sealing. Efficient and hygienic, the plastic tube is inserted into the package, then the attached pump is pressed to pump out all air.

Sealing can either be done with a paper-coated metal tie (don't use on dishes which will go into microwave cookers), or bags can be heat sealed. An electric heat-sealer can be bought, but a domestic iron can be used: exclude all air from bag, place brown paper over open ends and press with a warm iron. Freezer tape is sold in rolls and looks like ordinary sticky tape but has a special adhesive which can withstand low temperatures. Use for sealing polybags, foil packages, container tops and to stick on non-adhesive labels.

Labels are essential for identification as packages tend to look the same in a freezer. Freezer labels have a special glue to withstand low temperatures. Tie-on tags can be used for labelling, and some bags have their own printed on ones. Coloured labels are handy for they can be used to identify different foods (green for vegetables, red for meat). Label information should include quantity and/or servings, how it is to be cooked, and the date by which it should be eaten (the date of freezing is only helpful if you can remember the freezer life of the food).

A waxed pencil is needed for writing on labels so that your marks won't rub off in moist conditions.

A log or record book gives you a constant list of the freezer contents. It must however be kept up to date if it is to be of any use, and should guide you in rotating the food from the back or the bottom of the freezer. Keep it near the freezer.

Other useful equipment for freezer owners is: a *timer* which is needed for accurate blanching of vegetables; a *freezer knife* which efficiently cuts through frozen blocks of food; and a *thermometer* which if you freeze a lot of food is needed for establishing the internal temperature of the freezer for fast freezing (see page 9). Check the temperature of the fast freeze compartment before adding fresh foods by standing or hanging the thermometer in it overnight.

Below: the type of equipment that makes home freezing easy and efficient. The range of wrappings and containers available is wide, and different colours help you establish an identification plan. The timer ensures accurate blanching, the freezer knife will tackle frozen blocks of food

Labelling and packaging

Everything that goes into a home freezer should be labelled. Ideal are colour schemes which make the contents instantly recognizable (for example, green for vegetables) and both the date of making (and freezing) and the date it should be eaten by should be clearly stated. Use a pen that won't rub off in the moist conditions, and use specially designed freezer labels with a glue that takes as well to foil as it does to polythene and waxed containers. Overwrapping with cling film will ensure the label stays in place. Record all entries in a log book, including the same information that's on the labels so that you can tell at a glance what should be used up when. All packages should be well sealed, with a headspace left to allow for expansion of the liquid and as much air removed as possible. Freezer burn occurs when the wrapping has not been done carefully enough and the food becomes dehydrated through contact with the air. Wipe all packages dry before freezing so they don't stick to the walls of the freezer or baskets. Freezer life of each food is given on pages 16–25.

Choose labels in a variety of colours

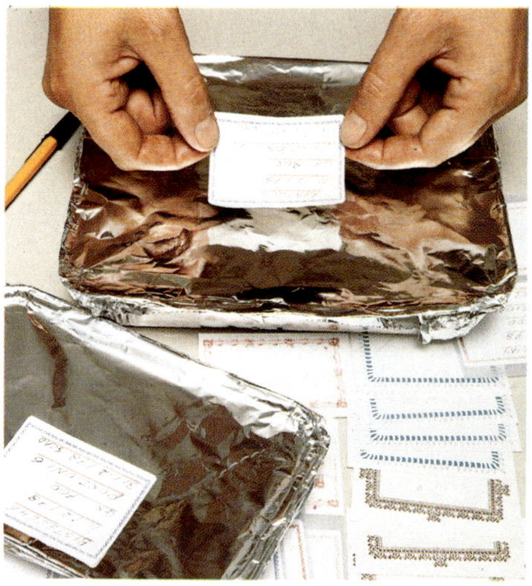

Stick labels on, then overwrap to secure

Kidneys

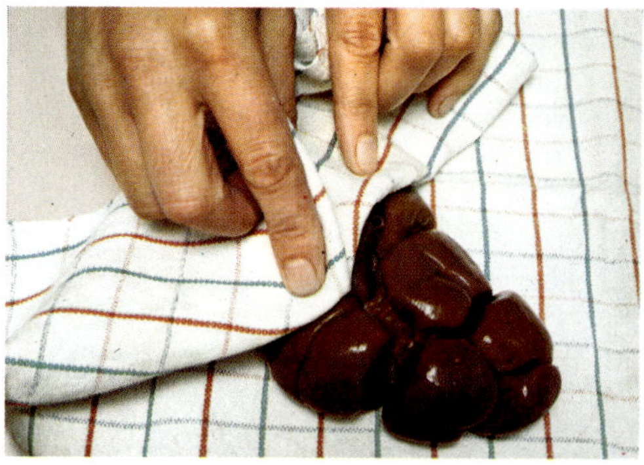

Wash fresh beef, calf or lamb kidneys well, then pat dry. Snip away core of lamb kidneys and remove transparent skin. Trim any fat

Finely slice beef or calf kidneys, removing central core if you prefer. Halve or quarter lamb kidneys or leave whole

Pack kidneys in layers in rigid containers holding meal-size amounts. Press on lid to seal, or wrap well in foil or polythene, then label and freeze.
As kidneys can go rubbery if overcooked, it's best to thaw them, then add them to other ingredients (for example, steak in steak and kidney) during the reheating

Eggs

Hard-boiled eggs go rubbery during freezing

Fresh yolks, whole eggs and whites should be lightly forked with salt or sugar ($\frac{1}{2}$ teasp/2.5ml to 6 eggs) to preserve them

Use small jars, plastic containers or ice-cube trays for storage. Label well so you don't use salted eggs in a cake

Hamburgers

Minced beef should be of best quality and frozen as soon as possible after mincing. Form into small, flat rounds or meatballs

Wrap each hamburger in cling film, pack in meal-size amounts in polybags, seal and label. Freeze cooked meatballs 1 month

Chops

Trim off all possible fat (it reduces freezer life). Wrap each chop in film

Overwrap bone ends with foil. Pack chops in meal-size amounts in polybags, seal

Steak

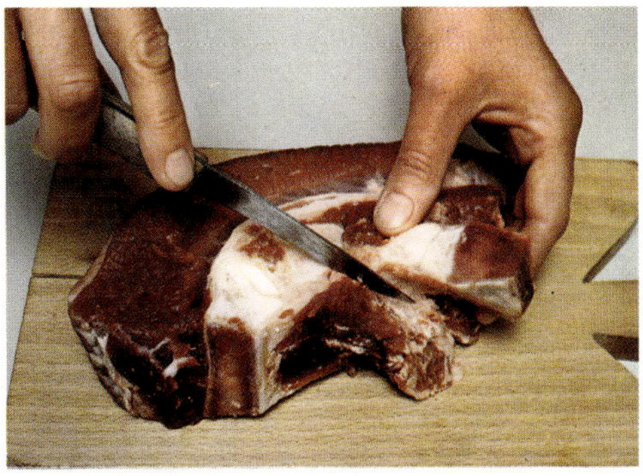

Steak, whether for braising, stewing, frying or grilling, must be well trimmed before freezing or freezer life is reduced

Use a sharp knife to cut away any fat on any part of the meat — render these down with other trimmings to make dripping

Steaks should not be more than 1 inch (2.5cm) thick. If preferred braising and stewing steak can be chopped

Wrap each steak in foil or thick plastic, then pack 2 or 3 in polybag. Seal. Place in coldest part of freezer to freeze rapidly. Thaw overnight in fridge in wrappings

Game

All game birds must be hung before they are prepared for the freezer. Pluck away all feathers being careful not to tear flesh

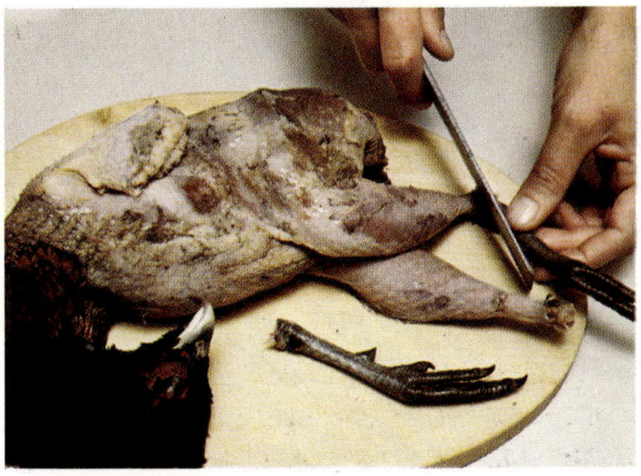

Trim off the feet, remove head and any shot that you can find. Wash bird well inside and out and dry with kitchen paper

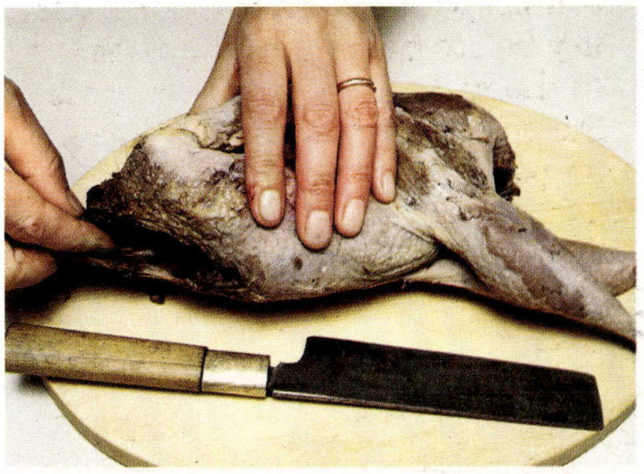

Game birds are best frozen raw without stuffing. They are also best trussed after stuffing and before cooking

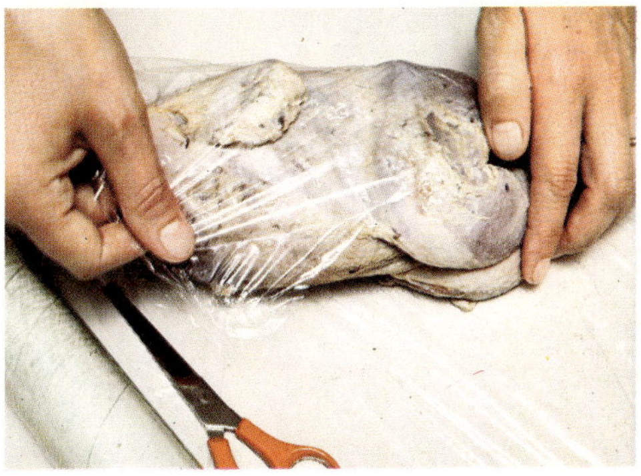

Cover ends of legs with foil, then wrap closely in plastic. Overwrap in foil or heavy polythene so smell can't spoil other foods in the freezer. Thaw before cooking

Fish

Only fish that has been out of water for up to 12 hours can be considered fresh enough to freeze. Remove scales with a scaler or knife

Slit the fish along belly and scrape out the innards. Wash and dry fish if freezing whole, or cut off head and tail

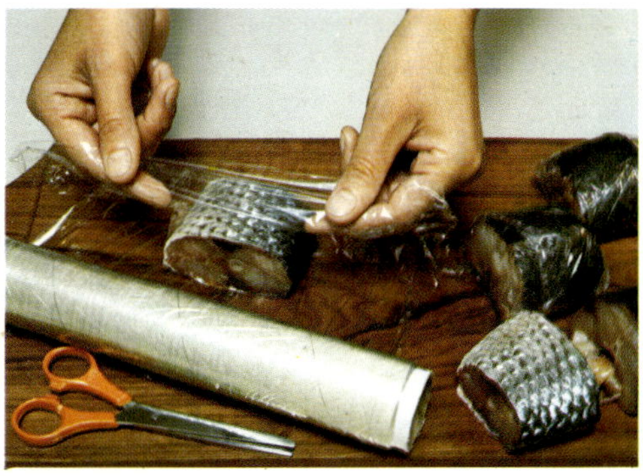

Cut fish into steaks or fillets and after washing and drying wrap each one closely in cling film. Do the same with whole fish

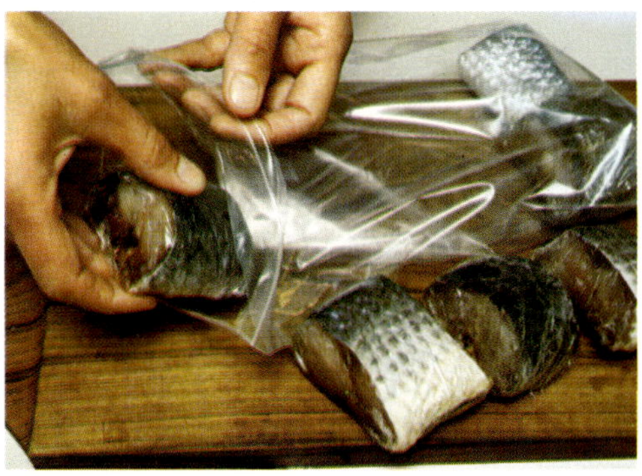

Pack steaks or whole fish in meal-size amounts in polybags and seal tightly. Cook from frozen allowing extra cooking time for centre to be thawed and cooked

Beans

Newly picked and crisp beans can be open frozen (freezer life 1 month) or blanched (french, 3 minutes, runner 2), then frozen

To open freeze, put topped and tailed beans, cut into short lengths of left whole, on shallow tray and place in freezer

When the beans are frozen, tip the tray into a polybag. Remember that meal-size amounts are handier than 1 big bag

Press out as much air as possible, then seal the top of the bag with wired tape (stick to a particular colour for vegetables). Label and store in freezer

Cauliflower

Small, compact and very fresh cauliflowers can be frozen either whole or cut into sprigs. Trim away all greenery and stalks

Wash and dry the cauliflower, then use a sharp knife to divide it into fairly equal sized florets. Or leave whole if liked

Pile cauliflower into blanching basket and blanch in boiling water for 3 minutes (4 minutes for small whole heads)

After immersing in ice-cold water for 3 (or 4) minutes, dry cauliflower well. Pack carefully in rigid containers to prevent florets being squashed in freezer

Stone fruit

Peaches, nectarines and plums should be firm, ripe, unbruised. Blanch in boiling water for 1 minute, then same time in cold

Peel away the skins with a sharp knife, then halve and remove stones. Apricots can be halved and stoned but don't need peeling

To prevent the fruit being bruised in the freezer, pack the halves (or slices) in rigid containers with self-seal lids

Pour cold sugar syrup (see page 23) over the fruit. Cover with layer of crumpled greaseproof to keep fruit under syrup and leave ¾ inch (2cm) headspace. Seal, freeze

Soft fruit

Raspberries, blackberries and strawberries should be free from dirt, insects, bruises. Pick over, but do not wash before freezing

Soft fruit can be "dry sugar packed". Sprinkle every 1lb (450g) fruit with 4oz (125g) caster or granulated sugar

Ease film or foil carefully over the fruit so it isn't pressed down. Rigid containers with self-seal lids protect fruit best

When open freezing raspberries, black and red currants, blackberries, etc, line tray with film before adding fruit. After freezing, lift film, tie ends together

Citrus fruit

Halve lemons, oranges, grapefruit, limes and squeeze juice. Do not press too hard – the pith will come off and spoil the juice

Pour juice into small cartons (individual drink size) or ice-cube trays. Juice can be sweetened – dissolve sugar before freezing

Cover the cartons with cling film or self-seal lids, then label and freeze.
The shells left after squeezing can also be frozen as a source of rind – just grate from frozen when needed.
Citrus fruits, especially those which have a short season, can be frozen whole (for later use in marmalade). Just wipe over and pack in polybags.
Slices of fruit should be open frozen and then packed into polybags for storage

HOW TO FREEZE

Fresh meat, fish and poultry

Major protein foods such as meat, fish and poultry have a definite place in a freezer, especially when bought in bulk to provide a reliable food source for several weeks. (In the process you save money and also reduce the time spent shopping.) Before buying in bulk, you must know how much fresh food your freezer can freeze at a time (usually 10% of the total capacity in 24 hours). If the amount you want is too great, or your freezer can't reach the state of coldness necessary, it is best to buy from a butcher or farmer who will blast freeze it for you after it's been divided, wrapped and labelled.

FOOD	PREPARATION
BEEF joints	Remove surplus fat. If possible, saw off protruding bone ends or bone whole joints to economize on space. Roll and tie boned joints, but do not stuff
steaks	Remove surplus fat. Cut no more than 1 inch (2.5 cm) thick, cut into serving pieces
boneless braising/ stewing meat	Remove surplus fat, sinews and gristle. Slice or cut into 1 inch (2.5 cm) cubes
mince	Only freeze lean mince. Leave loose, or shape into burgers or meatballs with onion, herbs, spices, etc
LAMB joints	Remove surplus fat. If possible, saw off protruding bone ends or bone whole joints to economize on space. Roll and tie boned joints, but do not stuff
chops	Trim bone ends. Remove skin and surplus fat
stewing meat and boneless leg or fillet	Chop scrag and neck into serving pieces, including bones. Cut leg or fillet into slices or 1 inch (2.5 cm) cubes. Remove surplus fat, skin and gristle
PORK joints	Remove surplus fat; leave skin on for crackling if wished. If possible, saw off protruding bone ends or bone whole joints to economize on space. Roll and tie boned joints, but do not stuff before freezing
chops/steaks/belly rashers	Remove surplus fat; leave skin on chops and belly rashers for crackling if wished
boneless fillet/ spare ribs	Remove surplus fat, sinews and gristle. Leave fillets whole or cut into 1 inch (2.5 cm) cubes. Cut spare rib into cubes or slices
mince	Only freeze very lean pork. Leave loose, or shape into burgers, patties or meatballs with onion, herbs, spices, etc

PACKAGING	STORAGE TIME	TO USE
Wrap individual joints in foil or cling film. Pad protruding bones. Overwrap in polybags. Seal, label and freeze	12 months	Thaw in wrappings in fridge for 8–10 hrs per lb/16–20 hrs per kg, or at room temp for 3–4/6–8 hrs. *Or* cook from frozen for approx twice normal time until 165F (74C) on meat thermometer at centre of joint
Wrap individually or interleave with foil/freezer tissue/greaseproof. Pack together in polybags. Seal, label and freeze	12 months	Thaw in wrappings in fridge overnight, or at room temp for 2–3 hrs. *Or* grill or fry thin steaks from frozen for approx twice normal time
Pack in usable quantities in polybags. Seal, label and freeze	8 months	Thaw in wrappings in fridge overnight. Use thawed juices with liquid in recipe. *Or* stew when partially thawed for slightly longer than normal time if searing is not required
Pack loose mince in usable quantities in polybags. Wrap burgers individually or interleave with foil/freezer tissue/greaseproof. Pack together in polybags. Open freeze meatballs, then pack together in polybags. Seal, label and freeze	3 months	Thaw mince in wrappings in fridge overnight, or cook when partially thawed for slightly longer than normal time. Cook burgers, etc from frozen
Wrap individual joints in foil or cling film. Pad protruding bones. Overwrap in polybags. Seal, label and freeze	12 months	Thaw in wrappings in fridge for 8–10 hrs per lb/16–20 hrs per kg, or at room temp for 3–4/6–8 hrs. *Or* cook from frozen for approx twice normal time until 185F (85C) on meat thermometer at centre of joint
Wrap individually or interleave with foil/freezer tissue/greaseproof. Pack together in polybags. Seal, label and freeze	12 months	Thaw in wrappings in fridge overnight, or at room temp for 2–3 hrs. *Or* grill or fry from frozen for approx. twice normal time
Pack in usable quantities in polybags. If scrag and neck have many bones, pack in rigid containers. Seal, label and freeze	8 months	Thaw in wrappings in fridge overnight. Use thawed juices with liquid in recipe. *Or* cook when partially thawed for slightly longer than normal time
Wrap individual joints in foil or cling film. Pad protruding bones. Overwrap in polybags. Seal, label and freeze	9 months	Thaw in wrappings in fridge for 8–10 hrs per lb/16–20 hrs per kg, or at room temp for 3–4/6–8 hrs. *Or* cook from frozen for approx twice normal time until 190F (87C) on meat thermometer at centre of joint
Wrap individually or interleave with foil/freezer tissue/greaseproof. Pack together in polybags. Seal, label and freeze	9 months (belly rashers: 6 months)	Thaw in wrappings in fridge overnight, or at room temp for 2–3 hrs. *Or* grill or fry from frozen for approx twice normal time
Wrap whole fillets individually in cling film/foil, then overwrap in polybags. Pack cubes and slices in usable quantities in polybags. Seal, label and freeze	9 months	Thaw in wrappings in fridge overnight. Use thawed juices in liquid in recipe. *Or* cook when partially thawed for slightly longer than normal time
Pack loose mince in usable quantities in polybags. Wrap patties individually or interleave with foil/freezer tissue/greaseproof. Pack together in polybags. Open freeze meatballs, then pack together in polybags. Seal, label and freeze	3 months	Thaw mince in wrappings in fridge overnight, or cook when partially thawed for slightly longer than normal time. Cook patties, etc from frozen

(continued)

Meat Whole carcasses can mean an expensive capital outlay so you want to be sure you're buying the best quality, as well as the sort of meat you like to eat. The butcher or farmer will divide it as you want, but with a pig you get a head (not something everyone appreciates), and with beef a lot of huge bones and fat which can be used for stock or rendered down for dripping (both activities requiring time which not every freezer owner has to spare).

The whole carcass works out less costly because prime and poorer grades of meat are included, and the price will probably be an average of both. Package deals can sometimes be arranged on just steaks, or chops, or joints – shop around to find the options. When freezing fresh meats in bulk, check the manufacturer's instructions about when the fast freeze button should be switched on. As to amount, allow 2 cu feet (56 litres) of space for every 20lb (9kg) boneless meat; twice the space for meat on the bone. Freezer centres and some supermarkets specialize in blast-frozen bulk packs which might not give the origin of the fresh product, but will have been frozen and stored by the best methods.

Poultry and game Unless you live in the country or have a source of supply which provides you with fresh birds, most poultry and game is bought already frozen. Before freezing, it is hung (if necessary), drawn, plucked or skinned, trussed, or divided into halves and joints. Never stuff poultry or game before freezing – because of its bulk it might not thaw sufficiently to allow heat penetration during cooking and any micro-organisms in the birds or stuffing will not be destroyed. Once poultry and game have thawed, cook immediately; never refreeze uncooked.

Fish These are among the most highly perishable of foods and must be frozen within 12 hours of being caught (or 24 at the very most if they have been stored on ice). Fish bought from a fishmonger should not be frozen as it may have been frozen and thawed once already. Scale, gut, wash and dry whole fish; ice glaze to preserve skin. Wash and dry fillets before freezing. Overwrap fish well to prevent cross-flavouring.

FOOD	PREPARATION
VEAL joints	Remove any surplus fat. If possible, saw off protruding bones or bone whole joints to economize on space. Roll and tie boned joints, but do not stuff
chops, escalopes (fillet)	Trim bones and any surplus fat. Bat out escalopes
mince	Leave loose, or shape into burgers, patties or meatballs
OFFAL	Clean and remove fat/suet, sinews, skin, gristle, etc. Wipe dry. Leave whole or slice/chop/cube according to type of offal and possible future use
SAUSAGES/ SAUSAGEMEAT	Only freeze when very fresh. Avoid highly seasoned or spicy products
BACON joints	Only freeze when very fresh, lean and mild-cured. Remove surplus fat if possible. Saw off any protruding bone ends or bone whole joints to economize on space. Roll and tie boned joints
rashers	Only freeze when very fresh, lean and mild-cured. Remove surplus fat if possible. Commercial vacuum packs are best for freezing
POULTRY AND GAME whole birds	Hang, pluck, draw and truss if necessary. Wash inside and out, then dry thoroughly
giblets	Remove from bird. Discard sac from gizzard. Separate liver. Wash and dry thoroughly
joints	Separate whole birds into halves, quarters, drumsticks, breasts, etc. Wash and dry thoroughly
game animals	Remove entrails as soon as possible. Hang, skin, draw and dress as required. Leave whole or joint.
FISH white fish	Only freeze very fresh fish, 12–24 hrs after catching. Gut, clean, remove scales and fins. Cut off heads, tails and remove skin if wished. Wash and dry thoroughly. Leave small fish whole, cut large fish into steaks or divide into fillets
oily fish	Only freeze very fresh fish, 12–24 hrs after catching (mackerel within 12 hrs). Gut, clean, remove scales and fins. Leave whole, or cut off heads and tails, split open and bone. Wash and dry thoroughly. Large fish can be cut into steaks
smoked and cured fish	Only freeze freshly-smoked fish that has not been previously frozen and thawed. Leave whole or separate into fillets, removing all visible bones. Skin if wished
SHELLFISH oysters, scallops	Freeze as soon as possible after removal from sea. Wash shells, open and remove meat. Discard inedible parts. Retain liquid. Wash edible meat quickly in lightly salted water
prawns, shrimps, scampi	Freeze as soon as possible after removal from sea. Cook in boiling salted water for 2–6 mins, shell and devein. Wash claws and tails of large shellfish in salted water, dry thoroughly, but do not cook
crabs, lobsters	Freeze as soon as possible from live state. Prepare and cook before freezing as for serving fresh

PACKAGING	STORAGE TIME	TO USE
Wrap individual joints in foil or cling film. Pad protruding bones. Overwrap in polybags. Seal, label and freeze	12 months	Thaw in wrappings in fridge for 8–10 hrs per lb/16–20 hrs per kg, or at room temp for 3–4/6–8 hrs. *Or* cook from frozen for approx twice normal time until 170F (77C) on meat thermometer at centre of joint
Wrap individually or interleave with foil/freezer tissue/ greaseproof. Pack together in polybags. Seal, label and freeze	12 months	Thaw in wrappings in fridge overnight, or at room temp for 2–3 hrs. *Or* grill or fry chops from frozen for approx twice normal time. Thin escalopes hardly need thawing: cook from frozen for a few minutes longer than usual
Pack loose mince in usable quantities in polybags. Open freeze/interleave burgers, etc, pack in polybags	3 months	Thaw mince in wrappings in fridge overnight, or cook when partially thawed for slightly longer than normal time. Cook burgers, etc from frozen
Wrap individually or interleave whole items, pieces or slices with freezer tissue or foil. Pack together in polybags. Pack chopped or cubed offal in usable quantities in polybags. Seal, label and freeze	3 months	Thaw in wrappings in fridge overnight, or at room temp for 2–3 hrs. *Or* cook from frozen, taking care not to overcook
Open freeze sausages, then pack together in polybags. Pack sausagemeat in usable quantities in polybags. Seal, label and freeze	2–3 months	Cook sausages from frozen or thaw in fridge overnight, whichever is most convenient. Thaw sausagemeat in wrappings in fridge overnight
Wrap individual joints in foil or cling film. Pad protruding bones. Overwrap in polybags. Seal, label and freeze	2 months (smoked); $1\frac{1}{2}$ months (unsmoked)	Thaw in fridge for 24 hrs or at room temp overnight. *Or* cook from frozen for approx twice normal time until 170F (77C) on meat thermometer at centre of joint
Wrap in usable quantities in foil or cling film, then pack in polybags. Seal, label and freeze. Place vacuum packs straight in freezer	2 months (smoked); 2–3 weeks (unsmoked); $2\frac{1}{2}$ months (vacuum packs)	Thaw in wrappings in fridge overnight, or 2–3 hrs at room temp
Pad protruding bones. Wrap whole birds in foil, then overwrap individually in polybags	12 months (turkey and chicken) 4–6 months (duck and goose) 6 months (game birds)	*All birds must be thawed before cooking.* Thaw in wrappings in fridge, allowing approx 5–6 hrs per lb/10–12 hrs per kg
Pack in polybags, keeping liver separate. Seal, label and freeze	2–3 months	Thaw in wrappings in fridge overnight. *Or* use from frozen to make stocks, gravies, etc
Wrap in individual pieces in foil/cling film, then pack together in polybags. Seal, label and freeze	As for whole birds (above)	Thaw in wrappings in fridge for 12–15 hrs. *Or* cook from frozen or partially thawed, allowing up to twice usual cooking time
Wrap whole small animals in foil, padding any protruding bones. Overwrap individually in polybags. Wrap individual joints in cling film/foil, then pack together in polybags	8 months	Thaw in wrappings in fridge, allowing approx 5–6 hrs per lb/ 10–12 hrs per kg for whole birds, 12–15 hrs total thawing time for joints
Wrap whole fish individually in cling film/foil, then pack several together in polybags. Wrap steaks and fillets individually or interleave with cling film/foil/ greaseproof, pack in polybags. Seal, label and freeze	3–4 months	Thaw whole fish in wrappings in fridge overnight. Cook steaks and fillets from frozen, allowing extra cooking time
Wrap large whole fish, boned fish and steaks individually or interleave with cling film/foil, then pack together in polybags. Pack small whole fish in usable quantities in polybags.	2 months	Thaw whole fish in wrappings in fridge overnight. Cook boned fish and steaks from frozen, allowing extra cooking time. Thaw small whole fish in fridge for 1 hr until separate
Wrap whole fish and fillets individually or interleave with cling film/foil/greaseproof. Pack together in polybags. Seal, label and freeze	3 months	Thaw in wrappings in fridge overnight
Pack meat and liquid together in usable quantities in rigid containers. Place crumpled greaseproof between surface of liquid and lid of container to keep fish submerged. Seal, label and freeze	3 months	Cook from frozen, taking care not to overcook. To serve oysters raw, thaw in fridge for 6 hrs. Eat as soon as possible after thawing
Pack in usable quantities in polybags. Seal, label and freeze	2 months	Cook from frozen, taking care not to overcook. To serve cold, thaw in wrappings in fridge for 2–3 hrs. Uncooked claws and tails can be cooked from frozen, then shelled
Pack lobsters and dressed crabs in shells. Cover with cling film, then overwrap in polybags. *Or* remove meat from shells and pack in rigid containers (pack white and brown crab meat separately). Seal, label and freeze	2 months	Cook from frozen, taking care not to overcook. To serve cold, thaw in wrappings in fridge for 2–3 hrs for crab, 6 hrs for lobster

HOW TO FREEZE

Vegetables

Nearly all vegetables will freeze successfully either in their natural raw state or in some other form. It is vitally important to freeze them at their freshest – after harvesting is ideal, or within a few hours at the most. Difficult vegetables are those with a high water content or a soft, delicate texture for their look and structure will alter on freezing.

Avocados should be frozen as pulp mixed with lemon juice or cream cheese, or as a soup.

Jerusalem artichokes should be boiled, then made into a purée.

Mushrooms can be frozen whole but keep longer if sliced and sautéed in butter, or made into duxelles.

Potatoes should be cut into chips and part cooked before freezing, or mashed and formed into croquettes or piped into duchesse shapes. New potatoes should be par-boiled.

Sweet potatoes and **pumpkin** should be baked, boiled or puréed for freezing.

VEGETABLE	BLANCHING TIME IN MINS	PACKAGING	STORAGE TIME IN MONTHS	TO USE
artichokes, globe, whole	5–7	RC/PB	6	thaw RT (4 hrs) use as fresh
hearts	2–5	RC/PB	6	thaw RT (4 hrs) use as fresh
asparagus, bundles	2–4	RC	9	thaw RT steam 2–4 mins
aubergines, sliced	4	RC/IL	12	thaw RT/F use as fresh
beans, broad, podded	2–3	PB	12	boil from frozen 3–5 mins
haricot/French, whole	1–2	PB	12	boil from frozen 5–7 mins
runner, sliced	1–2	PB	12	boil from frozen 5–7 mins
broccoli, spears	2–4	OF/PB	12	boil from frozen 3–7 mins
brussels sprouts, whole	2–4	OF/PB	12	boil from frozen 4–8 mins
cabbage, green/white, shredded	1	PB	6	boil from frozen 5–8 mins
red, shredded	1	PB	12	thaw RT use as fresh
capsicum, chopped/sliced	2	OF/PB	6	thaw RT (1–2 hrs)/use frozen in casseroles, salads
whole (deseeded)	3–4	OF/PB	6	thaw RT (1–2 hrs) use for stuffing/baking
carrots, baby new, whole	3	RC/PB	12	boil from frozen 4 mins
old, sliced	2	RC/PB	12	thaw RT add to casseroles
cauliflower, florets	3	OF/PB	6	boil from frozen 4 mins
celeriac, diced/sliced	1	PB	6	thaw RT/cook from frozen
grated	2	PB	6	add frozen to casseroles
celery, chunks	3	PB	6	add frozen to casseroles
chillies, split and deseeded	1	PB	6	thaw RT/use frozen in casseroles
courgettes, large sliced	1	OF/PB	12	thaw RT (2 hrs) use as fresh
small whole	1	OF/PB	12	boil from frozen 4 mins
fennel bulb, quartered	3–5	PB	6	boil from frozen
horseradish, grated	–	RC	6	thaw RT/F use as fresh
kale (curly), leaves	1	PB	12	boil from frozen 4–6 mins
kohlrabi, large sliced/diced	2	PB	12	thaw RT use as fresh
small whole	3	PB	12	thaw RT use as fresh
leeks, large sliced	3	PB	6	use frozen in casseroles
small whole	4	PB	6	boil from frozen 6–8 mins

VEGETABLE	BLANCHING TIME IN MINS	PACKAGING	STORAGE TIME IN MONTHS	TO USE
mange-tout, whole	½–1	PB	6	boil from frozen 3–4 mins
marrow, chunks	2	RC	6	steam from frozen 1–2 mins
mushrooms, whole	–	OF/RC	1	cook from frozen
okra, small whole	3	PB	12	cook from frozen/boil 6–8 mins
onions, chopped	1	PB/OW	3	add frozen to casseroles
small button (pickling)	2	OF/PB/OW	3	add frozen to casseroles
parnsips, sliced	2	PB	6	boil from frozen/thaw RT add to casseroles
peas, podded	1	OF/PB	12	boil from frozen 4 mins
salsify (scorzonera), cut into short lengths after blanching	2	PB	12	thaw RT (2 hrs) cook from frozen
shallots, whole	2	OF/PB/OW	3	thaw RT use as fresh
spinach, leaves	2	PB	12	cook from frozen
purée	–	PB	12	cook from frozen
swedes, diced	2	PB	12	boil from frozen/thaw RT add to casseroles
sweetcorn, cobs	2–8	OF/PB	12	thaw RT (5–6 hrs)/F overnight use as fresh
kernels	–	PB	12	cook from frozen
swiss chard (seakale beet), leaves	2	PB	12	boil from frozen 7 mins
ribs (stalks)	3	PB	12	boil from frozen 7 mins
turnips, large sliced	2	PB	12	boil from frozen/thaw RT add to casseroles
small whole	4	PB	12	boil from frozen 5–10 mins

NB: blanching and boiling times vary according to size of vegetable
Abbreviations: RC rigid container; PB polybag; IL interleave; OF open freeze; OW overwrap; RT room temperature; F fridge

cook's know-how

Salad vegetables have a high water content and go limp in a freezer. But if there is a glut you can freeze them to use other than raw.

Beetroot should be boiled and skinned and can be left whole, sliced or diced to be used later as a hot vegetable with a white sauce or spicy dressing.

Chicory should be blanched for 5 minutes, and left whole or sliced. It can be served hot, with sauce, or braised with other vegetables.

Cucumber can be frozen as a soup or as a purée for sauces, dips.

Lettuce hearts can be frozen to use later in soups.

Winter radishes are like turnips and should be diced and blanched for 2 minutes. Use as a hot vegetable with sauce.

Spring onions should be frozen whole and chopped for use in stir-fried dishes.

Tomatoes should be made into juice, purée or sauce for freezing.

HOW TO FREEZE

Fruit

Preserving fruit by freezing takes less time and effort than bottling. Their high water content causes a structure change but this can be used to advantage – soft fruits in a sugar pack, for example, produce juice during thawing and the mix can be folded into whipped cream to make a mousse, or poured over ice cream. Ripe, unblemished stone fruits can be halved or sliced straight into a cold sugar syrup (see cook's know-how right) and the flesh, though softened, retains enough texture to rival commercially canned fruit. Fruit must be of the best quality for sugar or syrup packs; squidgy or overripe ones should be puréed. Speed in preparation is especially important with fruits that have a pale-coloured flesh likely to brown when cut. Keep lemon juice handy to sprinkle over if necessary. Pears and guavas are so prone to discoloration that they are best cooked before freezing. Bananas can only be frozen if combined with other ingredients (eg, in ice cream, or cheesecake). Thaw fruit in its unopened pack and use when still slightly frozen.

FRUIT	METHOD OF FREEZING	PACKAGING	STORAGE TIME IN MTHS	TO USE
apples, cooking, pulp/purée		PB/RC	8	use from frozen/thaw RT (1 hr) reheat/use in cooked dishes
slices/rings	OF/MS	PB/RC	12	use from frozen/thaw RT (1 hr) use as fresh
apricots, peeled, halves	MS	RC	12	thaw F (3 hrs) use in fruit salads, etc
bilberries/blueberries, whole	OF/PD/M–HS	PB/RC	12	use from frozen/thaw RT (2 hrs) use as fresh
blackberries, whole	OF/PD/M–HS	PB/RC	12	use from frozen/thaw RT (2 hrs) use as fresh
cherries, black/red, stoned	M–HS	RC	12	thaw RT (3 hrs) use as fresh
citrus fruits, whole	PD	PB	12	thaw RT (1–2 hrs) use as fresh
segments/slices	OF/PD/L–MS	RC	12	thaw RT (2 hrs) use as fresh
cranberries, whole	OF/PD/M–HS	PB/RC	12	use from frozen/thaw RT (2 hrs) use as fresh
currants, black/red/white, whole	OF/PD	PB/RC	12	use from frozen/thaw RT (2 hrs) use as fresh
crushed/purée		PB/RC	12	thaw RT (1 hr) reheat/use in cooked dishes
damsons, whole	OF/PD	PB/RC	6	thaw RT (2–3 hrs) use as fresh
halved and stoned	PD/MS	RC	12	thaw RT (2 hrs) use as fresh
purée (cooked)		PB/RC	12	thaw RT (1 hr) reheat/use in cooked dishes
dates, fresh, stoned	OF/PD/LS	PB/RC	12	thaw RT (1 hr) use as fresh
elderberries, whole blanched (30 secs)	OF/PD	PB/RC	12	thaw RT (2 hrs) use as fresh
figs, fresh, whole unpeeled	OF/PD	PB/RC	12	thaw RT (1–2 hrs) use as fresh
whole peeled/sliced	L–MS	RC	12	thaw RT (1–2 hrs) use as fresh
gooseberries, whole	OF/PD	PB/RC	12	use from frozen/thaw RT (2 hrs) use as fresh
purée (cooked)		PB/RC	12	thaw RT (1 hr) reheat/use in cooked dishes
grapes, seedless, whole and in bunches	OF/PD	PB/RC	12	thaw RT (2 hrs) use as fresh
large, halved and seeded	LS	RC	12	thaw RT (2 hrs) use in fruit salads, etc
kiwifruit, skinned and sliced	PD	RC	6	use partially frozen in fruit salads, etc

Abbreviations: OF open freeze; LS light syrup; MS medium syrup; HS heavy syrup; PD pack dry, with or without syrup according to taste and future use; PB polybag; RC rigid container; CF cling film; RT room temperature; F fridge

FRUIT	METHOD OF FREEZING	PACK-AGING	STOR-AGE TIME IN MTHS	TO USE
loganberries, whole	OF/PD/MS	PB/RC	12	use from frozen/thaw RT (2 hrs) use as fresh
crushed/purée		PB/RC	12	thaw RT (1 hr) reheat/use in cooked dishes
lychees, shelled and stoned	HS	RC	12	use partially frozen in fruit salads, etc
mangoes, peeled and sliced	MS	RC	12	thaw F (3 hrs) use in fruit salads, etc
melon, balls/cubes	HS	RC	12	thaw F (1–2 hrs) use partially frozen in fruit salads, etc
mulberries, whole	OF/PD/HS	PB/RC	12	thaw RT use as fresh
nectarines, peeled and stoned, halves/slices	HS	RC	12	thaw F (3 hrs) use partially frozen in fruit salads, etc
peaches, peeled and stoned, halves/slices	HS	RC	12	thaw F (3 hrs) use partially frozen in fruit salads, etc
pears (firm eating)/cooking peeled, halved, cored, quarters/slices	HS	RC	12	thaw RT (3 hrs) use in fruit salads, etc
persimmons, chunks/slices	HS	RC	12	thaw F use partially frozen
purée (cooked)		PB/RC	12	thaw RT reheat/use in cooked dishes
pineapples, peeled, slices/cubes/wedges	PD/LS	RC	12	thaw RT (3 hrs) use as fresh
crushed with sugar		RC	12	thaw RT (3 hrs) use as fresh
plums, halved and stoned	M–HS/PD	RC	12	thaw RT (2 hrs) use as fresh
quinces, peeled, cored, sliced and poached		RC	12	thaw RT use partially frozen
raspberries, whole	OF/PD	PB/RC	12	use from frozen/thaw RT (3 hrs) use as fresh
purée (uncooked)		PB/RC	12	thaw RT (3 hrs) use as fresh
rhubarb, chunks blanched (1 min)	PD	PB/RC	12	use from frozen/thaw RT (3 hrs) use as fresh
strawberries, small whole	OF	PB/RC	12	use partially frozen
large sliced	PD	RC	12	thaw RT (1–2 hrs) use as fresh
purée (uncooked)		RC	12	thaw RT (1–2 hrs) use as fresh

cook's know-how

When making a sugar pack, layer the fruit in a rigid container with caster sugar – 4–6oz (125–175g) to each lb (450g) of fruit. Soft fruit, berries and fresh currants can be open frozen without sugar and put into polybags to make free-flow packs. Purées can either be cooked or uncooked, with or without sugar. Syrup packs can be light, medium or heavy. Light is made with 4–6oz (125–175g) sugar to 1 pint (560ml) water; medium, 8–12oz (225–350g); heavy, 16–20oz (450–600g). Heat sugar and water, stirring till dissolved, then boil for 2 minutes. Leave to cool before using. You need to make up quite a lot, well in advance, as the fruit must be completely covered in the rigid containers (leave $\frac{3}{4}$ inch/2cm headspace). Balls of crumpled greaseproof can be placed on top of syrup to prevent fruit rising.

HOW TO FREEZE

Useful standbys

Some foods need to be dealt with in a special way so they freeze well.
Eggs, hard-boiled (whole, chopped or sieved) go tough and rubbery in a freezer. **Fresh eggs** can't be frozen in their shells (they crack), but can be lightly mixed with a fork with salt or sugar – remember to note which on the label to prevent wrong use later. Mix egg yolks the same way; whites need no addition.
Cream, milk and yogurt should not be used to thicken soups or stews to be frozen – when boiled after thawing unsightly curdling will occur. All, however, can be frozen as part of a cooked or uncooked filling (quiche, cheesecake). Double cream (with a butter fat content of not less than 40%) can be lightly whipped with sugar to store, or piped into rosettes. Whipped cream can be used to coat a gâteau but only short term or it will be tacky.
Butter cream (made with butter and icing sugar) freezes well and is best for filling and decorating. Cakes filled with jam or lemon curd will go soggy in the freezer.
Cold soufflés and mousses made with cream and egg whites and set with gelatine freeze well, as gelatine stops large ice crystals forming.
Pastry, if it is to be served hot after freezing, has to be refreshed in the oven which can result in over-cooked pastry and filling. Uncooked pastry cases glazed with egg white (to prevent sogginess) are a good standby for filling when needed with a sweet or savoury mix. Storage times of pastry dishes vary. With pastry it is the same as the fat content; if filled, the filling governs the time. Bacon or smoked fish, for example, are high in salt (this causes rancidity) and storage time is less than a filling made with eggs and vegetables.
Most cooked **bread** stores splendidly (crusty loaves will lose their crust after 1 week). Doughs, however,

FOOD	PREPARATION	PACKAGING	STORAGE TIME	TO USE
biscuits, unbaked dough	pipe/shape on trays	OF/RC	6 months	bake from frozen
	form into long rolls	AF	6 months	thaw F (1–2 hours), slice, bake
baked	cool	IL/RC	6 months	thaw RT refresh in hot oven if necessary
bread loaves, unrisen dough	increase yeast by 50%, knead lightly, package immediately	PB (large greased)	1 month (white/brown) 1½ (enriched)	reseal bag to allow room for rising at RT (6 hrs), knock back, prove, bake
risen dough	increase yeast by 50% when making. After first rising, knock back, place in greased baking tin or foil	PB (large greased)	1 month	thaw RT, prove before baking
partially baked, home-made	cool	PB/AF	4 months	bake from frozen, allowing extra time
commercial	leave in original wrappings	OW/PB	2 months	bake from frozen to manufacturer's instructions
baked, home-made	cool	PB/AF	6 months (white/brown) 4 (enriched)	thaw RT (3 hrs)/refresh from frozen in AF hot oven for 45 mins
commercial (not crusty)	freeze as fresh as possible	PB/AF		
sliced	leave in original wrappings	OW/PB	6 months	thaw RT (3 hrs)/toast slices from frozen
baps/rolls, etc	cool/freeze as fresh as possible	IL/RC	1 month (white/brown) 1½ (enriched)	thaw RT (1 hr)/refresh from frozen in AF in hot oven for 15 mins
butter	keep in original wrapping	OW/PB	3 months (salted) 6 (unsalted)	thaw F (overnight)
cakes, plain and fruity, large and small	make in usual way, cool	PB/IL slices	4–6 months 10 (fat free)	thaw RT (1–4 hrs)
fancy, with butter cream or cream	avoid synthetic flavourings, don't decorate with nuts, fruit	OF/RC/IL slices	3 months 2 (cream)	thaw RT (1–4 hrs)
casseroles/stews, cooked	do not thicken, cool quickly	RC/PB/PF/AF	1–3 months	reheat from frozen/thaw F (overnight), then reheat
cheese, hard	divide into usable quantities	CF/OW/PB	3–4 months	thaw RT (overnight)
soft	divide into usable quantities	CF/OW/PB	6 months	thaw F (overnight), then RT
cottage/curd	keep in cartons	OW/PB	4–6 months	thaw F (overnight), stir before use
cream, double or whipping (at least 40% fat content)	chill and whip lightly with 2 teasp (2×5ml) sugar per ½ pint (300ml)	RC	6 months	thaw F stir/whip before use
rosettes	whip with sugar, pipe on to trays	OF/RC	3 months	thaw RT (30 mins)

need care. Yeast should be doubled for some of the cells will be killed before the dough freezes and extra ensures raising after the dough thaws. Dough allowed to rise before freezing is often not as successful as dough packed and frozen soon after making.

Casseroles, stews and soups are best without too much seasoning, or strong-flavoured root vegetables and aren't thickened (this should be done when reheating).

Unfreezables include: unstabilized yogurt, buttermilk, cream with less than 40% butter fat, milk that isn't homogenized, clear jellies (they go cloudy), blancmange or custard (they separate), mayonnaise (it curdles), aspic toppings (they become murky).

Right: a large chest freezer which filled to capacity can take 350lb (158kg) and can freeze 71lb (32kg) fresh food in 24 hours. The mains light flashes if temperature in freezer rises

FOOD	PREPARATION	PACKAGING	STORAGE TIME	TO USE
eggs, whole/yolks	mix with salt/sugar according to future use ($\frac{1}{2}$ teasp/2.5ml to 6 eggs)	RC	6 months	thaw RT
whites	no beating, no additions	RC	6 months	thaw RT
ice cream	divide into usable quantities	RC	3 months	do not allow to thaw, "soften" home-made ice creams, sorbets in main body of fridge before serving
lard/white fats	keep in original wrapping	OW/PB	6 months	thaw F (overnight)
margarine, hard and soft tub	keep in original wrapping	OW/PB	12 months	thaw F (overnight)
milk, homogenized	do not freeze in bottles	RC	1 month	thaw F (overnight)
pastry, uncooked dough	divide into usable quantities/blocks	PB	3–6 months	thaw F (overnight)/RT (2–3 hrs) use as fresh
uncooked pies, tarts, quiches, etc	prepare in foil dishes, brush pastry with egg white before filling	OF/PB/AF	1–3 months (according to filling)	cook from frozen in foil containers, allowing extra time
uncooked lids/shells, etc	make to fit pie dishes/flan cases	OF/IL/PB	3–6 months	cook from frozen/thaw RT, use as fresh
cooked pies, tarts, quiches, etc	make in foil containers, cool	PB/AF	1–6 months (according to filling)	thaw RT (3 hrs) refresh to serve hot, taking care not to overcook
puddings, baked (sponges, charlottes, crumbles, etc)	make in foil containers	PB/AF	3 months	reheat from frozen, allowing extra time
steamed (sponge and suet crust)	make in foil containers	PB/AF	3 months	reheat from frozen, allowing extra time
sauces, apple, sweet (fruit, chocolate), tomato, espagnole, white (béchamel, mornay, soubise) bread, meat	make in bulk/divide into usable quantities/keep seasoning and thickening to minimum	RC	12 months (sweet/fruit/tomato) 6 (espagnole/white) 3 (bread/meat)	thaw RT then reheat if necessary/reheat from frozen, beat vigorously during reheating before serving
soups	do not thicken/do not add eggs, cream, yogurt or milk/skim off all fat/keep seasoning to minimum	PF/RC	3 months	reheat from frozen/thaw RT/thicken or add cream or milk on reheating/adjust seasoning
stocks	make in usual way, skim off all fat, boil till reduced to one-third	RC/ICT	3 months	reheat from frozen/thaw RT/add cubes to casseroles, stews

Abbreviations: OF open freeze; RC rigid container; OW overwrap; PB polybag; CF cling film; AF aluminium foil; IL interleave; PF preform; ICT ice cube trays; F fridge; RT room temperature

Sauces and Stocks

Keep a basic white and brown sauce in your freezer, packed in small quantities ready to use. The basic sauces can be varied endlessly after thawing. A supply of richly flavoured home-made stocks will give you an excellent base for tasty soups, stews and sauces

Above: Espagnole – brown sauce for meats, with flavour improved by long cooking

Béchamel sauce

A classic white sauce, made with flavoured milk. Cook over a low heat so it doesn't colour

SAUCE Makes 1 pint (560ml)

Overall timing 25 minutes

Equipment 2 saucepans

Freezing Cool, pour into rigid container leaving ½ inch (12.5mm) headspace, cover, label and freeze. Freezer life: 6 months. To use: reheat from frozen in heavy-based saucepan or the top of a double boiler, beating continuously

Remove pan from heat and gradually stir in flavoured milk with a wooden spoon

Return pan to heat and bring to boil, stirring all the time, then add seasoning

INGREDIENTS

½	Small onion	½
½	Carrot	½
½	Stalk of celery	½
1	Bay leaf	1
1 pint	Milk	560ml
2oz	Butter	50g
2oz	Plain flour	50g
	Salt and pepper	
	Grated nutmeg	

METHOD

1 Peel the onion. Peel and chop the carrot. Wash and chop celery. Place in saucepan with bay leaf and milk and bring slowly to the boil. When bubbles break the surface remove from the heat and leave to infuse for 15 minutes. Strain and discard flavourings.

2 Melt the butter in another saucepan. Stir in the flour and cook for 1 minute, stirring with a wooden spoon. Remove from the heat and gradually stir in the strained milk to give a smooth lump-free mixture.

3 Return pan to the heat and bring to the boil, stirring continuously. Reduce heat and cook sauce for 3 minutes. Add salt, pepper and nutmeg to taste. The sauce is now ready to use.

Espagnole sauce

One of the basic sauces of French cuisine. It's made brown by cooking the roux over a high heat

SAUCE Makes 1 pint (560ml)

Overall timing 1¼ hours

Equipment Saucepan

Freezing Cool, pour into rigid container leaving ½ inch (12.5mm) headspace, cover, label and freeze. Freezer life: 6 months. To use: reheat from frozen in heavy-based saucepan or the top of a double boiler, beating continuously

INGREDIENTS

2	Streaky bacon rashers	2
1	Small onion	1
1	Carrot	1
2oz	Mushroom stalks	50g
2oz	Butter	50g
2oz	Plain flour	50g
1 pint	Beef stock	560ml
4 tbsp	Tomato paste	4×15ml
1	Bouquet garni	1
	Salt and pepper	
3 tbsp	Dry sherry	3×15ml

METHOD

1 Chop the bacon, leaving the rind on. Peel and chop the onion and the carrot. Chop the mushroom stalks.

2 Melt the butter in a saucepan and add the bacon and prepared vegetables. Fry gently for 5–10 minutes or until golden, stirring occasionally to release sediment which can gather on the base of the pan.

3 Stir in the flour and cook, stirring, until it is lightly browned. Remove from the heat and gradually stir in the stock (made up with 2 stock cubes if necessary).

4 Return to the heat and bring to the boil, stirring. Add the tomato paste and the bouquet garni. Season to taste. Reduce the heat, cover and simmer very gently for 45 minutes, stirring occasionally to prevent sticking (this can be done in a double boiler if you prefer).

5 Strain sauce and discard the flavourings. Add the sherry. Taste and adjust seasoning if necessary. Serve with roast or grilled meats especially lamb.

Brown stock

This is a rich, meaty stock with excellent colour and flavour. It can be clarified to make consommé and is essential in both Espagnole and Demi-glace sauce (see opposite and page 65). Use it in hearty soups and stews and for braising red meat and vegetables. Don't throw the meat away after straining; mince it, season well and use to stuff capsicums or pasta

Makes about $2\frac{1}{2}$ pints (1.5 litres)

Overall timing $4\frac{3}{4}$ hours plus cooling

Equipment Large heavy-based saucepan with lid, skimming spoon, muslin, sieve

Freezing Boil strained stock rapidly to reduce to 1 pint (560ml). Pour into ice-cube tray and freeze. Pack cubes into polythene bags, seal and label. Freezer life: 6 months. To use: add to soups, gravies, casseroles, diluting as required

INGREDIENTS

1	Marrow bone or veal knuckle	1
1lb	Shin of beef	450g
1	Carrot	1
1	Onion	1
1	Stalk of celery	1
3 pints	Cold water	1.7 litres
	Bouquet garni	
6	Black peppercorns	6

METHOD

1 Wipe the bone and saw into pieces (if using veal knuckle, split it in half). Wipe and trim the beef and cut into large pieces.
2 Place in a large saucepan and cook, stirring, over a high heat till browned.
3 Scrape and halve the carrot. Remove any papery or damaged skin from the onion, leaving the inner brown skin on, then cut the onion in half. Wash the celery and cut in half.
4 Add to the meat with the water, bouquet garni and peppercorns. Bring slowly to the boil.
5 Skim off any scum. Reduce the heat, almost cover the pan with a lid, then simmer for at least 4 hours without boiling.
6 Wring muslin out in hot water and use to line sieve. Strain stock and discard the flavourings. Leave the stock to cool completely.
7 Skim off any fat, then use the stock as required. Cover and refrigerate if not using immediately.

White stock

White stock, made entirely from veal, has a gelatinous quality and delicate flavour, making it superb for use in fine sauces or soups. Raw veal releases a great deal of grey scum, so it needs to be blanched in boiling water and then rinsed thoroughly under cold water before being used to make stock. Rather than waste the meat, remove it from the pan after about 2 hours and serve it separately

Makes $2\frac{1}{2}$ pints (1.5 litres)

Overall timing $4\frac{3}{4}$ hours plus cooling

Equipment Large heavy-based saucepan with lid, skimming spoon, muslin, sieve

Freezing Boil strained stock rapidly to reduce to 1 pint (560ml). Pour into ice-cube tray and freeze. Pack cubes into polythene bags, seal and label. Freezer life: 6 months. To use: add to soups, gravies, casseroles, diluting as required

INGREDIENTS

1lb	Boned, rolled shoulder of veal	450g
1	Veal knuckle	1
1lb	Breast of veal	450g
1	Carrot	1
1	Onion	1
1	Stalk of celery	1
	Bouquet garni	
6	White peppercorns	6
3 pints	Cold water	1.7 litres

METHOD

1 Wipe the meat and chop the knuckle and breast into pieces. Place in a pan, cover with cold water, bring to the boil and simmer for 5 minutes. Drain and rinse thoroughly under cold water, then return to rinsed pan.
2 Scrape and slice the carrot, peel and quarter the onion. Wash and chop the celery. Add vegetables to the pan with the bouquet garni, peppercorns and water.
3 Bring slowly to the boil. Skim off any scum, then reduce the heat, partially cover with the lid and simmer for at least 4 hours.
4 Wring muslin out in hot water and use to line sieve. Strain the stock and discard the flavourings. Leave the stock to cool completely.
5 Skim off any fat, then use the stock as required. Cover and refrigerate if not using immediately.

Poultry stock

Uncooked bones and giblets give the best results – when these are not available use a whole ovenready chicken instead. Prepare the stock as below and simmer till the chicken is tender. Remove from the heat and leave to cool, then lift the bird out, carve the flesh neatly and use as required. Crack the bones and carcass, then return to the pan with the skin and complete cooking, straining and skimming. For game stock, replace chicken trimmings with those from game birds

Makes $2\frac{1}{2}$ pints (1.5 litres)

Overall timing $3\frac{1}{2}$ hours plus cooling

Equipment Rolling-pin, large heavy-based saucepan with lid, skimming spoon, muslin, sieve

Freezing Boil strained stock rapidly to reduce to 1 pint (560ml). Pour into ice-cube tray and freeze. Pack cubes into polythene bags, seal and label. Freezer life: 6 months. To use: add to soups, gravies, casseroles, diluting as required

INGREDIENTS

1lb	Uncooked poultry carcass, bones, feet, giblets	450g
1	Carrot	1
1	Onion	1
1	Stalk of celery	1
	Blade of mace	
	Bay leaf	
6	White peppercorns	6
3 pints	Cold water	1.7 litres

METHOD

1 Wash the carcass, bones and feet and crush with a rolling-pin. Place in the saucepan. Wash the giblets and add to the pan.
2 Scrape and halve the carrot. Peel and halve the onion. Wash, trim and halve the celery. Add to the pan with the mace, bay leaf, peppercorns and water.
3 Bring slowly to the boil, then skim off any scum. Reduce the heat and partially cover with a lid, then simmer for at least 3 hours.
4 Wring muslin out in hot water and use to line sieve. Strain stock and discard the flavourings. Leave the stock to cool completely.
5 Skim off any fat and use as required. Cover and refrigerate if not using the stock immediately.

SOUPS

Soup from the freezer reheats quickly for a light lunch or supper and will solve the problem of what to serve as starter when you are entertaining. Don't forget to leave plenty of headspace in your container, as the liquid expands as it freezes

Chicken and mushroom soup with Calvados

Calvados adds a sophisticated apple flavour to this thick chicken and mushroom soup, while the egg/cream liaison gives a rich, smooth texture

STARTER Serves 6

Overall timing 50 minutes

Equipment 2 saucepans, 2 bowls, sieve

Freezing Complete Step 5, then cool completely, put into a rigid container, leaving 1 inch (2.5cm) headspace. Cover, label and freeze. Freezer life: 2 months. To use: place block of soup in pan, heat gently till thawed. Complete Steps 6 and 7

INGREDIENTS

8oz	Chicken breast	225g
	Bay leaf	
$1\frac{3}{4}$ pints	Milk	1 litre
6 tbsp	Calvados	6×15ml
8oz	Button mushrooms	225g
2oz	Butter	50g
4 tbsp	Plain flour	4×15ml
1 tbsp	Lemon juice	15ml
$\frac{1}{4}$ teasp	Freshly-grated nutmeg	1.25ml
1 tbsp	Chopped parsley	15ml
	Salt	
	Freshly-ground white pepper	
1	Egg yolk	1
4 tbsp	Single cream	4×15ml

METHOD

1 Wipe and trim the chicken breast, place in a saucepan with the bay leaf and milk and bring to the boil. Cover and simmer for about 15 minutes till tender.

2 Remove the chicken from the milk. Discard any bones and skin and cut the flesh into strips. Put into a shallow bowl and pour the Calvados over. Leave to marinate for 20 minutes.

3 Meanwhile, wipe, trim and thickly slice the mushrooms. Heat the butter in a large saucepan, add the mushrooms and fry gently for 5 minutes without browning.

4 Sprinkle the flour into the pan and cook for 1 minute. Strain the milk and gradually add to the roux. Bring to the boil, stirring constantly. Add the lemon juice and nutmeg and simmer for 5 minutes.

5 Add the chicken and marinade with the parsley. Simmer for a further 5 minutes and adjust seasoning to taste.

6 Lightly beat the egg yolk and cream in a bowl and pour a little of the soup into it, stirring constantly. Pour back into the soup and cook, stirring, for 3 minutes – do not boil.

7 Pour the soup into a warmed tureen and serve immediately.

Left: Chicken and mushroom soup with Calvados – serve with poppy seed rolls for crunchy contrast

Bortsch

One of the many versions of the famous soup which originated in Russia. In this one, meat makes the soup a substantial meal

STARTER OR LUNCH Serves 6

Overall timing $2\frac{1}{4}$ hours

Equipment Large casserole, small saucepan

Freezing When cold, ladle soup into a rigid container, allowing 1 inch (2.5cm) headspace. Cover, label and freeze. Freezer life: 3 months. To use: turn into a saucepan and gently bring to the boil

INGREDIENTS

1	Onion	1
3	Carrots	3
4	Stalks of celery	4
1	Leek	1
1lb	Braising steak	450g
6oz	White cabbage	175g
1oz	Butter	25g
1 tbsp	Plain flour	15ml
2 tbsp	Vinegar	2×15ml
2	Tomatoes	2
6oz	Cooked beetroot	175g
2 tbsp	Chopped parsley	2×15ml
4 tbsp	Soured cream	4×15ml

METHOD

1 Peel and roughly chop the onion. Scrape the carrots, then cut into matchstick lengths. Roughly chop the celery. Wash and chop the leek.

2 Place the vegetables in a large saucepan with the beef and $1\frac{3}{4}$ pints (1 litre) water. Cover and cook for $1\frac{1}{2}$ hours over a medium heat.

3 Meanwhile, wash and shred the cabbage and place in a small saucepan. Cook with the butter over a low heat until the cabbage softens, then stir in the flour and vinegar. Mix cabbage into the soup.

4 Blanch tomatoes, remove skins then peel and chop. Peel and dice beetroot. Remove the meat from the soup. Cut it into large cubes, discarding any fat. Return the meat to the soup with the tomatoes, beetroot and parsley.

5 Cover and simmer gently for a further 30 minutes or until all ingredients are cooked. The bortsch may be served with or without soured cream and chopped parsley.

Right: Bortsch – famous Russian soup made from beetroot and cabbage

Gazpacho

The world-famous iced soup of Spain. The colour will deepen according to the ripeness of the tomatoes used

STARTER Serves 6

Overall timing 20 minutes plus chilling

Equipment Blender, large bowl

Freezing Pack into rigid container, leaving 1 inch (2.5cm) headspace, cover, label and freeze. Freezer life: 2 months. To use: thaw in fridge overnight

INGREDIENTS

$1\frac{1}{4}$lb	Tomatoes	600g
$\frac{1}{2}$	Cucumber	$\frac{1}{2}$
1	Large onion	1
1	Green or red capsicum	1
2	Garlic cloves	2
4oz	Fresh white breadcrumbs	125g
3 tbsp	Olive oil	3×15ml
1 tbsp	Wine vinegar	15ml
1	Sprig of parsley or mint	1
	Salt	
	Freshly-ground white pepper	

METHOD

1. Blanch, peel and chop the tomatoes. Peel, deseed and chop the cucumber. Peel and chop the onion. Deseed and chop the capsicum, peel and chop the garlic.
2. Place in blender with breadcrumbs, oil, vinegar, parsley or mint, salt and pepper and 1 pint (560ml) water. Blend to a purée.
3. Place purée in a large bowl, add 1 pint (560ml) water, cover and chill for 3 hours. Before serving, add a few ice cubes. Serve with side dishes of chopped onion, hard-boiled eggs, tomatoes, capsicums and croûtons.

Below: Gazpacho – the perfect chilled soup for summer which tastes as good as it looks

Cream of chicken soup

There are various different ways of making chicken soup, such as using just the carcass, or utilizing the leftovers from a roast chicken, but this recipe, which calls for a whole bird, is in a completely different class. Quite simply, the flavour is superb. Lemon juice, nutmeg and cream add the finishing touches which enhance the goodness of the chicken

STARTER Serves 6–8

Overall timing $2\frac{1}{2}$ hours

Equipment 2 saucepans

Freezing Complete Step 3, then cool. Pour into rigid container, leaving 1 inch (2.5cm) headspace, cover, label and freeze. Freezer life: 3 months. To use: put block in saucepan and reheat gently till thawed. Complete Step 4

INGREDIENTS

1	Onion	1
2	Carrots	2
1	Stalk of celery	1
$2\frac{1}{2}$lb	Boiling chicken	1.1kg
3 pints	Water	1.7 litres
	Bouquet garni	
6	Peppercorns	6
2oz	Butter	50g
3 tbsp	Plain flour	3×15ml
$\frac{1}{4}$ pint	Milk	150ml
1 tbsp	Lemon juice	15ml
$\frac{1}{4}$ teasp	Freshly-grated nutmeg	1.25ml
$\frac{1}{4}$ pint	Carton of single cream	150ml
	Salt	
	Freshly-ground white pepper	

METHOD

1 Peel the onion. Wash and trim the carrots and celery. Put into a large saucepan with the chicken and water, bouquet garni and peppercorns. Bring to the boil, skim off any scum, then cover and simmer for 1½–2 hours till the chicken is tender.
2 Remove the chicken from the pan. Strain the stock and reserve. Remove the flesh from the chicken, discarding skin and bones, and cut into tiny pieces.
3 Heat the butter in a saucepan. Stir in the flour and cook for 1 minute. Gradually add the milk and the strained stock and bring to the boil, stirring constantly. Add the chicken flesh, lemon juice and nutmeg and simmer for 5 minutes.
4 Remove from the heat and stir in the cream. Taste and adjust seasoning, then heat through gently without boiling. Serve with croûtons or toast.

French onion soup

In France this soup, which is a speciality of the cafés of Paris, is called either *soupe à l'oignon* or *soupe au fromage*. It's thick, tasty and warming and a great favourite with students, market porters – and, of course, tourists

HOT STARTER Serves 4

Overall timing 45 minutes

Equipment Large saucepan, ovenproof tureen, casserole or individual bowls

Freezing Add wine and seasoning before simmering. Freeze in container leaving a 1 inch (2.5cm) headspace. Freezer life: 3 months. To use: thaw, then reheat in saucepan. Proceed as Step 4 of method, right.

INGREDIENTS

3	Large onions	3
2oz	Butter	50g
1 tbsp	Plain flour	15ml
½ teasp	Brown sugar	2.5ml
2½ pints	Stock	1.5 litres
8	Slices of French bread	8
2 tbsp	Dry white wine	2×15ml
	Salt and pepper	
2oz	Gruyère	50g

METHOD

1 Peel and slice onions. Melt half the butter in a large saucepan and cook onions over a gentle heat. Don't let them turn brown.
2 Sprinkle onions with flour. Stir over heat until flour colours. Add sugar and pour in stock a little at a time so soup keeps coming to the boil, then reduce heat and simmer for 20 minutes.
3 Preheat oven to 450F (230C) Gas 8.
4 Fry bread in remaining butter. Place bread slices in bottom of individual bowls or ovenproof soup tureen. Add wine, salt and pepper then pour soup over bread. Grate Gruyère and sprinkle it into the bowls then put them in oven for 5–10 minutes to melt the cheese.

Above: French onion soup – a warming and filling dish for a wintry day

shape saver

A serving of this soup would make a very satisfying main meal for anyone trying to slim. Cut out the butter used for frying and grill the bread instead – wholemeal rather than a French loaf will not only be better for you but will add a different, nutty flavour to the dish.

Thick chicken and vegetable soup

A chicken carcass and any leftover meat can be made into a delicious soup – such as this thick and creamy winter vegetable soup

STARTER OR LUNCH Serves 4

Overall timing $1\frac{1}{4}$ hours

Equipment Large heavy-based saucepan, bowl, sieve or blender

Freezing Complete Step 3, then cool. Remove fat from liquor. Pour liquor and purée into a container leaving 1 inch (2.5cm) headspace, cover, label and freeze. Freezer life: 3 months. To use: turn into pan and reheat. Complete Step 4

INGREDIENTS

8oz	Jerusalem artichokes	225g
8oz	Turnips	225g
1	Onion	1
8oz	Celery	225g
3oz	Butter	75g
1 tbsp	Oil	15ml
1	Leftover chicken carcass	1
5	Peppercorns	5
1 teasp	Salt	5ml
$1\frac{1}{2}$ pints	Water	850ml
2oz	Plain flour	50g
1 teasp	Celery salt	5ml
$\frac{1}{4}$ pint	Milk	150ml

METHOD

1 Peel and dice artichokes, turnips and onion. Dice celery. Heat 1oz (25g) of the butter and the oil in a pan and cook prepared vegetables for 4–5 minutes over a moderate heat, stirring. Do not allow to brown.

2 Add chicken carcass, peppercorns, salt and water to pan, cover and cook for 1 hour over a low heat.

3 Take carcass from pan and remove any pieces of flesh and peppercorns. Strain cooking liquor into a large bowl. Purée vegetables (press them through a sieve or put in a blender with a little stock and liquidize for a few seconds).

4 Heat remaining butter in pan. Stir in flour and celery salt and then the strained cooking liquor and the purée. Bring to the boil and cook for 5 minutes. Add milk and pieces of chicken. Taste and adjust seasoning. Cook for 5 minutes more, then pour soup into a warmed tureen and garnish with a swirl of cream and croûtons.

Rich asparagus soup

A hot soup that combines the delicate flavour of asparagus with the richness of cream and eggs. Made in a blender for smoothness, texture is added with croûtons fried till crisp in oil and butter

HOT STARTER Serves 4

Overall timing $1\frac{1}{2}$ hours

Equipment 2 saucepans, blender, bowl

Freezing Make as below but without the cream. Cool, place in a container leaving an inch (2.5cm) headspace, seal, label and freeze. Freezer life: 1 month. To use: thaw then heat. Whisk in the cream just before serving

INGREDIENTS

1lb	Asparagus	450g
	Salt and pepper	
2oz	Butter	50g
2oz	Rice flour or cornflour	50g
4 tbsp	Single cream	4×15ml
2	Egg yolks	2

METHOD

1 Prepare asparagus by lightly scraping off all the coarse scales below the tip with a potato peeler or the back of a knife. Cut or break off about an inch (2.5cm) of the stem end. Tie the asparagus in 2 inch (5cm) bundles and place them upright in a deep saucepan half-filled with boiling, salted water. Cook for about 10 minutes.

2 Lift out asparagus with draining spoon. Cut off tips and put aside for the moment. Chop stalks and return them to the saucepan for another 10 minutes.

3 Remove pan from heat. Lift out stems and place in a blender with $1\frac{3}{4}$ pints (1 litre) of the cooking liquid – add water if necessary to make up amount. Blend for a few seconds. Check taste and add salt and pepper if necessary.

4 Gently melt butter in a deep saucepan. Remove from heat and stir in the rice flour or cornflour. Gradually stir in the hot asparagus mixture. Return pan to heat and stir constantly. When about to boil, remove from heat.

5 Whisk together the cream and egg yolks in a bowl. Thin down with a little of the asparagus liquid then pour into the pan, stirring constantly. Adjust seasoning if necessary.

6 Add the asparagus tips. Return pan to the heat and cook gently for 2–3 minutes. Serve with crisp croûtons.

Avocado soup

A quickly prepared, delicate soup which can be made with avocados that are a little too ripe to eat *au naturel*. Enriched with cream and egg yolk, this soup can be served either hot or cold garnished with slices of fresh avocado, croûtons, thin lemon slices or parsley

HOT OR COLD STARTER Serves 4

Overall timing 15 minutes plus refrigeration time if serving cold

Equipment Saucepan, mixing bowl

Freezing Make as below but without the cream. Cool, place in a container leaving 1 inch (2.5cm) headspace and freeze. Freezer life: 1 month. To use: thaw then heat gently. Whisk in the cream before serving. Serve hot or cold as below

INGREDIENTS

$1\frac{3}{4}$ pints	Chicken stock	1 litre
2	Ripe avocados	2
1 tbsp	Lemon juice	15ml
1	Egg yolk	1
3 tbsp	Single cream*	3×15ml
	Salt and pepper	

METHOD

1 Heat chicken stock (made up with 3 cubes if necessary) in a saucepan to boiling point.

2 Cut open avocados and lift out stones. If intending to serve soup cold, cut out eight very fine slices, sprinkle with lemon juice to prevent discoloration and set aside. Scoop out remaining avocado flesh, place in a bowl and mash well with the egg yolk and cream.

3 Remove stock from heat. Gradually add the avocado mixture, whisking vigorously. Add salt and pepper to taste. Do not reheat.

TO SERVE

Serve hot with fried croûtons. If serving cold, refrigerate soup for at least one hour, then serve garnished with reserved avocado slices.

*To make this soup serve 6, use a 4fl oz (113ml) carton of single cream.

Right: Avocado soup – a creamy concoction garnished with slices of the fruit

Cream of mushroom soup

Open mushrooms would add the best flavour, but button or cup mushrooms give a paler, more attractive colour

STARTER Serves 4–6

Overall timing 30 minutes

Equipment Saucepan, frying pan, blender or sieve

Freezing Cool completely. Pour into a rigid container leaving 1 inch (2.5cm) headspace. Seal, label and freeze. Freezer life: 3 months. To use: place block of soup in pan, heat gently till thawed. Bring to boil, whisking. Serve with croûtons

INGREDIENTS

12oz	Mushrooms	350g
$2\frac{1}{2}$ pints	Chicken stock	1.5 litres
2oz	Fresh breadcrumbs	50g
	Salt	
	Freshly-ground black pepper	
1oz	Butter	25g
2 tbsp	Cornflour	2×15ml
4 tbsp	Water	4×15ml
	Croûtons or chopped parsley	

METHOD

1 Wipe and trim the mushrooms and slice thinly. Put two-thirds of the sliced mushrooms into a saucepan with the stock (made with cubes if necessary), breadcrumbs and a little salt and pepper. Bring to the boil and simmer for about 15 minutes.

2 Heat the butter in a frying pan. Finely chop the remaining mushroom slices and put into the pan. Fry over a low heat for 3 minutes, stirring.

3 Purée the soup in a blender or rub through a sieve. Return to the saucepan and add the fried mushrooms. Blend the cornflour with the cold water and stir into the soup.

4 Bring back, to the boil, stirring, and simmer for about 5 minutes. Taste and adjust the seasoning, then serve immediately with croûtons or chopped parsley sprinkled over.

Above: American-style fish soup – pepped up with tomatoes and Worcestershire sauce

American-style fish soup

A meal in itself – serve it with lots of fresh white or wholemeal bread

LUNCH OR SUPPER Serves 4

Overall timing $1\frac{1}{2}$ hours

Equipment Flameproof casserole

Freezing Cool, turn into rigid container, leaving 1 inch (2.5cm) headspace. Cover, label and freeze. Freezer life: 1 month. To use: reheat slowly from frozen

INGREDIENTS

2lb	Mixed white fish	900g
$1\frac{1}{2}$ pints	Fish stock (see page 51)	850ml
2oz	Streaky bacon	50g
1 tbsp	Oil	15ml
1	Large onion	1
4	Medium potatoes	4
4	Carrots	4
4	Stalks of celery	4
1 tbsp	Chopped parsley	15ml
14oz	Can of tomatoes	397g
2 tbsp	Tomato ketchup	2×15ml
2 tbsp	Worcestershire sauce	2×15ml
	Dried thyme	
	Salt and pepper	

METHOD

1 Skin and bone fish and cut into bite-size pieces. Prepare fish stock according to method on page 51. Dice bacon.

Add chopped potatoes, carrots and celery to casserole with parsley and tomatoes

The vegetables are cooked until soft, then the fish and bacon are added

2 Heat oil in casserole and fry bacon till crisp. Remove from pan. Peel and chop onion and add to casserole. Cook gently till transparent.

3 Wash, peel and chop potatoes and carrots. Finely chop celery. Add to casserole with chopped parsley, tomatoes and their juice.

4 Add the prepared fish stock, tomato ketchup, Worcestershire sauce, a pinch of thyme, salt and pepper. Cover and simmer gently for about 45 minutes.

5 Add the fish pieces and bacon, cover and cook for a further 15 minutes.

Artichoke soup

This is a classic soup using Jerusalem artichokes

STARTER Serves 6

Overall timing 1 hour

Equipment Saucepan, blender or food mill

Freezing Make as Steps 1–4. Pack in rigid container, leaving 1 inch (2.5cm) headspace, cover, label and freeze. Freezer life: 3 months. To use: reheat slowly from frozen, then proceed as Step 5

INGREDIENTS

1lb	Jerusalem artichokes	450g
1	Large onion	1
1	Garlic clove	1
2	Stalks of celery	2
2oz	Bacon	50g
2oz	Butter	50g
$2\frac{1}{2}$ pints	Strong chicken stock	1.5 litres
	Salt and pepper	
1	Egg yolk	1
6 tbsp	Double cream	6×15ml
2 tbsp	Chopped parsley	2×15ml

METHOD

1 Prepare and slice artichokes. Peel and chop onion. Peel and crush garlic. Trim and chop celery. Derind and chop bacon.

2 Heat half the butter in a large saucepan, add vegetables and bacon and cook, covered, over medium heat for 10 minutes, stirring occasionally.

3 Add stock and seasoning and simmer, covered, for 30 minutes, or until vegetables are tender.

4 Purée mixture in a blender or food mill.

5 Reheat soup. Lightly beat the egg yolk and cream together and whisk into the soup. Cook gently for 3 minutes but do not boil. Adjust seasoning. Stir in the parsley. Pour soup into warmed tureen and serve immediately with croûtons.

Fresh pea soup

Sweet fresh peas cooked in stock with bacon and onion are puréed and flavoured with parsley

STARTER Serves 4

Overall timing 1 hour

Equipment Large saucepan, blender

Freezing Pour into a rigid container, leaving 1 inch (2.5cm) headspace. Seal, label and freeze. Freezer life: 1 month. To use: place block in a saucepan, heat gently till thawed. Bring to the boil and adjust seasoning

INGREDIENTS

$1\frac{1}{2}$lb	Unshelled fresh peas	700g
1	Large onion	1
2oz	Smoked bacon rashers	50g
2oz	Butter	50g
2 pints	Stock	1.1 litres
1 tbsp	Chopped parsley	15ml
	Salt and pepper	
	Croûtons	

METHOD

1 Shell and wash the peas. Peel and finely chop the onion. Derind and dice the bacon. Heat the butter in a saucepan and fry the bacon and onion for about 5 minutes until transparent but not browned.

2 Add the peas and stir over a low heat for 5 minutes. Stir in the stock (made with cubes if necessary) and bring to the boil. Simmer for 25 minutes.

3 Purée in a blender or press through a sieve. Return to the saucepan, add the chopped parsley, and salt and pepper to taste. Bring to the boil and pour into a warmed tureen. Garnish with fried croûtons and serve immediately.

VARIATION

If fresh peas aren't available, use 1lb (450g) frozen peas instead, but reduce simmering time to 5 minutes.

cook's know-how

Although there are many varieties of garden pea, all should be plump and green, and so tender that the juicy pods "pop" when gently pressed between the fingers. At this stage they are very sweet. As the peas pass their prime, they fit the pods tightly and lose their strong green colour; they also need longer cooking to become tender. They are best cooked till they soften and then sieved and served as a purée. Special varieties of pea have been developed for home growing and freezing. They should be picked young, shelled, blanched for 1 minute, then cooled and drained. Open freeze till hard and then pack into polythene bags. Freezer life is 1 year.

Oxtail soup

A hearty nourishing soup livened up with dry sherry. It is thickened with flour towards the end of the cooking time. An alternative but more difficult way to add the flour would be to mix it with cold water first, then stir in well

STARTER Serves 6

Overall timing 5 hours plus overnight chilling

Equipment 2 large saucepans

Freezing Cool, pour into rigid container leaving 1 inch (2.5cm) headspace, cover, label and freeze. Freezer life: 3 months. To use: reheat from frozen

INGREDIENTS

1	Small onion	1
3oz	Butter	75g
2lb	Chopped oxtail	900g
3 pints	Beef stock	1.7 litres
14oz	Can of tomatoes	397g
1 teasp	Salt	5ml
4	Black peppercorns	4
1	Bay leaf	1
8oz	Carrots	225g
4	Stalks of celery	4
3 tbsp	Chopped parsley	3×15ml
1 teasp	Dried basil	5ml
2oz	Plain flour	50g
4 tbsp	Dry sherry	4×15ml

METHOD

1 Peel and chop the onion. Melt 1oz (25g) of the butter in a large saucepan, add the onion and oxtail, and brown.

2 Add the stock (made up with 3 stock cubes if necessary), tomatoes, salt, peppercorns and bay leaf. Bring to the boil, cover and simmer for about 4 hours or until the meat is falling off the bones. Cool, remove bones, then leave mixture overnight in the fridge.

3 The next day, peel and chop carrots. Chop celery. Skim cold fat from surface of oxtail mixture, then add carrots, celery, parsley and basil. Bring to the boil and cook for about 30 minutes or until vegetables are tender.

4 Strain mixture (or purée it if you want a smooth textured soup).

5 In another pan, melt the remaining 2oz (50g) butter and stir in the flour. Cook for 1 minute. Gradually add strained stock and bring to the boil, stirring. Cook for 10 minutes.

6 Place oxtail and vegetables in the pan and add sherry. Taste and adjust seasoning if necessary.

Potatoes in soups

Cooked puréed potato thickens soups, adds more substance and also absorbs fat. A raw potato, discarded before serving, improves oversalted soups

Above: Cooked potato is put through a fine sieve and blended into soups to thicken them

Irish potato soup

Hearty, nourishing country soup – use soured cream or buttermilk as a change instead of single cream

STARTER Serves 6

Overall timing 1 hour

Equipment 2 saucepans, potato masher, tureen

Freezing Prepare to end of Step 3. Pour into a rigid container, leaving 1 inch (2.5cm) headspace, cover, label and freeze. Freezer life: 3 months. To use: place block in a pan, heat gently till thawed, complete Steps 4–6

INGREDIENTS

2	Large onions	2
1oz	Butter	25g
1oz	Dripping	25g
2lb	Floury potatoes	900g
1 pint	Milk	560ml
1½ pints	Chicken stock	850ml
	Salt	
	Freshly-ground white pepper	
6	Streaky bacon rashers	6
¼ pint	Carton of single cream	150ml
1 tbsp	Chopped chives	15ml

METHOD

1 Peel and thinly slice the onions. Heat the butter and dripping in a saucepan and fry the onions gently for 10 minutes without browning.

2 Meanwhile, peel and slice the potatoes. Add to the onions and fry, stirring, without browning for 3 minutes.

3 Add the milk and stock (made with cubes if necessary) and bring to the boil. Season, cover and simmer for 15 minutes.

4 Meanwhile, grill the bacon till very crisp.

5 Strain the liquid into a clean saucepan and add half the vegetables. Mash the remaining vegetables to a smooth purée and return to the soup. Reheat till just simmering.

6 Stir in the cream. Cook, stirring, for 2 minutes, without boiling. Add the chives, taste and adjust the seasoning. Pour into a warmed tureen and crumble the bacon over. Serve immediately.

Crème Parmentier

Antoine-Auguste Parmentier made the potato popular in 18th century France and many dishes were named after him. This thick soup is a hot form of vichyssoise

STARTER Serves 4–6

Overall timing 50 minutes

Equipment Saucepan, blender or sieve, tureen

Freezing Prepare soup to end of Step 2. Pour into a rigid container, leaving 1 inch (2.5cm) headspace, cover, label and freeze. Freezer life: 6 months. To use: place block of soup in pan, heat gently till thawed, complete Steps 3 and 4

INGREDIENTS

1lb	Floury potatoes	450g
2	Large leeks	2
2oz	Butter	50g
1½ pints	Chicken stock	850ml
	Salt	
	Freshly-ground white pepper	
½ pint	Hot milk	300ml
¼ pint	Carton of single cream	150ml
2 teasp	Chopped chervil	2×5ml
	Fried croûtons	

METHOD

1 Peel and dice the potatoes, wash, trim and thinly slice the leeks. Heat the butter in a saucepan and add the potatoes and leeks. Cover and sweat over a low heat for 10 minutes.

2 Add the stock (made with cubes if necessary), season and bring to the boil. Simmer for 15 minutes till the potatoes are tender. Purée in a blender or press through a sieve.

3 Return to the saucepan and add the milk and cream. Heat through gently but do not allow to boil.

4 Taste and adjust seasoning and pour into a warmed tureen. Sprinkle the chervil over and serve immediately with a dish of croûtons.

Crème Du Barry

Egg yolks and single cream whisked into puréed potato and cauliflower – a luscious soup named after Louis XV's favourite who loved cauliflower

STARTER Serves 6

Overall timing 50 minutes

Equipment Saucepan, blender or sieve, tureen

Freezing Prepare to end of Step 3. Pour into a rigid container, leaving 1 inch (2.5cm) headspace, cover, label and freeze. Freezer life: 3 months. To use: place block of soup in pan, heat gently till thawed, complete Steps 4 and 5

INGREDIENTS

12oz	Floury potatoes	350g
1	Medium-size cauliflower	1
2oz	Butter	50g
2½ pints	Milk	1.5 litres
	Blade of mace	
	Salt	
	Frcshly-ground white pepper	
2	Egg yolks	2
5 tbsp	Single cream	5×15ml
1 tbsp	Chopped chervil or parsley	15ml

METHOD

1 Peel and dice the potatoes, wash and trim the cauliflower and divide into florets.

2 Heat the butter in a saucepan, add the potatoes and cauliflower, cover and sweat over a low heat for 10 minutes.

3 Add the milk and mace and bring to the boil. Season, cover and simmer for 15 minutes till the potatoes are tender. Cool slightly, then remove mace. Purée mixture in a blender or press through a sieve.

4 Return to the pan and reheat till just simmering. Mix together the egg yolks and cream and whisk into the soup.

5 Cook, stirring constantly, for 2–3 minutes but do not allow to boil. Taste and adjust the seasoning and pour into a warmed tureen. Sprinkle with chopped chervil or parsley and serve immediately.

Tomato and pesto soup

The addition of pesto, a popular Italian and southern French sauce made with fresh basil, cheese and garlic, makes this very special

STARTER Serves 6

Overall timing 50 minutes

Equipment Large saucepan, bowl, pestle and mortar

Freezing Cool completely, pour into a rigid container, leaving 1 inch (2.5cm) headspace. Cover, label and freeze. Freezer life: 3 months. To use: place block of soup in pan, heat gently till thawed. Bring to boil, adjust seasoning

INGREDIENTS

2	Medium-size carrots	2
1	Medium-size leek	1
1	Medium-size onion	1
1oz	Butter	25g
1½lb	Large ripe tomatoes	700g
1 tbsp	Tomato paste	15ml
	Bouquet garni	
	Salt	
	Freshly-ground black pepper	
2½ pints	Chicken stock	1.5 litres
8	Fresh basil leaves *or*	8
1 teasp	Dried basil	5ml
2	Garlic cloves	2
2 tbsp	Grated Parmesan	2×15ml
2 tbsp	Olive oil	2 tbsp
3	Large floury potatoes	3

METHOD

1 Scrape the carrots, wash and trim the leek, peel the onion. Chop finely. Heat the butter in a large saucepan, add the vegetables and fry over a low heat for 5 minutes.

2 Blanch, peel and chop the tomatoes. Add to the pan with the tomato paste, bouquet garni, salt, pepper and stock (made with cubes if necessary). Bring to the boil, mash vegetables with potato masher. Cover and simmer for 20 minutes.

3 Meanwhile, make the pesto. Pound the basil leaves with the peeled and crushed garlic and ¼ teasp (1.25ml) salt in a mortar. Gradually add the cheese and oil, pounding between each addition till the mixture is creamy.

4 Peel and wash the potatoes and grate coarsely. Add to the soup and simmer for a further 10 minutes.

5 Discard the bouquet garni. Stir the pesto into the soup and simmer for 2–3 minutes. Adjust seasoning. Pour into a warmed tureen and serve.

Below: Tomato and pesto soup – the basil brings out the full flavour of the tomatoes

Iced tomato soup

This refreshing summer starter, served with crisp croûtons, is made in minutes and needs no cooking

STARTER Serves 6

Overall timing 15 minutes plus chilling

Equipment Blender, nylon sieve, bowl, frying pan

Freezing Complete Step 2. Pour into a rigid container, leaving 1 inch (2.5cm) headspace, cover, label and freeze. Freezer life: 3 months. To use: thaw at room temperature for about 4 hours, then complete Steps 3–4

INGREDIENTS

2lb	Ripe tomatoes	900g
2	Stalks of celery	2
1	Small onion	1
1 teasp	Sugar	5ml
¼ pint	Dry white wine	150ml
¼ pint	Water	150ml
2 tbsp	Chopped parsley	2×15ml
1 teasp	Lemon juice	5ml
	Salt	
	Freshly-ground black pepper	
2	Thick slices of bread	2
1	Garlic clove	1
2oz	Butter	50g
3 tbsp	Oil	3×15ml

METHOD

1 Blanch, peel and chop the tomatoes and put into a blender. Wash, trim and chop the celery, peel and chop the onion. Add to the blender with the sugar, wine, water and half the parsley.

2 Blend till smooth, then rub through a nylon sieve into a bowl. Add the lemon juice and season to taste. Cover and chill for 3–4 hours.

3 Meanwhile, cut the bread into ½ inch (12.5mm) cubes, removing the crusts. Heat the butter and oil in a frying pan, add the peeled and crushed garlic and bread cubes and fry till crisp and golden. Drain on kitchen paper, then sprinkle with parsley and salt and leave to cool.

4 Scatter the croûtons into the soup and serve immediately.

leftovers in soup

Leftover meats and vegetables in too small quantities to be served again are ideal for soups. With a blender as basic equipment you never need throw food away. A chicken carcass will make good stock (recipe page 27), and the meat can also be added. All leftover vegetables – potatoes, peas, carrots, spinach – can be puréed and added to stock for a thick tasty soup. Hard heels of cheese, finely grated, will convert into fondue-like soups, while leftover bread can be crumbled and used as a thickener. Limp salad ingredients – onions, cucumber, tomatoes, capsicums – can be made into a purée to transform Gazpacho.

STARTERS

A starter from the freezer will simplify the preparations for any dinner party or celebration meal. Either prepare the dish ahead, to be thawed and if necessary reheated on the day, or use ingredients from the freezer as in the recipe below

Prawn cocktail

Use the top quality frozen prawns for this favourite starter

STARTER Serves 4

Overall timing 15 minutes plus thawing

Equipment 2 bowls, 4 glasses*

Freezing Not recommended for the finished dish

INGREDIENTS

12oz	Frozen shelled prawns	350g
	Salt	
	Freshly-ground black pepper	
1 tbsp	Lemon juice	15ml
¼ pint	Thick mayonnaise	150ml
2 tbsp	Tomato ketchup	2×15ml
½ teasp	Worcestershire sauce	2.5ml
2	Lettuce hearts	2
1 teasp	Chopped parsley	5ml
4	Lemon slices	4
4	Frozen whole prawns	4

METHOD

1 Thaw the prawns and put the shelled fish into a bowl with salt, pepper and lemon juice. Chill until ready to serve.

2 Put the mayonnaise into a bowl, add the tomato ketchup, Worcestershire sauce and salt and pepper.

3 Wash the lettuce hearts, separate into leaves and dry thoroughly. Use to line the glasses.

4 Arrange the shelled prawns on top of the lettuce and spoon the sauce over. Sprinkle with parsley. Make a cut to the centre of each slice of lemon and place on the side of each glass with an unpeeled prawn. Serve immediately with brown bread and butter.

*The special cocktail glasses for prawns and other seafoods have two parts. The food and its dressing are put into the top bowl which then fits neatly inside the goblet-like glass. Between the two there is room for crushed ice which will keep all the ingredients cool.

Above: Prawn cocktail – assemble at last minute so lettuce doesn't have time to wilt

Menai pride mussel pâté

Wales, with its 750–mile long coastline, has many delicious seafood dishes, both traditional and contemporary. This particular pâté is the creation of the Glantraeth Restaurant in Bodorgan, near the Menai Strait, in Anglesey

STARTER Serves 4–6

Overall timing 1 hour

Equipment Saucepan, mincer, ovenproof dish, foil, roasting tin

Freezing Allow to cool completely. Foil wrap, seal, label and freeze. Freezer life: 1 month. To use: thaw overnight in fridge

Below: Menai pride mussel pâté – a mixture of minced herring roe, mussels, vegetables and herbs, held together and enriched by egg yolks, brandy and cream, and baked for 30 minutes to make a delicious and unusual seafood pâté that was created in Wales

INGREDIENTS

2 pints	Mussels	1.1 litres
5 tbsp	Water	5×15ml
1	Stalk of celery	1
1	Small carrot	1
2oz	Herring roe	50g
¼ teasp	Dried mixed herbs	1.25ml
	Pinch of dill weed	
1oz	Fresh breadcrumbs	25g
½	Garlic clove	½
4	Egg yolks	4
2 tbsp	Brandy	2×15ml
2 tbsp	Double cream	2×15ml
	Salt	
	Freshly-ground black pepper	

METHOD

1 Preheat the oven to 350F (180C) Gas 4.

2 Scrub and wash the mussels and put into a saucepan with the water. Cook over a high heat till the shells open. Discard any that remain closed.

3 Drain and remove the mussels from the shells. Wash, trim and chop the celery, scrape and chop the carrot. Push twice through the mincer with the mussels and roe till finely minced.

4 Add the dried herbs, dill, breadcrumbs and peeled and crushed garlic. Mix in the egg yolks, brandy, cream and plenty of seasoning.

5 Pour into an ovenproof dish and smooth the top. Cover with foil. Stand the dish in a roasting tin containing 1 inch (2.5cm) of hot water and bake on the centre shelf of the oven for 30 minutes.

6 Remove from the bain-marie and allow to cool. Garnish with slices of lemon and sprigs of parsley. Serve cold, cut into slices, with fresh toast.

Chicken liver pâté

A very strong, creamy pâté flavoured with sherry. Made in a blender, it goes quite a long way and keeps well in the fridge if covered. If you prefer more texture, set aside a few of the chicken livers before blending. Chop them roughly and stir them into the creamed mixture

STARTER Serves 6–8

Overall timing 1½ hours

Equipment 10 inch (25cm) frying pan, blender, small dish or individual ramekins

Freezing When cold, wrap, label and freeze. Freezer life: 3 months. To use: thaw overnight in fridge or for 2 hours at room temperature

INGREDIENTS

4oz	Butter	125g
2	Garlic cloves	2
5oz	Onion	150g
2oz	Mushrooms	50g
2×8oz	Cartons of chicken livers	2×225g
1 teasp	Sweet mixed herbs	5ml
	Salt and pepper	
2 tbsp	Double cream	2×15ml
2 tbsp	Amontillado sherry	2×15ml
	Bay leaves	
	Freshly-ground black pepper	

METHOD

1 In frying pan, melt half the butter and cook crushed garlic and chopped onion till golden.
2 Add the wiped, chopped mushrooms and drained chicken livers and cook for 5 minutes. Mix in herbs, season to taste and cook for a further 5 minutes. Remove from heat and stir in cream and sherry. Leave till cold.
3 Blend mixture until it is smooth and creamy, then scoop out into a small earthenware dish or distribute between small ramekins. Decorate with one or two bay leaves and sprinkle with freshly-ground black pepper. Melt remaining butter and pour over. Place dish or ramekins in fridge for at least an hour before serving (the longer you can leave it the better).

TO SERVE

Serve with hot toast or fresh crusty bread and butter curls.

Pâté de foie de porc

Above: Pâté de foie de porc – an easy pâté that's full of flavour, and is fine-textured

Pigs liver pâté that's a speciality of Alsace where the excellent local wines would be used – extra flavour comes from plum spirit or slivovitz*

STARTER OR LUNCH Serves 8–10

Overall timing 2½ hours plus marination and overnight chilling

Equipment Mincer, bowl, 2lb (900g) loaf tin or mould, foil, roasting tin

Freezing Cool the pâté and leave in the tin. Wrap in foil, overwrap, seal and label. Freezer life: 1 month. To use: remove wrappings, thaw overnight in the fridge and turn out of the tin to serve

INGREDIENTS

1lb	Pigs liver	450g
1lb	Streaky bacon rashers	450g
1	Slice of bread	1
2 teasp	Salt	2× 5ml
	Freshly-ground black pepper	
¼ teasp	Ground allspice	1.25ml
	Pinch of dried thyme	
1 tbsp	Plum spirit or brandy	15ml
¼ pint	Medium-dry white wine	150ml
	Thin slices of pork back fat	

METHOD

1 Wipe liver and cut into pieces, discarding any blood vessels or membranes. Derind the bacon and push through a mincer with the liver into a large bowl. Add crustless bread to clean mincer. Add salt, pepper and allspice to mixture in bowl, with thyme, spirit and wine. Mix well. Marinate in the fridge for 2 hours.
2 Preheat the oven to 400F (200C) Gas 6.
3 Line the loaf tin or mould with some of the pork fat. Spread the liver mixture into the tin, press down and cover with the remaining pork fat.
4 Cover the tin with foil and stand in a roasting tin containing 1 inch (2.5cm) of hot water. Bake in the centre of the oven for about 1¾ hours.
5 Remove the tin from the oven and leave to cool. Chill in the fridge overnight.
6 Turn pâté out on to a serving dish, cut into thick slices and serve with crusty bread and a green salad.

*Slivovitz, a strong spirit or brandy, is made from plums and comes mainly from Central Europe and the Balkan states. The Czechs call it slivovice and serve it in brandy glasses or special long-stemmed glasses, with coffee. In Yugoslavia it is known as sljivovica and is offered as a greeting to guests. There are two types – the "soft" one has only 25% alcohol while the strong type is distilled twice and has over 40% alcohol.

Pâté de campagne

A rich, glazed country pâté – pork, bacon and chicken are flavoured with Cognac, allspice, nuts and truffle

STARTER OR LUNCH Serves 8–10

Overall timing 3½ hours plus marination and overnight chilling

Equipment Mincer, bowls, terrine with lid, roasting tin, saucepan, foil, weights

Freezing Make to end of Step 7, remove from terrine and discard fat. Wrap in double thickness of foil, label and freeze. Freezer life: 1 month. To use: remove wrappings, replace pâté in terrine and thaw overnight in fridge. Glaze with gelatine mixture and leave to set before serving

INGREDIENTS

1lb	Belly of pork rashers	450g
1lb	Lean pork	450g
4oz	Streaky bacon rashers	125g
2 tbsp	Cognac	2×15ml
	Salt	
	Freshly-ground black pepper	
¼ teasp	Ground allspice	1.25ml
1lb	Chicken breasts	450g
1	Boneless pork chop	1
	Thin slices of pork back fat	
2	Eggs	2
2	Slices of black truffle (optional)	2
½oz	Chopped pistachios (optional)	15g
1	Bay leaf	1
	Luting paste (see page 45)	
¼ pint	Light stock	150ml
1 teasp	Gelatine	5ml

METHOD

1 Wipe and trim belly of pork, removing skin and bones. Cut into small pieces. Cut 4 thick strips from the lean pork and reserve. Cut the rest into small pieces. Derind and dice the bacon.

2 Mince the pork and bacon pieces into a large bowl. Add the Cognac, salt, pepper and allspice. Mix well and leave to marinate for 2 hours, stirring occasionally.

3 Meanwhile, wipe and bone the chicken breasts, discarding the skin, and cut into thick strips. Wipe the pork chop and cut into strips. Cut a little of the pork back fat into strips and reserve. Use the rest to line the terrine, leaving enough overhanging to cover the pâté.

4 Preheat the oven to 375F (190C) Gas 5. Add the eggs to the minced meat and mix well. Spread half the mixture in the terrine, pressing it down well. Arrange the strips of pork, chicken and fat on top and sprinkle with the sliced truffle and pistachios if using.

5 Spread the remaining minced meat over, smooth the top and place the bay leaf in the centre. Fold the overhanging fat over the top to enclose the meat.

6 Cover with the lid, sealing it with luting paste according to the instructions on page 45. Stand the terrine in a roasting tin containing 1 inch (2.5cm) hot water and bake in centre of oven for 2 hours.

7 Remove luting paste and pour the liquid from the terrine into a bowl and reserve. Leave the pâté to cool.

8 Lift the pâté out of the terrine. Remove and discard the fat. Wash the terrine and replace the pâté. Put 3 tbsp (3×15ml) of the stock (made with a cube if necessary) in a bowl, sprinkle the gelatine over and leave to sponge. Place bowl in a pan of simmering water and stir till gelatine dissolves. Add to remaining stock and liquid from the terrine.

9 Pour over the pâté, cover with foil and place weights on top. Chill overnight. Serve, cut into slices, from the terrine with crusty bread and gherkins or sliced dill pickles.

Mince pork and bacon pieces then marinate in Cognac, salt, pepper and allspice for 2 hours. Add eggs to the mince and mix well

Line terrine with pork back fat and spread half the minced mixture in. Press down well. Arrange the pork and chicken strips on top

Sprinkle chicken and pork strips with sliced truffle and pistachios (if used). Spread the remaining minced meat over and add bay leaf

Fold overhanging fat to enclose meat. Cover, seal and bake for 2 hours. Pour out liquid, cool pâté and discard fat. Glaze with stock and gelatine, cover, add weights and chill

Left: Pâté de campagne – tasty pâté that takes time to make but is well worth it. Serve with crusty bread and gherkins

Using a sharp knife cut fish into thin strips. Have bowl of milk and separate dish of seasoned flour at hand

Dip the strips of fish in the milk first in order to give the flour something to adhere to

Carefully but thoroughly coat each strip with seasoned flour, shaking off any excess — the fish is now ready for frying

Right: Goujonettes de poisson — strips of fried white fish, garnished with lemon, served with tartare sauce

Goujonettes de poisson

Strips of mixed white fish are given a light coating of milk and flour, then deep fried. A simple and delicious fish dish good as a starter or as an easy-to-prepare snack for a party

STARTER Serves 6

Overall timing 20 minutes

Equipment Deep-fryer, 2 bowls

Freezing Fry fish till just golden. Drain well, then open freeze. Pack into freezer bags, seal and label. Freezer life: 1 month. To use: cover and reheat from frozen in the oven at 375F (190C) Gas 5 for about 30 minutes

INGREDIENTS

	Oil for frying	
2lb	Mixed white fish fillets	900g
¼ pint	Milk	150ml
	Salt and pepper	
3oz	Plain flour	75g
	Fresh parsley	
2	Lemons	2

METHOD

1 Heat the oil for frying to 340F (170C) or until a cube of stale bread browns in one minute.

2 Wipe fish and pat dry. Remove skin. Cut fish into thin strips. Dip into milk, then roll in seasoned flour to coat.

3 Fry the strips of fish in the oil till golden brown. Remove from pan with a draining spoon and drain on kitchen paper. Garnish with sprigs of parsley and lemon wedges and serve with tartare sauce.

Stuffed mushrooms

When you see large cup mushrooms, buy them to fill with this simple breadcrumb, egg and Parmesan stuffing flavoured with herbs. They make a good starter for an Italian-style dinner party

Above: Stuffed mushrooms – the cheesy filling is flavoured with marjoram

STARTER Serves 4

Overall timing 1 hour

Equipment Pestle and mortar or blender, bowl, shallow ovenproof dish

Freezing Cool, then pack in rigid container. Cover, label and freeze. Freezer life: 3 months. To use: thaw overnight in fridge, then place in shallow dish, cover with foil and heat through in oven at 375F (190C) Gas 5 for 10 minutes

INGREDIENTS

8	Cup mushrooms	8
2oz	Fresh breadcrumbs	50g
¼ pint	Warm milk	150ml
1	Garlic clove	1
	Salt	
	Freshly-ground black pepper	
1	Egg	1
1	Egg yolk	1
4oz	Grated Parmesan	125g
2 teasp	Finely chopped marjoram	2×5ml
8 teasp	Oil	8×5ml

METHOD

1 Carefully detach the mushroom caps from the stalks. Wipe the caps and reserve. Trim the stalks and cut into small pieces.

2 Preheat the oven to 350F (180C) Gas 4.

3 Soak the breadcrumbs in warm milk, then squeeze out well, reserving milk. Peel the garlic and place in mortar or blender with stalks, salt, pepper and a little of the reserved milk. Pound or blend till well combined. Put the mixture into a bowl, add the eggs, grated Parmesan, marjoram and 2 teasp (2×5ml) of oil. Mix well until creamy, then add salt.

4 Spread the stuffing into the hollow of each mushroom cap using a wetted knife. Lightly oil the dish and arrange the stuffed mushrooms in it. Sprinkle the top with a little oil and freshly-ground pepper and bake in the oven for about 30 minutes. Garnish with parsley and serve while still hot.

Mushroom pasties

Crisp puff pastry encases a slightly tangy and moist filling of sliced mushrooms, onion and breadcrumbs

STARTER/PARTY SNACK Makes 9

Overall timing 45 minutes

Equipment Saucepan, bowl, baking tray

Freezing Open freeze till firm. Pack into rigid container, seal and label. Freezer life: 3 months. To use: thaw for 1 hour at room temperature, then refresh in the oven at 400F (200C) Gas 6 for about 20 minutes

INGREDIENTS

13oz	Packet of frozen puff pastry	375g
	Filling	
12oz	Mushrooms	350g
1	Small onion	1
3oz	Butter	75g
2oz	Fresh breadcrumbs	50g
1 tbsp	Chopped parsley	15ml
	Salt	
	Freshly-ground black pepper	
¼ teasp	Paprika	1.25ml
¼ teasp	Grated nutmeg	1.25ml
3	Eggs	3
3 tbsp	Lemon juice	3×15ml

METHOD

1 Thaw the pastry and roll out on a floured surface to a rectangle 18×12 inches (45×30cm). Cut into 9 even rectangles 6×4 inches (15×10cm).

2 Preheat the oven to 425F (220C) Gas 7.

3 Wipe and trim the mushrooms and slice thickly. Peel and chop the onion. Heat the butter in a saucepan and fry the onion till transparent. Add the mushrooms and fry for 3–4 minutes.

4 Remove from the heat. Add the breadcrumbs to the pan with the chopped parsley, salt, pepper, paprika and nutmeg. Lightly beat 2 of the eggs and add with the lemon juice to the pan. Mix well.

5 Put a little of the filling into the centre of each pastry rectangle. Beat the remaining egg and brush around the edges of the pastry rectangles.

6 Fold the top corners down and the bottom corners up over the filling for each rectangle. Arrange on a wetted baking tray and glaze with the egg. Bake near the top of the oven for 15–20 minutes till well risen and golden. Serve hot.

Above: Artusi bean cake — slices beautifully

Add blanched French beans to fried chopped celery, onion and parsley. Cover, then let the mixture cook very gently in its own steam

Meanwhile, make a thick, well-flavoured sauce with Gruyère. When bean mixture is cooked, drain off excess liquid and add sauce

Beat the eggs lightly with a balloon whisk and then stir them into the bean and sauce mixture with a wooden spoon

Grease sides and bottom of ovenproof dish and coat with crisp breadcrumbs. Add bean and egg mixture. Cook, set in tin of water

Artusi bean cake

An unusual oven-cooked egg dish delicately flavoured with Gruyère

STARTER OR LIGHT LUNCH Serves 4

Overall timing $1\frac{1}{4}$–$1\frac{1}{2}$ hours

Equipment 2 saucepans, frying pan with lid, 2 pint (1.1 litre) ovenproof dish, roasting tin

Freezing Cook cake in foil dish. Leave to cool, then wrap, label and freeze. Freezer life: 3 months. To use: thaw for about 3 hours then reheat in oven at 300F (150C) Gas 2 for 30 minutes

INGREDIENTS

1lb	Green beans	450g
1	Celery stalk	1
3oz	Butter	75g
2 tbsp	Oil	2×15ml
1 tbsp	Chopped onion	5 ml
1 tbsp	Chopped parsley	15ml
1oz	Plain flour	25g
9fl oz	Milk	250ml
	Salt and pepper	
4oz	Gruyère	125g
2 tbsp	Crisp breadcrumbs	2×15ml
3	Eggs	3

METHOD

1 Wash beans and remove strings. Blanch for 5 minutes in lightly salted, boiling water. Drain.

2 Chop celery. Heat 2oz (50g) of the butter, and the oil, in a frying pan and brown the onion, celery and chopped parsley. Add beans, cover and cook very gently for 10 minutes. (See step-by-step pictures, right.)

3 Meanwhile, make a well-flavoured sauce: heat the remaining butter in a pan, remove from heat and stir in flour, then milk. Return to heat and cook for 2 minutes. Add salt, pepper and grated Gruyère and cook for further 5 minutes. Remove from heat.

4 Preheat the oven to 425F (220C) Gas 7. Grease ovenproof dish and coat bottom and sides with breadcrumbs. Lightly beat eggs.

5 Drain bean mixture and mix it into sauce until well combined, then mix in eggs. Spoon mixture into ovenproof dish. Stand dish in roasting tin of water and cook in oven for 25 minutes. Reduce heat to 400F (200C) Gas 6 and cook for 10 more minutes.

6 Remove dish from oven, leave to stand for 5 minutes then invert on to serving plate. Serve either hot or cold.

Toss sliced courgettes in flour, fry till golden and tender, drain and season

Cut Mozzarella into thin slices and layer into dish with remaining courgettes

Ladle over the tomato, onion and garlic dressing and chill for 2–3 hours

Courgettes with tomato and Mozzarella

Courgettes layered with Mozzarella, one of Italy's best cooking cheeses, in a fragrant, herby tomato sauce. Instead of basil, a good pinch of dried oregano gives extra flavour. To make this a main meal, add minced cooked meat between the layers of courgettes

STARTER OR LUNCH Serves 4

Overall timing 30 minutes plus chilling

Equipment Frying pan, ovenproof dish

Freezing Cool, cover, label and freeze. Freezer life: 2 months. To use: bake from frozen in moderate oven 350F (180C) Gas 4 for about 45 minutes till bubbling hot

INGREDIENTS

1	Onion	1
1	Garlic clove	1
3 tbsp	Oil	3×15ml
1oz	Butter	25g
1lb	Fresh or canned tomatoes	450g
4	Basil leaves *or*	4
½ teasp	Dried basil	2.5ml
6	Courgettes	6
3 tbsp	Flour	3×15ml
	Salt and pepper	
8oz	Mozzarella	225g

METHOD

1 Peel and finely chop onion. Peel and crush garlic. Heat 1 tbsp (15ml) oil and the butter in a frying pan. Cook onion and garlic till onions are transparent.

2 Blanch, peel and chop fresh tomatoes or drain can of tomatoes. Add to pan with chopped basil and cook over a low heat for 20 minutes. Purée mixture in a blender or push through a sieve.

3 Heat rest of oil in pan. Wash courgettes and trim ends, then slice. Coat slices with flour and fry in oil till lightly golden and tender. Drain on kitchen paper and season with salt and pepper.

4 Thinly slice Mozzarella. Place in dish layers of courgettes, Mozzarella, then tomato dressing. Place in the fridge and chill for 2–3 hours. Serve with hot garlic bread or toast and butter curls.

Above: Courgettes with tomato and Mozzarella – a tasty starter or lunch

cook's know-how

Luting paste is used to provide an airtight seal between the lid and the rim of a casserole or terrine in order to trap steam inside. Mix 4oz (125g) plain flour with 4–5 tbsp (4–5×15ml) cold water to make a stiff paste. Shape into a long sausage and press firmly over the outside edge of the lid and rim of the dish to seal it well. Scrape off the paste before pressing the terrine with weights after cooking.

Caponata

This dish could be called the Sicilian answer to France's ratatouille. It's a splendidly piquant mix and it's served cold

STARTER Serves 4–6

Overall timing 45 minutes

Equipment 2 frying pans

Freezing When cold, pack into rigid container, seal, label and freeze. Freezer life: 3 months. To use: thaw overnight in fridge or for 2–3 hours at room temperature

Stir salt, pepper, sugar, vinegar and water into cooked vegetable mixture

INGREDIENTS

8oz	Green capsicums	225g
$1\frac{1}{2}$lb	Aubergines	700g
4 tbsp	Olive oil	4×15ml
1	Large onion	1
3	Stalks of celery	3
8oz	Tomatoes	225g
4oz	Pitted green olives	125g
1 tbsp	Pine nuts (optional)	15ml
2 tbsp	Capers	2×15ml
	Salt and pepper	
1 teasp	Caster sugar	5ml
6 tbsp	Vinegar	6×15ml

METHOD

1 Wipe capsicums and deseed. Cut into narrow strips. Wipe the aubergines and chop roughly without peeling.
2 Heat 2 tbsp (2×15ml) of the oil in a frying pan. Add aubergines and green capsicums, gently fry for 15 minutes.
3 Meanwhile, peel and chop the onion finely, chop the celery. Scald tomatoes, then peel and cut into quarters. Heat the rest of the oil in the other frying pan. Add the onion and cook till brown. Add celery, tomatoes, olives, pine nuts (optional) and capers. Cook 5 minutes.
4 Mix in the contents of the other frying pan and then add salt, pepper, sugar, vinegar and 6 tbsp (6×15ml) water. Cook, covered, for 15 minutes over low heat. Leave to go cold before serving.

Bean ramekins

This is a very good way of using up leftover lamb, either to make a starter or a light lunch. Canned flageolet beans are quick, but dried ones can be used if you prefer. Either soak them overnight or pour boiling water over them and leave them to stand for two hours, then use as you would the canned ones

STARTER OR LIGHT LUNCH Serves 4

Overall timing 35 minutes

Equipment Sieve, mincer, bowl, four $\frac{1}{2}$ pint (300ml) ramekins

Freezing Prepare ramekins then cover with foil or polythene, label and freeze. Freezer life: 1 month. To use: place in cold oven set at 400F (200C) Gas 6. Heat through for 1 hour.

Below: Bean ramekins are flavoured with garlic, topped with buttery breadcrumbs

INGREDIENTS

14oz	Can of flageolet beans	397g
2oz	White bread	50g
	Milk	
1	Garlic clove	1
2	Sprigs of parsley	2
8oz	Leftover cooked lamb	225g
1	Egg	1
	Salt and pepper	
$\frac{1}{4}$ pint	Stock or leftover gravy	150ml
3 tbsp	Dried breadcrumbs	3×15ml
2oz	Butter	50g

METHOD

1 Preheat oven to 400F (200C) Gas 6.
2 Drain beans. Place in sieve and pour hot water over to rinse.
3 Prepare the stuffing: dip the bread in milk, then squeeze it out and put it through a mincer with peeled garlic, parsley and leftover lamb. Place in a bowl and mix with the egg, salt, pepper and stock.
4 Butter ramekin dishes and make alternate layers of beans and stuffing. Sprinkle with breadcrumbs and dot with knobs of butter.
5 Cook for 20 minutes in oven.

Left: individual Onion tartlets – to make a larger number of smaller tartlets use a bun tray instead of individual moulds

Cheddar croquettes

England's all-purpose cheese, named after the Somerset town in which it was first made, gives a good flavour to these croquettes which are shallow rather than deep fried. Mature Cheddar is more than 6 months old, and at 9 months is at its best in texture and taste

STARTER OR PARTY SNACK Makes 12

Overall timing 30 minutes

Equipment Bowl, frying pan

Freezing Make as Steps 1 and 2. Open freeze, then pack in rigid container, cover and label. Freezer life: 3 months. To use: proceed as Step 3, but lengthen cooking time to 3–4 minutes

INGREDIENTS

6oz	Mature Cheddar	175g
4oz	Fresh white breadcrumbs	125g
2 tbsp	Chopped chives or spring onions	2×15ml
2 tbsp	Chopped parsley	2×15ml
½ teasp	Powdered mustard	2.5ml
½ teasp	Salt	2.5ml
	Freshly-ground black pepper	
2	Eggs	2
1 tbsp	Water	15ml
3 tbsp	Plain flour	3×15ml
3oz	Dried breadcrumbs	75g
4 tbsp	Oil	4×15ml

METHOD

1 Grate cheese and mix together in a bowl with the fresh breadcrumbs, chives or spring onions, parsley, mustard, salt and pepper. Separate the eggs and add yolks and water to bowl. Mix to a firm paste, divide into 12 equal pieces and roll into firm balls.

2 Roll each ball into a cylinder about ¾ inch (2cm) thick by 2 inches (5cm) long. Roll each one in flour till coated, then dip first in lightly beaten egg whites and then in dried breadcrumbs.

3 Heat the oil in a frying pan. Fry croquettes for 2–3 minutes, turning them over with tongs, until golden brown all over. Remove from pan, drain on kitchen paper and serve hot.

Onion tartlets

Try this recipe next time you have a party – it comes from Franche-Comté, a French region which boasts a variety of culinary specialities

STARTER Serves 4

Overall timing 40 minutes

Equipment Saucepan, eight 2½ inch (6.5cm) tartlet moulds, pastry cutter, bowl

Freezing Cool completely, then open freeze till firm. Remove from tins, wrap in foil, seal and label. Freezer life: 2 months. To use: replace in tins and reheat from frozen at 425F (220C) Gas 7 for 10 minutes

INGREDIENTS

7oz	Packet of frozen puff pastry	212g
12oz	Onions	350g
4oz	Smoked bacon	125g
2oz	Butter	50g
3	Eggs	3
½ pint	Milk	300ml
	Salt	
	Freshly-ground black pepper	

METHOD

1 Thaw the pastry. Preheat the oven to 425F (220C) Gas 7. Grease tartlet moulds.

2 Peel and thinly slice the onions. Derind and dice the bacon. Heat the butter in a saucepan and fry the bacon and onions till lightly browned. Cover and sweat for 15 minutes.

3 Roll out the pastry on a lightly floured surface. Stamp out 8 circles with a pastry cutter and use to line tartlet moulds. Prick the base of each several times with a fork.

4 Using a fork, beat the eggs, milk and onion mixture in a bowl. Season and divide between pastry cases. Bake in the centre of the oven for 10–15 minutes till lightly set and golden.

TO SERVE

Garnish with fried onion rings if liked, arrange on a plate with lettuce leaves and serve hot.

VARIATION

Use cream instead of milk, or a mixture of half milk and half cream.

Crêpes au Camembert

Savoury pancakes filled with blended Camembert and topped with spicy tomatoes and grated Gruyère or Emmenthal

STARTER OR LIGHT LUNCH Serves 4

Overall timing 45 minutes

Equipment 1 bowl, small frying pan, blender or sieve, ovenproof dish

Freezing Prepare as Steps 1–4, but assemble dish in foil container. Seal, label and freeze. Freezer life: 2 months. To use: bake from frozen in oven at 400F (200C) Gas 6 for 30–40 minutes

INGREDIENTS

4oz	Plain flour	125g
	Pinch of salt	
2	Eggs	2
¼ pint	Milk	150ml
1 teasp	Brandy (optional)	5ml
4oz	Butter	125g
½	Ripe Camembert	½
8oz	Can of tomatoes	227g
	Worcestershire sauce	
4oz	Grated Gruyère or Emmenthal	125g

METHOD

1 Put flour, salt, eggs and milk into a bowl and whisk well together. Add the brandy (optional), cover and chill for 2 hours.

2 Fry the batter in a small frying pan to make 8 pancakes, adding a nut of butter between each so they brown evenly. Preheat the oven to 400F (200C) Gas 6. Grease ovenproof dish.

3 Mash Camembert and remaining butter with a fork until well blended. Spread a little of the cheese mixture over each pancake. Roll up and arrange in ovenproof dish, seam-side underneath.

4 Blend tomatoes and juice for a few seconds with a dash of Worcestershire sauce or press through a sieve. Pour over crêpes and sprinkle with grated cheese and freshly-ground black pepper.

5 Cook in oven for 20 minutes. Serve immediately with a mixed green salad or peas flavoured with mint.

Ham and chicken beignets

Minced ham, chicken and cheese coated with choux paste and fried

STARTER OR PARTY SNACK Makes about 30

Overall timing 1½ hours

Equipment 2 bowls, mincer, saucepan, deep-fryer

Freezing Freeze uncooked paste in rigid container after completing Step 4. Freezer life: 2 months. To use: thaw in fridge, then use as below

INGREDIENTS

3oz	Dried breadcrumbs	75g
	Milk	
4oz	Cooked boneless chicken	125g
5oz	Ham	150g
2oz	Grated Parmesan	50g
	Salt and pepper	
	Choux paste	
4oz	Plain flour	125g
	Pinch of powdered mustard	
8fl oz	Water	220ml
3oz	Unsalted butter	75g
¼ teasp	Salt	1.25ml
3	Eggs	3
	Oil for frying	

METHOD

1 Soak breadcrumbs in a little milk, then squeeze dry. Mince chicken and ham and mix in a bowl with the Parmesan and breadcrumbs. Add salt and pepper to taste and mix well. Shape mixture into about 30 small balls.

2 Sift flour and mustard on to sheet of greaseproof paper. Put water, butter, cut into small pieces, in a saucepan and heat gently till the butter has melted. Bring rapidly to the boil, remove pan from heat and add the flour all at once.

3 Beat vigorously with a wooden spoon, then return pan to heat.

4 Continue beating until the paste is a single smooth mass, leaving the sides of the pan cleanly (about 45 seconds). Remove pan from heat immediately, cool paste slightly, then add the eggs, one at a time, beating till each egg is mixed in and forms a soft, glossy mass, before adding the next.

5 Heat oil in deep-fryer to 350F (180C). Using 2 teaspoons, coat 4 or 5 chicken balls at a time with choux paste and drop them immediately into the hot fat. Cook for about 5–10 minutes till golden.

6 Remove from pan with a draining spoon and drain well on kitchen paper. Keep hot till all the choux balls have been fried. Arrange on hot serving dish and serve immediately with tomato or tartare sauce.

Above: Ham and chicken beignets – crispy on the outside with a flavourful filling

Chinese spring rolls

A tribute to the fresh vegetables available in the spring, deep fried Chinese rolls make excellent eating

STARTER OR SNACK Makes 12

Overall timing $1\frac{1}{2}$ hours plus resting

Equipment Bowl, deep-fryer

Freezing Interleave the pastry squares with non-stick paper, overwrap in foil. Seal, label and freeze. Freezer life: 6 months. To use: thaw in wrappings, fill and cook as below

INGREDIENTS

8oz	Strong flour	225g
$\frac{1}{2}$ teasp	Salt	2.5ml
3	Eggs	3
	Cornflour	
	Oil for frying	

METHOD

1 Sift the flour and salt into a bowl. Make a well in the centre and break the eggs into it. Mix with fingers to make a soft dough.
2 Knead the pastry on a large board for at least 10 minutes till smooth and elastic. Wrap it in cling film and leave to rest for 2 hours.
3 Divide the pastry into 2, keeping one part covered. Dredge board with cornflour and roll out half of the pastry till very thin. Stretch it further by stroking the underside with the back of the hands till transparent. Cut the pastry into six 6 inch (15cm) squares.
4 Place a square with one corner towards you. Put a little of the filling across the centre of the pastry. Fold bottom corner up and the side corners in over the filling so the pastry looks like an open envelope. Brush the open flap with beaten egg.
5 Starting from the side nearest you, roll up pastry square, finishing with the point underneath. Repeat with remaining pastry to make 12 rolls.
6 Heat the oil in a deep-fryer to 350F (170C) and fry the spring rolls, 3 at a time, for 3–4 minutes till crisp and golden. Drain on kitchen paper and keep hot, uncovered, in a warm oven till the rest are cooked.

FILLING

Fillings should be meaty and flavoursome with a crisp texture – there are many variations.

Wipe and thinly slice 8oz (225g) lean pork across the grain, cut into strips and fry in 2 tbsp (2×15ml) oil for 2 minutes. Wash, trim and slice 4 spring onions and 2oz (50g) mushrooms. Add to the pan with 4oz (125g) peeled shrimps, 8oz (225g) bean sprouts and 2 tbsp (2×15ml) soy sauce, and stir-fry for 2 minutes. Add 1 teasp (5ml) each of sugar and salt, mix well and leave to cool before using.

Sardine mousse

Anchovy essence gives an extra fishy taste to this layered mousse. Serve as a hot starter with buttered toast or cold with fresh crusty bread

STARTER Serves 6

Overall timing $1\frac{1}{2}$ hours

Equipment Blender, 2 pint (1.1 litre) soufflé dish, foil, roasting tin

Freezing Cool, wrap dish in foil, seal, label and freeze. Freezer life: 1 month. To use: thaw in fridge, serve cold

INGREDIENTS

2×11$\frac{1}{2}$oz	Cans of sardines	2×326g
1	Medium-size onion	1
1oz	Butter	25g
1 teasp	Lemon juice	5ml
	Salt	
	Black pepper	
2	Eggs	2
2oz	Fresh breadcrumbs	50g
3 tbsp	Milk	3×15ml
1 teasp	Anchovy essence	5ml
1 tbsp	Chopped parsley	15ml

METHOD

1 Preheat the oven to 325F (170C) Gas 3.
2 Drain sardines, remove skin and bones. Reserve half the flesh, purée rest in blender. Peel and finely chop onion and fry in the butter. Add to purée with remaining ingredients and mix well.
3 Grease soufflé dish. Put in layer of purée then half sardines. Repeat layers, finishing with purée. Cover with foil, place in roasting tin with 1 inch (2.5cm) hot water. Bake for 1 hour, topping up water as necessary.
4 Run a knife round sides of dish, turn mousse on to serving dish.

Left: Chinese spring rolls – neat, fried parcels with tasty fillings

FISH

These dishes can all be made using either fresh or frozen fish. There is no need to thaw fish before cooking unless it is to be coated for frying; but if cooking from frozen, add a little extra cooking time

Fish au gratin

A classic way of cooking fish – with a cheese (mornay) sauce and fresh leaf spinach, prepared separately, then topped with cheese and crumbs

LUNCH OR SUPPER Serves 4

Overall timing 45 minutes

Equipment 3 saucepans, flameproof dish

Freezing Open freeze till firm, then wrap and label. Freezer life: 1 month. To use: remove wrappings and cook for 20 minutes in oven at 425F (220C) Gas 7, then reduce heat to 350F (180C) Gas 4 and bake for a further 20–30 minutes

INGREDIENTS

2lb	Fresh spinach	900g
4oz	Butter	125g
	Salt and pepper	
	Grated nutmeg	
1lb	Mixed white fish fillets	450g
$\frac{3}{4}$ pint	Milk	400ml
1oz	Plain flour	25g
4oz	Parmesan or Cheddar	125g
1 tbsp	Fresh breadcrumbs	15ml

METHOD

1 Wash spinach well in several lots of water. Remove any coarse stalks. Put into a saucepan with only the water that still clings to the spinach after washing. Add 3oz (75g) of the butter, salt, pepper and a pinch of nutmeg. Bring to the boil gently and cook for 5–10 minutes till tender. Drain well.

2 Put the fish fillets in a pan with the milk and a little salt. Bring to the boil, then cover and simmer for about 10 minutes or until the fish is tender. Drain, reserving poaching milk, and flake fish. Preheat the grill.

3 Melt the remaining 1oz (25g) butter in a pan. Stir in the flour and cook for 2 minutes. Gradually stir in the reserved milk and bring to the boil, stirring. Cook for 3 minutes, then remove from the heat.

4 Grate the cheese. Stir three-quarters of it into the sauce. Season with salt, pepper and nutmeg to taste.

5 Mix together the spinach, fish and half the sauce. Place in an ovenproof dish and cover with the rest of the sauce. Sprinkle with the remaining cheese and the breadcrumbs.

6 Place under the hot grill and cook till the top is crisp and golden.

Left: Fish au gratin – a tasty fish and spinach dish for lunch or supper

Fish hot-pot

A fish dish from Brittany, similar to the Mediterranean bouillabaisse, but with the broth served first as soup and the fish and vegetables following as a main meal. Bretons vary their choice of fish according to local availability but mullet, cod, bream, whiting, conger, even sardines, can all be included

SOUP AND MAIN MEAL — Serves 6

Overall timing 1 hour

Equipment Large, heavy-based saucepan

Freezing Omit garlic. Cool quickly, then pack fish into rigid containers and pour liquid over, leaving $\frac{3}{4}$ inch (2cm) headspace. Cover, label and freeze. Freezer life: 1 month. To use: reheat from frozen in a heavy-based saucepan, then add garlic and boil for 5 minutes

Below: Fish hot-pot, a nourishing two-course meal in one

INGREDIENTS

3lb	Mixed fish	1.4kg
2 pints	Water	1.1 litres
2lb	Potatoes	900g
2	Onions	2
2oz	Sorrel *or* spinach	50g
3	Leeks	3
2oz	Butter	50g
1 tbsp	Chopped fresh chervil *or*	15ml
1 teasp	Dried chervil	5ml
1 tbsp	Plain flour	15ml
$\frac{3}{4}$ pint	Muscadet	400ml
	Bouquet garni	
2 teasp	Salt	2×5ml
$\frac{1}{2}$ teasp	White pepper	2.5ml
2	Garlic cloves	2
2 tbsp	Chopped parsley	2×15ml
2 tbsp	Oil	2×15ml
2 tbsp	Wine or cider vinegar or lemon juice	2×15ml
6	Slices of brown bread	6

METHOD

1. Scale, gut and wash fish. Remove heads, fins and tails. Put fish trimmings in a pan with the water. Bring to the boil.
2. Cook for 10 minutes to make a fish stock. Strain and save the liquid.
3. Cut the fish into pieces. Peel and thickly slice the potatoes. Peel and finely chop the onions. Wash well, then chop the sorrel or spinach. Trim and chop leeks. Heat the butter in a heavy-based pan. Add the onions, sorrel or spinach, chervil and leeks. Cook gently for 2 minutes.
4. Sprinkle flour into pan and cook, stirring, for 2 minutes. Gradually stir in the fish stock and Muscadet and bring to the boil. Add potatoes, bouquet garni, salt and pepper, cover and simmer for 20 minutes.
5. Add the fish and the peeled and crushed garlic. Boil, uncovered, for 10 minutes or until the fish is tender but still attached to bones.

TO SERVE

Remove fish from pan with a draining spoon. Surround with the drained potato slices. Sprinkle with chopped parsley, oil and vinegar or lemon juice and keep warm. Place bread slices in a warmed tureen and pour over the fish stock and vegetables. Serve the soup and fish as separate courses.

Quenelles de poisson

Delicately-flavoured fish dumplings served in a creamy cheese sauce

STARTER OR LUNCH Serves 4

Overall timing 45 minutes plus chilling

Equipment Blender, bowl, 2 saucepans, piping bag with plain nozzle (optional), ovenproof dish

Freezing Pack into rigid container, cover, label and freeze. Freezer life: 1 month. To use: reheat from frozen in oven at 350F (180C) Gas 4

INGREDIENTS

1lb	Mixed fish fillets	450g
2	Egg whites	2
	Salt and pepper	
	Cayenne pepper	
2 tbsp	Single cream	2×15ml
	Sauce	
2½oz	Butter	65g
1 tbsp	Plain flour	15ml
1 pint	Cold milk	560ml
2oz	Grated Gruyère	50g
1 tbsp	Single cream	15ml
	Salt and pepper	

METHOD

1 Skin and wipe fish fillets. Cut into small pieces and put into a blender for a few seconds to make a thick purée.

2 Turn mixture into a bowl and beat in egg whites with a wooden spoon. Season with salt, pepper and a pinch of cayenne, then beat in the cream. Place in fridge for at least 1 hour.

3 Preheat oven to 425F (220C) Gas 7. Bring a pan of salted water to the boil. Using 2 spoons, make egg shapes from the fish mixture and carefully lower them, one at a time, into the simmering water. Alternatively, you can use a piping bag and then pipe mixture in short lengths into the water. Cook for 8–10 minutes, turning once. Remove from pan with a draining spoon, drain on kitchen paper and arrange in an ovenproof dish.

4 To make the sauce, melt 2oz (50g) of the butter in a pan. Stir in the flour and cook for 2 minutes. Gradually add the milk and bring to the boil, stirring. Cook over a low heat for 5 minutes. Remove from heat and stir in the cheese and cream. Season with salt and pepper.

5 Pour sauce into the ovenproof dish. Dot with remaining butter and bake in oven for about 10 minutes, or until the top is golden brown and bubbling.

Flemish-style haddock

Haddock baked with white wine and topped with crispy breadcrumbs

MAIN MEAL Serves 4

Overall timing 45 minutes

Equipment Ovenproof dish

Freezing Make as Steps 1–3. Open freeze, wrap and label. Freezer life: 3 months. To use: cook from frozen as Step 4, adding 15 minutes to cooking time

INGREDIENTS

2lb	Haddock fillets	900g
2	Lemons	2
3	Onions	3
1 tbsp	Chopped parsley	15ml
1 tbsp	Chopped fresh dill	15ml
	Salt and pepper	
¼ pint	Dry white wine	150ml
6 tbsp	Fresh breadcrumbs	6×15ml
2oz	Butter	50g

METHOD

1 Preheat the oven to 425F (220C) Gas 7. Grease ovenproof dish.

2 Wash haddock and pat dry on kitchen paper. Cut into 2 inch (5cm) pieces and place in bottom of dish.

3 Cut away the peel and pith and thinly slice the lemons. Peel and slice onions. Arrange lemon and onion slices on top of fish. Sprinkle with herbs, salt and pepper. Pour wine over and sprinkle breadcrumbs on top.

4 Dot with butter and bake in the oven for 25–30 minutes. Serve hot with buttered boiled potatoes and salad.

cook's know-how

Preheat the oven to 350F (180C) Gas 4. Put 4×6oz (175g) frozen haddock pieces into an ovenproof dish with a peeled and chopped onion. Season with salt and pepper. Add 2 tbsp (2×15ml) tomato paste mixed with ½ pint (300ml) dry white wine. Cover with lid or foil and bake for 30–40 minutes until tender. Serve with boiled potatoes or Jerusalem artichokes, and broccoli or other greens. **Serves 4**

Cod mornay

Cod fillets poached in white wine and lemon juice, then covered with a cheesey sauce and grilled to a beautiful golden brown

MAIN MEAL Serves 4

Overall timing 45 minutes

Equipment 2 saucepans, flameproof serving dish

Freezing Make the sauce as in Step 3, cool, then pour into rigid container. Cover, leaving headspace, label and freeze. Freezer life: 1 month. To use: cook frozen cod fillet without thawing. Reheat sauce gently from frozen in double saucepan. Complete as Step 4

INGREDIENTS

1¾ pints	Water	1 litre
½ pint	Dry white wine	300ml
1	Stalk of celery	1
1	Carrot	1
1	Slice of lemon	1
	Salt	
1¼lb	Cod fillet	600g
	Mornay sauce	
3oz	Butter	75g
2oz	Plain flour	50g
1 pint	Milk	560ml
	Pepper	
5oz	Grated Cheddar	150g

METHOD

1 In a large saucepan, put the water, wine, celery, carrot, washed and scraped, lemon and a little salt.

2 Wash and dry cod fillet and add to saucepan when water is boiling. Cover and simmer gently for about 20 minutes.

3 Meanwhile, make the sauce. Put 2oz (50g) of the butter in a small saucepan, heat gently till melted, then stir in flour and cook for 2 minutes. Gradually add milk, stirring all the time, until smooth. Add pepper to taste and bring to the boil. Boil for 3 minutes, then remove from heat and stir in 4oz (125g) of the cheese till well combined.

4 Preheat the grill. Lift cod from pan with draining spoon and place in serving dish. Cut fish in small pieces. Pour the sauce over, then sprinkle with the remaining cheese and dot with rest of butter. Place under grill for 5 minutes. Serve with sauté potatoes and broccoli.

Cod with cream sauce

Bite-size squares of cod simmered in a creamy sauce and served on a bed of crisp toast. This is a quick and easy recipe which would work well with frozen cod fillets

SUPPER Serves 4

Overall timing 40 minutes

Equipment Saucepan

Freezing After completing Step 3, cool, then pour into rigid container, cover, label and freeze. Freezer life: 1 month. To use: reheat gently from frozen in double saucepan till hot. Continue from Step 4

INGREDIENTS

$1\frac{1}{2}$lb	Cod fillets	700g
2oz	Butter	50g
2oz	Plain flour	50g
$\frac{1}{2}$ pint	Milk	300ml
8fl oz	Carton of single cream	227ml
2	Egg yolks	2
	Freshly-ground white pepper	
$\frac{1}{4}$ teasp	Nutmeg	1.25ml
$\frac{1}{4}$ teasp	Salt	1.25ml
8	Slices of bread	8
2 tbsp	Chopped parsley	2×15ml

METHOD

1 Remove skin from cod and cut cod into small squares.
2 To make the sauce, heat butter in a saucepan, stir in the flour, then add the milk all at once. Stir with a wooden spoon or whisk until sauce boils, then add cream and simmer for 5–10 minutes over a low heat.
3 Add cod pieces to sauce and cook gently for 15 minutes, stirring frequently.
4 Remove from heat, beat in egg yolks, pepper to taste, nutmeg and salt.
5 Cut crusts off bread and toast it. Arrange toast on hot serving dish, tip cod and sauce on to the toast and sprinkle with chopped parsley. Serve with boiled new potatoes and spinach.

VARIATION

This makes an ideal meal when time is short. Try adding 4oz (125g) lightly sautéed mushrooms to the sauce. A little white wine can also be used to add extra flavour.

Above: Halibut Dugléré – firm halibut steaks served with a creamy tomato-flavoured sauce

Halibut Dugléré

Named after a famous 18th century French chef, *à la dugléré* refers to a method of cooking white fish in white wine with shallots and tomatoes. The cooking liquor is thickened, cream is added, then the sauce is poured over the cooked steaks

MAIN MEAL Serves 4

Overall timing 45 minutes

Equipment Frying pan, ovenproof dish, small saucepan

Freezing Cook as Steps 1–3, then place in foil container. Cool, cover, label and freeze. Freezer life: 2 months. To use: reheat from frozen in oven at 425F (220C) Gas 7 for 30 minutes, then complete as Step 4

INGREDIENTS

1oz	Butter	25g
1	Chopped onion	1
1	Chopped shallot	1
2	Tomatoes	2
4	Halibut steaks	4
$\frac{1}{4}$ pint	Dry white wine	150ml
$\frac{1}{4}$ pint	Water	150ml
	Salt and pepper	
1 teasp	Cornflour	5ml
2 tbsp	Single cream	2×15ml
1 tbsp	Chopped parsley	15ml

METHOD

1 Preheat oven to 425F (220C) Gas 7.
2 In a frying pan, melt the butter, add onion and shallot and cook gently until golden. Blanch, peel and chop tomatoes. Add to the pan and cook for 5 minutes.
3 Pour mixture into ovenproof dish and place halibut steaks on top. Add wine and water and season with salt and pepper. Cover and cook in oven for 20–30 minutes.
4 Place halibut steaks on serving dish and keep warm. Pour sauce into small saucepan. Blend the cornflour with 1 tbsp (15ml) water and stir into the sauce. Boil for 2 minutes, stirring all the time. Remove from heat and stir in cream and parsley. Adjust seasoning. Pour the sauce over the fish and serve immediately with boiled potatoes and a green salad.

Trout topped with almonds

One of the most popular dishes on a menu – and very easy to prepare at home with frozen trout. The almonds are fried with the trout to add taste as well as texture

MAIN MEAL Serves 2

Overall timing 20 minutes

Equipment Large frying pan, serving dish

Freezing Not recommended for finished dish

INGREDIENTS

2	Frozen trout	2
1oz	Flour	25g
2oz	Butter	50g
	Freshly-ground salt and pepper	
2 tbsp	Chopped parsley	2×15ml
2oz	Flaked almonds	50g
2	Lemon slices	2

METHOD

1 Thaw and dry trout. Dust with flour.
2 Melt butter in frying pan. Add trout and cook gently on one side for 5 minutes.
3 Turn trout over with a fish slice. Add salt, pepper, half the parsley and the almonds.
4 Cook for a further 7–8 minutes until fish is tender and almonds are golden brown (turn them as they cook).

TO SERVE

Place on a warm serving dish and garnish with lemon slices and remaining chopped parsley. Serve with boiled potatoes and a side dish of mixed salad.

Below: Trout topped with almonds – very easy to prepare and to cook

Curried prawns

This dish is quickly made with prawns from the freezer, or you can keep a stock of the curry sauce frozen, ready to use. But in that case do not add the yogurt until the sauce is thawed

MAIN MEAL Serves 4

Overall timing 30 minutes

Equipment Flameproof casserole, bowl

Freezing Make as Steps 1 and 2. Cool, pack into rigid container, cover, label and freeze. Freezer life: 1 month. To use: reheat slowly from frozen and complete as Step 3

INGREDIENTS

1	Onion	1
1oz	Butter or ghee	25g
1lb	Frozen peeled prawns	450g
½ teasp	Ground turmeric	2.5ml
	Freshly-ground black pepper	
2 tbsp	Ground coriander	2×15ml
¼ teasp	Cayenne pepper	1.25ml
½ teasp	Salt	2.5ml
½ pint	Fish stock (page 51)	300ml
5oz	Carton of natural yogurt	141g

METHOD

1 Peel and thinly slice the onion. Heat the butter or ghee in the casserole and fry the onion gently, stirring occasionally, till golden brown.
2 Add the prawns to the casserole and fry for 2 minutes. Put the turmeric, black pepper, coriander, cayenne pepper and salt in a bowl and mix well. Sprinkle over the prawns and fry gently for 2 more minutes. Pour the stock over the prawns and bring to the boil.
3 Stir in the yogurt and simmer uncovered for 10 minutes. Adjust the seasoning and serve immediately with plain boiled rice and a side dish of mango chutney.

Kedgeree

In the days when a huge breakfast was a major event, kedgeree was a common sight on the sideboard. The dish is Anglo-Indian in origin, its name coming from the Indian word *khicharhi*

BRUNCH OR SUPPER Serves 4

Overall timing 40 minutes

Equipment 2 saucepans, frying pan

Freezing Cool, pack into rigid container, cover, label and freeze. Freezer life: 1 month. To use: reheat slowly from frozen

INGREDIENTS

6oz	Long grain rice	175g
	Salt	
1lb	Smoked haddock fillets	450g
3	Eggs	3
1	Onion	1
1	Green capsicum	1
3oz	Butter	75g
2 tbsp	Chopped parsley	2×15ml
¼ teasp	Cayenne pepper	1.25ml
	Pepper	

METHOD

1 Cook the rice in boiling salted water for 15–20 minutes until tender. Drain well.
2 Poach the haddock fillets in water in a frying pan for 10 minutes or until tender. Drain and flake, discarding skin.
3 Hard boil the eggs, drain and chop.
4 Peel and chop the onion. Wipe, deseed and chop capsicum. Heat the butter in a large pan and fry onions until just soft. Add capsicum and cook for 5 minutes.
5 Add the rice, flaked fish, chopped eggs, parsley and cayenne. Stir over a moderate heat for 5 minutes, season to taste and pile on to a warmed serving plate. Serve immediately.

VARIATION

For a mildly curried flavour, add 2 teasp (2×5ml) curry paste to the melted butter. Stir in 2 tbsp (2×15ml) each of sultanas, toasted flaked almonds and chopped mango chutney with the rice and omit the cayenne and parsley.

Russian fish pie

LUNCH OR SUPPER Serves 4

Overall timing 1 hour

Equipment 2 saucepans, baking tray

Freezing Make as Steps 1–5. Open freeze, then wrap and label. Freezer life: 1 month. To use: bake from frozen in oven at 425F (220C) Gas 7 for 30 minutes, then reduce heat to 350F (180C) Gas 4 and cook for a further 10–20 minutes

INGREDIENTS

7½oz	Packet of frozen puff pastry	212g
1lb	Fish fillets	450g
2 tbsp	Lemon juice	2×15ml
½ pint	Milk	300ml
2oz	Butter	50g
2 tbsp	Plain flour	2×15ml
4oz	Grated cheese	125g
1	Hard-boiled egg	1
	Salt and pepper	
1	Egg	1

METHOD

1 Thaw pastry. Preheat oven to 400F (200C) Gas 6.
2 Put fish, lemon juice and milk in a pan. Bring to the boil, then cover and poach gently for 10 minutes or until the fish is just tender. Drain, saving poaching liquor, and flake fish.
3 Heat butter in a saucepan. Stir in the flour and cook for 1 minute. Gradually stir in the reserved poaching liquor (made up to ½ pint/300ml with extra milk if necessary). Bring to the boil and cook for 3 minutes, stirring.
4 Remove from heat and stir in the grated cheese, chopped hard-boiled egg and flaked fish. Season well.
5 Roll out pastry on a floured surface to a large square. Place on baking tray. Put the fish mixture in the centre and brush the pastry edges with a little beaten egg. Draw corners up to the centre to form an envelope shape. Press together. Brush with beaten egg.
6 Bake for 30–40 minutes, until golden.

English fish pie

LUNCH OR SUPPER Serves 4

Overall timing 1¼ hours

Equipment 3 saucepans, ovenproof dish

Freezing Make as Steps 1–4, then wrap well, label and freeze. Freezer life: 1 month. To use: bake in oven at 425F (220C) Gas 7 for 20 minutes, then reduce heat to 350F (180C) Gas 4 and cook for a further 10–20 minutes

INGREDIENTS

2lb	Potatoes	900g
	Salt	
3 tbsp	Milk	3×15ml
3oz	Butter	75g
2lb	Fish fillets	900g
½ pint	Milk	300ml
2 tbsp	Plain flour	2×15ml
2 tbsp	Chopped parsley	2×15ml
	Salt and pepper	
3oz	Grated Red Leicester	75g

METHOD

1 Peel potatoes and cut into large chunks. Put into a pan of salted water, bring to the boil and cook for 15 minutes or until tender. Drain, then add the 3 tbsp (3×15ml) milk and 1oz (25g) of the butter and mash well.
2 Preheat oven to 400F (200C) Gas 6. Put the fish fillets in a pan with the remaining milk. Bring to the boil and poach gently for 10 minutes or until the fish is just tender. Drain, saving poaching milk, and flake fish.
3 Melt remaining 2oz (50g) butter in a pan. Stir in flour and cook for a minute. Gradually add reserved poaching liquor (made up to ½ pint/300ml with extra milk if necessary) and bring to the boil, stirring. Cook for 3 minutes.
4 Remove sauce from heat and stir in the flaked fish, chopped parsley, salt and pepper. Turn mixture into an ovenproof dish and cover with the mashed potato. Sprinkle with grated cheese.
5 Bake near the top of the oven for about 30 minutes until the top is golden brown. Serve immediately.

cook's know-how

White fish are the best to use for making pies. Mix several types of fish if you like, use up pieces you have left over or buy packets of frozen white fish fillets. It's best to use cheap fish such as coley because, in pies, it is flaked and mixed with other flavours which would be a waste of more expensive fish. Potatoes and cheese, which are popular additions to fish pies, make them into more substantial meals.

Fish lasagne

Although grey mullet is recommended in this recipe, you can substitute any flavourful oily fish – such as mackerel

MAIN MEAL Serves 4

Overall timing $1\frac{1}{4}$ hours

Equipment 2 flameproof dishes, saucepan, shallow ovenproof dish

Freezing Cook in rigid foil container. Cool, seal, label and freeze. Freezer life: 3 months. To use: cook from frozen at 350F (180C) Gas 4 for 1 hour until heated through

INGREDIENTS

$1\frac{1}{2}$lb	Grey mullet	700g
1	Onion	1
3fl oz	Oil	90ml
2	Garlic cloves	2
2 tbsp	Tomato paste	2×15ml
	Salt	
	Freshly-ground black pepper	
1lb	Fresh peas	450g
4oz	Mushrooms	125g
8oz	Lasagne	225g
2 tbsp	Grated Parmesan	2×15ml
2 tbsp	Chopped parsley	2×15ml
2 tbsp	Pinenuts	2×15ml

Left: Fish lasagne – fish is not normally associated with lasagne but it does make a tasty change. Here the pasta is layered with fish, tomatoes, onions, peas, mushrooms and pinenuts

1 Lightly fry onion in oil, add fish, fry for 5 minutes, then add tomato and season

2 Cook peas and mushrooms in another dish, add water and seasoning and bring to boil

3 Remove fish from its tomato sauce and cut into pieces, discarding bones

4 Return fish to tomato sauce. Mix with vegetables, pinenuts, parsley and Parmesan

5 Put third of lasagne in ovenproof dish, add third of fish mixture, another third of lasagne

6 Continue to make layers, sprinkling each with a little oil. Finish with a fish layer

METHOD

1 Clean and trim fish and cut into large pieces. Peel and chop onion.
2 Heat 3 tbsp (3×15ml) of oil in flameproof dish, add onion and fry until golden, then add fish and cook over medium heat for 5 minutes, turning once.
3 Peel and crush garlic cloves. Stir tomato paste into ¼ pint (150ml) of water and add to the dish with half the garlic, salt and pepper. Cover and cook gently for 10 minutes.
4 Shell peas. Wipe and slice mushrooms. Heat 2 tbsp (2×15ml) of oil in another flameproof dish, add peas, mushrooms and other half of garlic and cook over medium heat for 5 minutes. Add 3fl oz (90ml) of water, salt and pepper, cover and cook for 10 minutes.
5 Meanwhile, cook the lasagne in boiling salted water for 10–15 minutes or until al dente. Drain thoroughly and spread out on a damp cloth. Preheat oven to 350F (180C) Gas 4. Grease ovenproof dish.
6 Remove fish from flameproof dish and cut into pieces, discarding bones. Return to dish with mushroom mixture. Gradually stir in Parmesan, parsley and pinenuts. Adjust seasoning.
7 Line ovenproof dish with one-third of lasagne, cover with one-third of fish mixture and sprinkle with a little oil. Repeat layers, finishing with fish mixture. Sprinkle with oil and bake for 20 minutes or until heated through. Serve with green salad.

Above: Fish croquettes – small balls of white fish served with lemon wedges

Fish croquettes

Crisp on the outside, soft and tasty inside, these fish croquettes are a good freezer standby for a meal or snack. If you have a lot of fresh white fish make up a few batches and freeze them in meal-size amounts

LUNCH OR SUPPER Serves 8

Overall timing 45 minutes

Equipment Bowl, frying pan

Freezing Cool completely, then open freeze till hard, put in polythene bag or rigid container, seal and label. Freezer life: 1 month. To use: thaw overnight in fridge. Reheat in oven at 375F (190C) Gas 5 for about 20 minutes or fry for 5–10 minutes

INGREDIENTS

6	Slices of bread	6
½ pint	Warm milk	300ml
1¼lb	White fish fillets	600g
2oz	Softened butter	50g
2 tbsp	Chopped parsley	2×15ml
2	Eggs	2
	Salt and pepper	
¼ teasp	Grated nutmeg	1.25ml
3 tbsp	Plain flour	3×15ml
1oz	Butter	25g
3 tbsp	Oil	3×15ml
1	Lemon	1
	Fresh parsley	

METHOD

1 Soak the bread in the milk for about 10 minutes. Meanwhile, place fish in pan and cover with water or milk. Bring to the boil, then remove from heat.
2 Mash bread with a fork. Drain fish and flake, then add to the bread. Stir in softened butter and chopped parsley. Add the eggs and mix well together. Season with salt, pepper and grated nutmeg.
3 Shape the fish mixture into small balls, then roll in flour to coat.
4 Heat the butter and oil in a frying pan and cook the croquettes in batches until golden brown on all sides.
5 Remove from pan with a draining spoon. Drain on kitchen paper, arrange on serving plate and serve garnished with lemon wedges and parsley sprigs.

Put bread slices in a bowl and pour warm milk over. Leave to soak for 5 minutes

Add eggs to bind the mixture of bread, fish, butter and parsley and season well

Shape the fish mixture into small balls, then roll in flour to coat and shallow fry

Normandy fish stew

A prawn and mushroom sauce enhances the taste of the fish

MAIN MEAL Serves 6–8

Overall timing 2 hours

Equipment 2 saucepans

Freezing Make as Steps 1–5. Pack fish and stock in rigid container, cover, label and freeze. Freezer life: 1 month. To use: reheat slowly from frozen, then complete as Steps 6–8

INGREDIENTS

3lb	Mixed fish	1.4kg
$\frac{1}{2}$ pint	White wine	300ml
2	Onions	2
3	Leeks	3
	Bouquet garni	
	Salt and pepper	
$1\frac{1}{2}$ pints	Mussels	850ml
1	Stalk of celery	1
1oz	Butter	25g
$\frac{1}{4}$ pint	Water	150ml
	Sauce	
1oz	Butter	25g
1oz	Plain flour	25g
	Fish stock (page 51)	
8fl oz	Carton of single cream	227ml
4oz	Mushrooms	125g
4oz	Cooked prawns	125g
	Salt and pepper	
	Garnish	
2 tbsp	Chopped chervil	2×15ml

Above: Normandy fish stew – a dish of mixed seafood from Dieppe, on the Normandy coast of France

METHOD

1 Scale, gut and wash fish. Remove heads, fins and tails. Put fish trimmings in a saucepan with $3\frac{1}{2}$ pints (2 litres) water, white wine, peeled and chopped onions, 2 trimmed and chopped leeks, bouquet garni, salt and pepper. Bring to the boil, cover and cook for 30 minutes. Strain.

2 Scrub mussels under running water. Wash and chop celery. Trim and chop remaining leek.

3 Heat butter in a pan, add celery and leek and cook till soft. Add the mussels, water and salt. Cover and cook for 5 minutes, shaking pan occasionally. Remove mussels from pan with a draining spoon. Tap any which are closed; if they don't open, discard them. Strain cooking juices.

4 Combine fish stock and cooking juice from mussels in a large saucepan. Cut fish into pieces.

5 Cook fish in stock, starting with the fish with the firmest flesh and adding the others as you go along. When the fish are all cooked, remove from pan with a draining spoon, place in tureen and keep warm.

6 Strain stock and return to pan. Cook rapidly, uncovered, to reduce the quantity by half.

7 To make the sauce, melt the butter in a pan. Stir in the flour and cook for one minute. Gradually stir in stock. Bring to boil, stirring, and cook for 3 minutes.

8 Remove pan from heat and stir in cream, sliced mushrooms and most of the prawns, shelled (reserve a few unshelled for garnish). Return to heat and heat through gently for 3 minutes. Do not boil. Taste and adjust seasoning.

9 Pour sauce into tureen and garnish with reserved prawns and chopped chervil. Serve immediately.

Scallops in citrus sauce

Orange and lemon juice give the sauce its fruitiness and they are well set off by the spiciness of cloves and mace. Use frozen scallops if you prefer

MAIN MEAL Serves 4

Overall timing 40 minutes

Equipment Saucepan, bowl

Freezing Pack into rigid foil container, cover, label and freeze. Freezer life: 1 month. To use: remove lid, cover with foil and cook at 350F (180C) Gas 4 for 30 minutes

INGREDIENTS

$\frac{1}{4}$ pint	Dry white wine	150ml
$\frac{1}{4}$ pint	Water	150ml
2 teasp	White vinegar	2×5ml
2	Cloves	2
	Blade of mace	
6	Black peppercorns	6
$\frac{1}{4}$ teasp	Salt	1.25ml
16	Scallops on half shells	16
2oz	Butter	50g
2 teasp	Plain flour	2×5ml
2 tbsp	Orange juice	2×15ml
1 tbsp	Lemon juice	15ml
2 tbsp	Single cream	2×15ml

METHOD

1 Put the wine, water, vinegar, cloves, mace, peppercorns and salt into a saucepan. Bring to the boil and boil for 10 minutes.

2 Meanwhile, remove scallops from shells and gently wash and dry.

3 Add scallops to pan and simmer for 10 minutes till tender. Remove scallops with draining spoon and put into a serving dish. Keep hot.

4 Strain the liquid and measure it – it should be $\frac{1}{2}$ pint (300ml). If more, boil to reduce.

5 Mash the butter and flour in a bowl. Whisk small lumps of the mixture into the simmering liquid and cook till the sauce thickens.

6 Stir in the orange and lemon juice and the cream, then taste and adjust seasoning. Reheat without boiling. Pour over the scallops and serve immediately with creamed potatoes and broccoli.

Below: Scallops in citrus sauce – smooth and creamy fish and fruit combination

MEAT

With a few exceptions, meat dishes are best frozen with generous amounts of sauce or gravy. When reheating, thaw completely, bring to the boil and maintain the temperature at boiling point for at least 10 minutes

Braised fruity pork

Pork goes particularly well with sweet, fruity flavourings. Here it is cooked with apricots and sultanas and served with a nourishing, creamy vegetable purée – a pleasant change, worth trying with lamb or chicken

MAIN MEAL Serves 6

Overall timing 1½ hours plus overnight soaking

Equipment Bowl, flameproof casserole, saucepan, blender

Freezing Make as Steps 1–3. Cool, pack into rigid container, leaving ½ inch (12.5mm) headspace. Cover, label and freeze. Freezer life: 2 months. To use: reheat slowly from frozen, then complete from Step 4

INGREDIENTS

8oz	Dried apricots	225g
2lb	Lean pork	900g
1oz	Butter	25g
2 tbsp	Oil	2×15ml
	Salt	
	Freshly-ground black pepper	
	Bouquet garni	
½ pint	Light stock	300ml
5 tbsp	White wine vinegar	5×15ml
4oz	Sultanas	125g
	Vegetable purée	
1lb	Celeriac	450g
1	Large leek	1
8oz	Carrots	225g
1½lb	Large potatoes	700g
	Salt	
2oz	Butter	50g
¼ pint	Carton of single cream	150ml
	Freshly-ground white pepper	

METHOD

1 Cover the apricots with cold water and leave to soak overnight.
2 The next day, wipe and trim the pork and cut into bite-size pieces. Heat the butter and oil in the casserole and fry the pork till brown on all sides. Add salt, pepper, bouquet garni, stock (made with a cube if necessary) and vinegar and bring to the boil. Cover and simmer for 30 minutes.
3 Drain the apricots and add to the pork with the sultanas. Cover and simmer for a further 30 minutes.
4 Meanwhile, wash and prepare the vegetables. Chop into even-size pieces and put into a saucepan. Cover with cold salted water, bring to the boil and simmer for 20–25 minutes till tender.
5 Drain thoroughly, then mash well till creamy. Add the butter and cream and heat through, stirring, without boiling. Adjust the seasoning and put into a warmed serving dish.
6 Taste the pork and adjust seasoning. Serve from the casserole with the vegetable purée.

Gingered pork and apple casserole

The sweetness of the apple provides good contrast for the fiery taste of the ginger in this unusual casserole cooked on top of the stove. Ginger beer is the cooking liquor and the pork is simmered in it till tender. Capsicums are added at the end for crunch and colour

MAIN MEAL Serves 4

Overall timing 1½ hours

Equipment Large saucepan or flameproof casserole

Freezing Make as Steps 1–3. Cool, pack into rigid container, leaving ½ inch (12.5mm) headspace. Cover, label and freeze. Freezer life: 6 months. To use: reheat slowly from frozen, then complete as Step 4

INGREDIENTS

1½lb	Lean pork	700g
3 tbsp	Plain flour	3×15ml
1 teasp	Ground ginger	5ml
	Salt and pepper	
2	Large onions	2
3 tbsp	Oil	3×15ml
¾ pint	Ginger beer	400ml
1	Green capsicum	1
2	Medium-size cooking apples	2
¼ pint	Carton of soured cream	150ml

METHOD

1 Wipe and trim meat and cut into 1 inch (2.5cm) cubes. Sift the flour, ginger and seasonings on to a plate. Toss meat in the flour to coat evenly, shaking off any excess.
2 Peel and slice the onions. Heat the oil in a large saucepan or casserole and fry onions till just golden. Add pork, a few pieces at a time, and brown quickly on all sides.
3 Sprinkle any of the leftover flour mixture into the pan and cook, stirring, for 2 minutes. Gradually add the ginger beer and bring to the boil, stirring. Cover and simmer for 45 minutes.
4 Wipe, deseed and thinly slice capsicum. Peel, core and thickly slice apples. Add capsicum and apples to pan with the soured cream. Simmer gently for a further 15 minutes, but do not allow contents to boil.
5 Adjust seasoning and serve immediately with boiled rice or creamed potatoes.

Above: Sweet and sour pork with cucumber, an Indonesian-style dish full of flavour

Scrape carrots and cut into small chunks. Peel and chop the onions and the cucumber

Add prepared vegetables to the frying pan with the garlic and stir-fry for 5 minutes

Sweet and sour pork and cucumber

Pieces of pork marinated in sherry or Marsala, lightly coated with egg and flour, then cooked and served with vegetables and a rich sauce

MAIN MEAL Serves 4

Overall timing 40 minutes plus marination

Equipment 2 bowls, plate, large frying pan

Freezing Pack into rigid container, cover, label and freeze. Freezer life: 3 months. To use: reheat slowly from frozen

INGREDIENTS

1lb	Lean pork	450g
2 tbsp	Dry sherry or Marsala	2×15ml
	Salt and pepper	
1	Egg	1
3 tbsp	Plain flour	3×15ml
3 tbsp	Oil	3×15ml
2	Carrots	2
2	Onions	2
1	Large cucumber	1
1	Garlic clove	1
4 tbsp	Tomato ketchup	4×15ml
2 teasp	Soy sauce	2×5ml
2 tbsp	Vinegar	2×15ml
1 tbsp	Brown sugar	15ml
½ pint	Water	300ml
1 tbsp	Cornflour	15ml

METHOD

1 Cut meat into ½ inch (12.5mm) cubes or into wafer-thin slices. Put into a bowl with the sherry or Marsala, season with salt and pepper and leave to marinate for 30 minutes.

2 Lightly beat egg in a bowl. Put the flour on a plate.

3 Heat the oil in a large frying pan. Dip the pork pieces in the egg, then coat with flour. Add to frying pan and cook for 8 minutes till golden brown on all sides. Remove from pan.

4 Scrape and chop carrots. Peel and chop onions and cucumber. Add to frying pan with peeled and crushed garlic and stir-fry for 5 minutes over fairly high heat.

5 Reduce heat to moderate. Add ketchup, soy sauce, vinegar, sugar, water and reserved marinade to the pan. Blend the cornflour with a little cold water and stir into sauce. Bring to the boil and cook for 3 minutes, stirring.

6 Return pork to pan and cook for 3 minutes more till heated through.

TO SERVE

Serve with plain boiled rice and side dishes of tomato wedges, chunks of cucumber and a little desiccated coconut for sprinkling over the finished dish.

France's famous cassoulet

Various regions of southern France have differing versions of this great dinner-party meal and the flavours vary mainly according to which regional speciality has been added – tasty sausages or goose fat. If you're in France, check food stores for canned cassoulet beans which are preserved in goose fat. With these you'll be able to give your cassoulet an authentic flavour without all the cooking and soaking time

MAIN MEAL Serves 8

Overall timing 3½ hours plus soaking

Equipment Bowl, 2 large saucepans, large ovenproof casserole

Freezing Prepare cassoulet as Steps 1–5. Assemble in a suitable container. Cover, label and freeze. Freezer life: 2 months. To use: thaw overnight then proceed as Step 6

INGREDIENTS

1lb	Dried haricot beans	450g
1lb	Belly pork	450g
2	Medium onions	2
6	Cloves	6
2	Carrots	2
2	Garlic cloves	2
	Bouquet garni	
2 pints	Stock	1.1 litre
1 teasp	Salt	5ml
1lb	Boned shoulder of lamb	450g
2	Onions	2
1oz	Lard	25g
14oz	Can of tomatoes	397g
2 tbsp	Tomato paste	2×15ml
2	Bay leaves	2
	Pepper	
1lb	Garlic sausage *or*	450g
1lb	Pork ring	450g
4oz	Fresh breadcrumbs	125g

METHOD

1 Put the beans into a bowl, cover with cold water and leave to soak overnight.

2 Drain beans. Remove rind and dice belly pork. Peel onions and spike each one with 3 cloves. Scrape carrots and and cut in half. Crush garlic. Put them all into a large saucepan with the bouquet garni and stock (made with 3 cubes if necessary). Bring to the boil, then cover and simmer for 1 hour. Add salt.

3 Cut lamb into small pieces. Peel and chop onions. Melt the lard in a saucepan and when hot add the lamb and onions and fry until brown. Remove from heat and stir in the tomatoes, tomato paste, bay leaves and pepper. Bring to the boil. Cover and simmer for 30 minutes. Preheat oven to 325F (170C) Gas 3. Lightly grease ovenproof casserole.

4 Remove spiked onions and bouquet garni from the bean and pork mixture and discard. Remove carrots, cut into small pieces and return them to bean mixture.

5 Using a draining spoon, place a layer of beans and pork on the bottom of greased ovenproof casserole. Cover with half the lamb mixture. Dice sausage or slice pork ring and put half on top. Continue the layers finishing with a layer of beans (it should be no higher than two-thirds of casserole depth.) Pour over half the stock from pork and beans mixture and reserve the rest.

6 Sprinkle the breadcrumbs on top and cook, uncovered, in oven for 1 hour 40 minutes. Add a little more of the stock from the pork and beans if the cassoulet starts becoming too dry during cooking.

cook's know-how

The name of this famous Languedoc haricot bean stew came from the earthenware pot, the *cassol d'Issel*, in which it was cooked. There are many variations of the traditional cassoulet and in France you will find ingredients such as goose, duck, calves foot, pigs cheek and highly spiced local sausages added to the pork and lamb (or mutton). Outside mainland Europe it is less easy to buy portions of duck and goose, though if you have them you can incorporate them into the recipe. When these heavy, fatty meats are included, the fat is absorbed by the breadcrumbs and a thick, golden crust forms during the cooking. This crust should be broken up and gently mixed in a few times so that the taste and goodness goes through the whole dish. More breadcrumbs and stock can be added – a perfect cassoulet is succulent, not dry.

Below: Cassoulet – a marvellous combination of beans, pork, lamb and strong sausage

Iowa skillet chops

From the heart of America's corn belt comes this recipe for casseroling chops and sweet corn over an open fire. The secret is to use a skillet, which is a lidded frying pan (a heavy-based casserole will do just as well)

MAIN MEAL Serves 8

Overall timing 1 hour

Equipment Heavy-based flameproof casserole with lid, or deep frying pan with lid, blender

Freezing Cool, pack chops well covered by sauce in rigid container. Cover, label and freeze. Freezer life: 3 months. To use: thaw overnight in fridge, then heat gently but thoroughly

INGREDIENTS

8	Pork loin chops	8
	Salt	
	Freshly-ground black pepper	
3 tbsp	Oil	3×15ml
1lb 12oz	Can of tomatoes	794g
1 tbsp	Worcestershire sauce	15ml
1 tbsp	Tomato paste	15ml
1	Onion	1
11½oz	Can of sweet corn kernels	326g
1 tbsp	Arrowroot (optional)	15ml
	Parsley	

METHOD

1 Sprinkle chops with salt and pepper. Heat oil in casserole or frying pan and cook chops in 2 batches for 2 minutes on each side. When all chops are cooked, return first batch to casserole. Remove from heat.

2 Purée the tomatoes, juice, Worcestershire sauce and tomato paste in a blender, then pour over chops. Finely chop the onion and add with the drained corn (use some of the corn water if the mixture is too thick). Bring back to the boil and add salt and pepper.

3 Cover the casserole or frying pan and cook over moderate heat for 25 minutes. Remove lid to reduce sauce a little and cook for a further 10 minutes. Thicken with arrowroot, if you like, blended with a little hot water, and cook till clear. Garnish with parsley and serve straight from the casserole.

Above: Iowa skillet chops – pan fried pork chops in a rich tomato and corn sauce

Braised pork chops with cider

Cider, like beer or wine, comes into its own when used in a dish that's slowly cooked. And, as the flavours go on developing, this dish can be made the day before, then reheated thoroughly

MAIN MEAL Serves 4

Overall timing 2 hours

Equipment Flameproof casserole with tight-fitting lid

Freezing Cool, remove fat from surface, turn into rigid container. Cover with crumpled greaseproof to keep meat under liquid and prevent from drying out. Cover, label and freeze. Freezer life: 2 months. To use: reheat gently from frozen in flameproof pan until hot

INGREDIENTS

2	Onions	2
6	Tomatoes	6
2oz	Lard	50g
4	Pork chump chops	4
	Salt and pepper	
¼ pint	Dry cider	125ml

METHOD

1 Preheat oven to 325F (170C) Gas 3.

2 Peel and chop onions. Blanch, peel and slice tomatoes. Heat lard in casserole, add chops and brown on both sides. Remove from casserole.

3 Fry onions for about 3 minutes, add tomatoes and seasoning and cook for a few more minutes.

4 Place meat on vegetables and pour cider over. Cover and cook in the oven for about 1½ hours. Serve with jacket potatoes – cooked near top of oven.

cook's know-how

Cider can be used in any recipe which calls for wine – substitute dry cider for dry wine, and sweet for sweet wine. It doesn't matter whether the cider is still, effervescent or even flat as it's the flavour that counts. This becomes more concentrated when the cider is boiled so that it reduces and thickens (the alcohol evaporates at the same time). When cooking with cider, use enamelled or aluminium pans – tin or unlined cast iron turns the liquid black.

Left: Pork chops charcutière – fried pork in a wine and tomato sauce with gherkins

Pork chops charcutière

French *charcutiers* are cooked meat specialists handling mainly pork products. The charcutière sauce, therefore, is a sauce to accompany fried or grilled pork, and its principal ingredients are white wine and gherkins (or *cornichons*), sliced into rounds

MAIN MEAL Serves 4

Overall timing 30 minutes

Equipment Large frying pan

Freezing Prepare sauce as Steps 2 and 3. Pour into rigid container, cool, cover, label and freeze. Freezer life: 3 months. To use: reheat sauce gently from frozen, cook chops as Step 1 and complete

INGREDIENTS

1oz	Butter	25g
4	Pork chops	4
	Salt and pepper	
1	Onion	1
3fl oz	Dry white wine	90ml
3fl oz	Water	90ml
1 tbsp	Tomato paste	15ml
6	Gherkins	6
1 tbsp	Chopped parsley	15ml
1 teasp	Prepared mustard	5ml

METHOD

1. Melt the butter in the frying pan and cook the pork chops gently for 10–12 minutes on each side. Season. Place on warmed serving dish and keep warm.
2. Peel and finely chop onion, add to pan and leave to soften for a few minutes without browning. Add wine, water, tomato paste, salt and pepper and bring to boil, stirring. Simmer for 3 minutes.
3. Remove pan from heat. Finely slice 2 of the gherkins and stir into the sauce with the parsley and mustard.

TO SERVE
Pour sauce over chops. Garnish with remaining gherkins, cut into fan shapes, and serve with macaroni or noodles.

Curried chops

This is a mild and fruity curry rather than a hot and pungent one, and it is accompanied by fried pineapple rings and a sweet, lemony sauce. There is no curry powder in the sauce – the yellow colour comes from the turmeric

MAIN MEAL Serves 6

Overall timing $1\frac{1}{4}$ hours

Equipment Large frying pan with lid, blender or sieve, small frying pan

Freezing Make as Steps 1–4, but omit cream from sauce. Cool, pack chops in the sauce and uncooked pineapple rings into separate rigid containers, cover, label and freeze. Freezer life: 3 months. To use: thaw overnight in fridge. Reheat gently for 15–20 minutes, stirring occasionally, then proceed as Step 5

Below: Curried chops – pork, mildly curried, and sweetened with canned fruit

INGREDIENTS

6	Pork loin or rib chops	6
	Salt and pepper	
2 teasp	Curry powder	2×5ml
1½oz	Coconut oil	40g
1	Onion	1
½ pint	Chicken stock	300ml
1 tbsp	Lemon juice	15ml
	Sauce	
	Pineapple juice (see garnish)	
	Grated rind of ½ a lemon	
1 teasp	Sugar	5ml
1 teasp	Turmeric	5ml
2 tbsp	Cornflour	2×15ml
2 tbsp	Water	2×15ml
2 tbsp	Single cream	2×15ml
	Garnish	
15oz	Can of pineapple rings	425g
1oz	Butter	25g
½oz	Coconut oil	15g
4oz	Bottle of sweet cocktail cherries	110g
	Parsley	

METHOD

1 Sprinkle chops with salt, pepper and curry powder. Heat coconut oil in a frying pan till very hot, add chops, cooking them 3 at a time, and brown for 3 minutes on each side.

2 Peel and chop onion and add to pan. Cook till transparent, then pour in the stock (made with a stock cube if necessary) and lemon juice, cover and simmer for 30 minutes. Remove chops from pan and keep warm.

3 To make the sauce, drain pineapple and make up can juice to ½ pint (300ml) with water. Add juice to the pan and bring to the boil. Blend sauce for a few seconds or press through a sieve. Return to pan and add the finely grated lemon rind.

4 Simmer for a few minutes and add sugar and turmeric. Mix the cornflour with the water in a cup and stir into the sauce. Heat through well, then remove from heat and stir in cream. Keep the sauce warm.

5 Dry pineapple rings on kitchen paper. Heat butter and oil in a small frying pan and fry pineapple rings on both sides till golden.

TO SERVE

Arrange chops on a serving dish with boiled rice down the sides. Garnish with pineapple rings, cherries and a few sprigs of parsley. Pour some of the sauce over and serve the rest separately.

Espagnole-based sauces

Use the basic Espagnole sauce, page 26, to make these rich sauces for grilled or fried chops and steaks. The quantities given are for 1 pint (560ml) Espagnole sauce

BOURGUIGNONNE Cook 1 small chopped onion in 1oz (25g) butter till transparent. Add ½ pint (300ml) red wine and a bouquet garni and boil till reduced to one-third. Add to **Espagnole sauce,** strain and stir in 1oz (25g) butter.

NAPOLITAINE Add 1 tbsp (15ml) each of grated horseradish and chopped lean ham to **Espagnole sauce** with 4 tbsp (4×15ml) each Madeira and consommé and a bouquet garni. Simmer for 30 minutes, strain and add 2 tbsp (2×15ml) redcurrant jelly.

PORTUGAISE Add one strip each of orange and lemon rind to **Espagnole sauce** with 1 teasp (5ml) each of coriander seeds and sugar and 4 tbsp (4×15ml) consommé. Simmer for 30 minutes, strain and add 4 tbsp (4×15ml) Malaga wine, a few drops lemon juice and 1oz (25g) butter.

RAVIGOTE BRUNE Fry 1 chopped onion in 1oz (25g) butter. Add to **Espagnole sauce** with a peeled and crushed garlic clove, 6 tbsp (6×15ml) Chablis, 1 tbsp (15ml) each of capers and consommé and 1 teasp (5ml) crushed peppercorns. Simmer for 30 minutes, strain and add 1 teasp (5ml) Dijon mustard.

VENAISON Put ¼ pint (150ml) Burgundy into a saucepan with 2 tbsp (2×15ml) each of vinegar and sugar, 4 tbsp (4×15ml) redcurrant jelly and the flesh of ½ a lemon. Simmer for 10 minutes, strain and add to **Espagnole sauce.**

VICTORIA Add ¼ pint (150ml) port, 3 tbsp (3×15ml) redcurrant jelly and a strip of orange rind to **Espagnole sauce** with 3 cloves, 6 peppercorns and a cinnamon stick. Simmer for 30 minutes, and add juice of 1 orange. Strain and add pinch of cayenne.

Demi-glace

Espagnole sauce with the addition of a rich, brown stock and Madeira. Using a good bone stock ensures full strength of flavour and a gelatinous quality which is lacking in stock made with cubes. Poultry carcasses, together with a few giblets, can be used as can game trimmings

Wipe and chop 1lb (450g) marrow bone or knuckle of veal. Wipe 1lb (450g) shin of beef, cut into cubes. Heat 1oz (25g) dripping in large pan, add bones, meat, 1 sliced carrot and 1 sliced onion and fry, stirring, till the meat is browned all over

Add 2 pints (1.1 litres) water, bay leaf, bouquet garni and seasoning. Bring to the boil, cover and simmer for 2 hours. Pour off stock into large pan, boil rapidly till reduced by half. Sprinkle 1 tbsp (15ml) plain flour over meat in pan

Fry, stirring, for 2 minutes, then gradually add reduced stock. Bring to boil, stirring. Remove from heat and lift out bones. Rub through a sieve into Espagnole sauce. Boil till reduced by half. Add 4 tbsp (4×15ml) Madeira, then season to taste

Ham and stout roast

A succulent joint which is given colour with stout and taste with caraway – a herb often used in dishes cooked with beer

MAIN MEAL Serves 6

Overall timing $2\frac{1}{2}$ hours plus cooling time

Equipment Ovenproof casserole, saucepan

Freezing Cool meat and sauce separately. Slice meat, place in foil container with slices overlapping. Pour sauce over and cover securely. Label and freeze. Freezer life: 2 months. To use: heat from frozen in moderate oven

INGREDIENTS

3lb	Lightly salted ham or bacon (collar, slipper, or gammon)	1.4kg
2	Onions	2
$\frac{1}{2}$ pint	Stout	300ml
1oz	Margarine	25g
1oz	Plain flour	25g
$\frac{1}{4}$ teasp	Crushed caraway seed	1.25ml
	Freshly-ground black pepper	

METHOD

1 Preheat oven to 400F (200C) Gas 4.

2 Wash and dry ham. If using bacon joint, remove rind. Place in an ovenproof casserole. Peel onions and slice into rings. Cover ham with onion rings. Pour stout over. Roast, uncovered, for 2 hours, turning meat once during cooking.

3 Remove meat from casserole, place on serving dish and sieve liquor from casserole. Cool quickly, then skim fat from surface. Place liquor in measuring jug and make up to $\frac{1}{2}$ pint (300ml) with water if necessary.

4 Heat margarine in saucepan. Stir in flour and allow to brown lightly. Gradually add liquid, stirring mixture to make a smooth, thick sauce. Season with crushed caraway seed and black pepper. Cook for 5 minutes then pour over the roast and serve.

Above: Ham and stout roast – a beautiful thick sauce flavoured with caraway is made from the liquor in which the ham is cooked

Bacon and onion pie

Layers of fried onion and bacon in a puff pastry case – with cabbage and potatoes, this savoury pie makes a simple, filling winter meal

MAIN MEAL Serves 4

Overall timing $1\frac{1}{4}$ hours

Equipment Baking tray, frying pan, 8 inch (20cm) flan tin or deep pie plate, bowl

Freezing Open freeze till firm. Remove from tin or plate, foil-wrap, seal and label. Freezer life: 1 month. To use: replace in tin or plate, cover with foil, and reheat at 350F (180C) Gas 4 for about 25 minutes, uncovering for last 5 minutes

INGREDIENTS

13oz	Packet of frozen puff pastry	375g
$1\frac{1}{2}$lb	Onions	700g
3oz	Butter	75g
12oz	Back bacon rashers	350g
	Salt	
	Freshly-ground black pepper	
1	Egg yolk	1

METHOD

1 Thaw the pastry. Preheat the oven to 400F (200C) Gas 6. Put a baking tray near the top of the oven to heat up.

2 Peel and thinly slice the onions into rings. Heat 2oz (50g) of the butter in a frying pan and fry the onions till golden. Remove from the pan and reserve. Derind the bacon and lightly fry the rashers in the remaining butter.

3 Roll out two-thirds of the pastry on a floured surface and use to line the flan tin or plate. Prick the base with a fork.

4 Spread half the reserved onions over the pastry base and cover with half the bacon rashers. Repeat the layers, seasoning between each one.

5 Roll out the remaining pastry and cover the pie, sealing the edges well. Beat the egg yolk and brush over the pastry. Stand the pie on the baking tray and cook for 20 minutes.

6 Reduce oven temperature to 350F (180C) Gas 4. Cover pie lightly with foil if top is golden brown and cook for a further 15–20 minutes till well risen and golden. Serve hot, cut into wedges, with creamed potatoes and wedges of buttered cabbage.

Cider-glazed ham

Special occasion party dish – the ham is first simmered in cider until nearly cooked, then skinned, glazed with cider and mustard and roasted

MAIN MEAL Serves 6–8

Overall timing $2\frac{1}{2}$ hours plus overnight soaking

Equipment Large saucepan, meat thermometer (optional), roasting tin, pastry brush

Freezing Cut ham into thick slices. Separate each slice with greaseproof paper and pack in polythene bag. Seal, label and freeze. Freezer life: 1 month. To use: thaw in wrapping in fridge for about 3 hours

INGREDIENTS

$4\frac{1}{2}$lb	Gammon joint	2kg
6	Peppercorns	6
1	Bay leaf	1
$2\frac{1}{2}$ pints	Dry cider	1.5 litres
2oz	Molasses or raw cane sugar	50g
1 tbsp	Prepared coarse-grained mustard	15ml

METHOD

1 Soak the ham overnight in water.

2 Drain ham and place in saucepan with the peppercorns and bay leaf. Cover with the cider.

3 Bring slowly to the boil and simmer for $1\frac{1}{2}$ hours (or until internal temperature reaches 350F/180C). Skim fat from surface from time to time. When the ham has been cooking for $1\frac{1}{4}$ hours, preheat the oven to 450F (230C) Gas 8.

4 Remove ham from saucepan and cut off the rind (if necessary, insert skewer and tie ham with string to get a good shape). Dry ham on kitchen paper and place in roasting tin.

5 Mix the sugar and mustard with 2 teasp (2×5ml) of the cider stock to make a stiffish paste. Brush it over the ham and bake at the top of the oven for 8–10 minutes, or until the sugar bubbles and becomes dark and glossy. (Chill the remaining cider stock overnight, then skim the surface to remove the fat, it can then be used as a well-flavoured base for sauces, soups and glazes.)

6 Baste ham with juices in roasting tin. Move to the bottom shelf of the oven and cook for a further 10 minutes. Serve hot or cold with peach halves stuffed with cream or cottage cheese and a green salad.

Wiener schnitzel

Crisply crumbed escalopes of veal make a simple, attractive meal. Serve with lemon for added flavour

MAIN MEAL Serves 4

Overall timing 25 minutes plus chilling time

Equipment 3 shallow bowls, large flat dish, large frying pan

Freezing Prepare and freeze raw. Wrap in polythene with foil separating slices. Exclude air, seal, label and freeze. Freezer life: 3 months. To use: leave to thaw and cook for 2–3 minutes on each side

INGREDIENTS

4×5oz	Slices of veal	4×150g
	Salt	
2 tbsp	Plain flour	2×15ml
1	Egg	1
2oz	Breadcrumbs	50g
1oz	Butter	25g
2oz	Pork dripping	50g
2	Lemons	2
	Sprigs of parsley	

METHOD

1 Rinse veal slices and dry well on kitchen paper. Mix salt and flour together in a bowl. Beat egg in another bowl. Place breadcrumbs in a third bowl.

2 Dip veal slices into flour, then into the egg and finally coat both sides with breadcrumbs. If possible, chill for 30 minutes on a large flat dish to help the egg and crumb layer adhere.

3 Heat butter and pork dripping in a large frying pan. Add slices two at a time and cook for 2–3 minutes on each side. Place on a warmed serving plate and garnish with lemon slices and parsley. Serve wedges of lemon separately.

cook's know-how

Fresh breadcrumbs need to be made from a whole loaf, and you will find them easier to make if you have a blender. Dried crumbs can be made from stale bread slices. Leave them in an oven to dry then grate them or put them in a blender.
Fresh or dried crumbs keep well in the freezer, packed in a polythene bag. Thaw them for 30 minutes before use. Mix with chopped fresh herbs or grated Parmesan for extra flavour.

Above: Escalopes in ginger sauce – a splendidly different dish for a midweek meal

Escalopes in ginger sauce

Tender pieces of veal are enhanced by a sauce flavoured with ground ginger, thyme and lemon. You can use pork or fish fillets if you prefer

MAIN MEAL Serves 4

Overall timing 40 minutes

Equipment Bowl, frying pan

Freezing Cool, then pack into rigid container. Cover, label and freeze. Freezer life: 2 months. To use: heat from frozen in oven at 325F (170C) Gas 3

INGREDIENTS

2	Onions	2
4 tbsp	Oil	4×15ml
2 tbsp	Lemon juice	2×15ml
½ teasp	Dried thyme	2.5ml
	Salt and pepper	
1 teasp	Ground ginger	5ml
1lb	Escalopes of veal	450g
3 tbsp	Plain flour	3×15ml
1oz	Butter	25g
1 tbsp	Tomato paste	15ml
½ pint	Stock	300ml
2oz	Tongue	50g
1oz	Ham	25g
1oz	Button mushrooms	25g

METHOD

1 Peel and chop the onions. Put into a bowl with 2 tbsp (2×15ml) of the oil, the lemon juice, thyme, salt, pepper and ginger. Mix together, then add the slices of veal, cut in half. Marinate in fridge for 15–30 minutes.

2 Remove veal from marinade and dry with kitchen paper. Coat well with 2 tbsp (2×15ml) of the flour. In frying pan, heat remaining oil with butter, add veal and cook gently on both sides till brown but not crisp.

3 Remove veal with draining spoon and set aside. Stir remaining flour into pan, and gradually add tomato paste, strained marinade and stock (made with cube if necessary). Cut the tongue, ham and mushrooms into fine strips and add to the pan with the veal. Cook for 10 minutes till sauce is thick.

TO SERVE

Place in warmed serving dish and serve with rice or thick slices of crusty bread and a crisp green salad.

cook's know-how

Choose Emmenthal or Gruyère when you want a cheese that will melt creamily and remain tasty when hot. Their smooth, creamy texture is ideal in a dish such as Escalopes cordon-bleu, below.

Above: Escalopes cordon-bleu – crispy crumbed coating and Emmenthal melting inside

Escalopes cordon-bleu

Veal escalopes filled with ham and cheese – a culinary speciality invented by a Swiss master chef. Louis XV first bestowed the "blue band" *(cordon bleu)* on Madame Du Barry's cook and since then the title has been awarded to cooks of special merit. The escalopes must be thick and a sharp knife is essential for slicing each one through

MAIN MEAL Serves 4

Overall timing 35 minutes plus chilling time

Equipment 3 shallow dishes, baking tray, frying pan

Freezing Make to Step 3. Open freeze, then wrap escalopes in polythene, with foil to separate each one. Seal and label. Freezer life: 3 months. To use: thaw overnight in fridge, remove wrappings and cook as Step 4

INGREDIENTS

4×7oz	Thick veal escalopes	4×200g
	Salt	
	White pepper	
4	Slices of ham	4
4	Slices of Emmenthal	4
2 tbsp	Flour	2×15ml
2	Eggs	2
3 tbsp	Breadcrumbs	3×15ml
2oz	Butter	50g
2 tbsp	Oil	2×15ml
1	Lemon	1
1	Tomato	1

Slice veal almost through, season, insert ham and cheese. Close with cocktail sticks

Coat escalopes first with flour, then beaten eggs and finally with crumbs. Pat them on well

METHOD

1. Slice each piece of veal lengthways leaving them attached at one side. Season inside with salt and pepper. Put a slice of ham and a slice of cheese inside each and close one side with cocktail sticks.
2. Put flour in one dish, beaten egg in another and breadcrumbs in the other.
3. Coat the veal pieces first in flour, then in egg and finally in breadcrumbs. Place on baking tray and chill if possible for 30 minutes.
4. Heat butter and oil in a frying pan. Cook escalopes, two at a time, for 6–8 minutes on each side. Keep them warm on the serving dish then, when all are cooked, remove cocktail sticks, garnish with lemon and tomato and serve.

Chill for 30 minutes, cook two at a time in heated oil and butter for 6–8 minutes a side

Veal chops milanese

From Milan in Italy comes this method of preparing meat. Here veal is used but any chop can be cooked in the same way. Grated Parmesan is mixed with breadcrumbs but Gruyère, or any other hard, strong cheese can be used instead

MAIN MEAL Serves 4

Overall timing 25 minutes

Equipment 2 bowls, large frying pan

Freezing Complete Step 3. Open freeze chops till firm. Pack in rigid container, interleaving each chop with foil or greaseproof, cover, label, freeze. Freezer life: 6 months. To use: thaw overnight in fridge. Continue from Step 4

INGREDIENTS

4	Veal chops	4
2	Eggs	2
	Salt and pepper	
3 tbsp	Oil	3x15ml
4oz	Breadcrumbs	125g
2oz	Grated Gruyère or Parmesan	50g
	Flour	
2oz	Butter	50g
	Sprigs of parsley	

METHOD

1 Remove excess fat from chops. Wash and dry them on kitchen paper.

2 Beat eggs in a bowl with salt and pepper to taste and 1 tbsp (15ml) of the oil. Put breadcrumbs and grated cheese in another bowl.

3 Lightly flour the chops and dip first in the beaten egg and then in the breadcrumb mixture to cover them completely. Turn them several times and press breadcrumbs on to chops with a knife to help them stick.

4 Heat butter and remaining oil in a large frying pan. Add chops and cook for 5–6 minutes on each side over a moderate heat. Transfer to a warmed serving plate, garnish with sprigs of parsley and serve at once with boiled potatoes and broccoli.

1 Carefully trim the chops, removing any excess fat with a sharp knife. Rinse the chops under running water, then dry and lightly flour both sides

2 In a shallow dish beat eggs with salt, pepper and oil till well combined. Dip chops, one at a time, into the mixture, making sure both sides are coated

3 Place chops in mixture of breadcrumbs and grated cheese and turn several times till well coated

4 Heat butter and oil in frying pan and cook chops on both sides over moderate heat – cook 2 at a time if pan is small

Right: Veal chops milanese – a cheese and crumb coating for crispy, fried veal chops

Veal Marengo

This dish which gets its name from a Napoleonic battle features a rich sauce made with white wine, tomatoes, herbs and vegetables

MAIN MEAL Serves 4

Overall timing 2 hours

Equipment Large pan or flameproof casserole

Freezing Cool quickly after cooking, seal in a foil container, label and freeze. Freezer life: 1 month. To use: thaw at room temperature for about 6 hours, heat in oven at 375F (190C) Gas 5

INGREDIENTS

1lb	Stewing veal	450g
1oz	Butter	25g
1 tbsp	Oil	15ml
3	Shallots	3
1	Carrot	1
1oz	Plain flour	25g
4	Ripe tomatoes	4
4oz	Button onions	125g
1 teasp	Tomato paste	5ml
4fl oz	Dry white wine	120ml
4fl oz	Water	120ml
2	Garlic cloves	2
	Bouquet garni	
1 teasp	Salt	5ml
	Freshly-ground black pepper	
4oz	Mushrooms	125g

METHOD

1 Cut the veal into pieces. Heat the butter and oil in pan or flameproof casserole. Add the veal and brown on all sides over a high heat. Chop the shallots, scrape and slice carrots and add to pan.

2 Sprinkle with flour. Stir with wooden spoon until flour turns golden.

3 Blanch, peel and chop the tomatoes, peel the onions and add to the pan with tomato paste, white wine, water, crushed garlic, bouquet garni, salt and pepper. Cover and simmer for $1\frac{1}{2}$ hours over a low heat.

4 Wipe and slice mushrooms and add to pan. Cover and cook for a further 15 minutes, stirring occasionally.

5 Remove bouquet garni. Either serve in the casserole or transfer meat and sauce to a warmed serving dish. Serve with buttered noodles, mashed potatoes or plain, boiled rice.

CHICKEN MARENGO

The original dish prepared by Napoleon's cook contained only the foods he could find in Marengo, in Northern Italy, at the time. Use $1\frac{1}{2}$lb (700g) chicken pieces and follow the recipe for Veal Marengo. To make it truly traditional, steam crayfish above the chicken while cooking and serve it together with fried eggs as a garnish – rather hefty but obviously just the thing to follow a strenuous battle.

Right: Veal Marengo – variation on a theme. The original dish was made with chicken

Beef stew

Fry vegetables like onions, celery and carrots with the meat to ring the changes on this basic beef stew. Or, replace some of the stock with wine or beer, adding tomato paste, mustard, Worcestershire sauce or horseradish for a touch of piquancy

MAIN MEAL Serves 6

Overall timing 1 hour 45 minutes

Equipment Flameproof casserole

Freezing Reduce cooking time to 1 hour. Cool completely and pour into foil container, ensuring meat is covered with gravy. Cover, label and freeze. Freezer life: 6 months. To use: place frozen stew in casserole, heat gently till thawed. Adjust seasoning

INGREDIENTS

2lb	Chuck steak	900g
	Salt	
	Freshly-ground black pepper	
3 tbsp	Plain flour	3×15ml
2oz	Dripping	50g
1 pint	Beef stock	560ml
	Bouquet garni	

METHOD

1 Wipe and trim the meat and cut into 1 inch (2.5cm) cubes. Season the flour and toss the meat in it till lightly coated. Reserve any excess flour.

2 Heat the dripping in the casserole, add the meat and fry, stirring, over a moderate heat till browned all over. Sprinkle in reserved flour and fry for 3 minutes till lightly browned.

3 Gradually add the stock (made with cubes if necessary) and bring to the boil, stirring constantly. Add the bouquet garni, season and mix well.

4 Cover and simmer for 1½ hours, or cook in the centre of the oven preheated to 350F (180C) Gas 4 for 1½ hours.

5 Remove the bouquet garni, adjust the seasoning to taste and serve immediately with creamed potatoes and wedges of buttered cabbage.

Goulash

As *gulyàs*, it is the national dish of Hungary; as goulash it is better known as a tasty beef stew. The capsicums, paprika and caraway seeds give it its special flavour

MAIN MEAL Serves 6

Overall timing 2¼ hours

Equipment Large saucepan or casserole with tight-fitting lid

Freezing Cool rapidly, pack in freezer container leaving 1 inch (2.5cm) headspace. Seal, label and freeze. Freezer life: 3 months. To use: thaw over gentle heat, bring to boiling point and simmer for 10 minutes

INGREDIENTS

2lb	Stewing beef	900g
2oz	Pork dripping	50g
8oz	Onions	225g
2	Garlic cloves	2
1 tbsp	Plain flour	15ml
1	Beef stock cube	1
1 pint	Boiling water	560ml
	Salt	
	Freshly-ground black pepper	
½ teasp	Marjoram	2.5ml
½ teasp	Caraway seed	2.5ml
	Brown sugar	
2 teasp	Paprika	2×5ml
8oz	Potatoes	225g
2	Green capsicums	2
5	Tomatoes	5
¼ pint	Red wine	150ml
¼ pint	Carton of soured cream (optional)	150ml

METHOD

1 Wash, dry and cube beef. Heat dripping in a large saucepan or casserole. Add beef and sauté, stirring continuously, till meat is brown on all sides. Peel and chop onion and garlic. Add to meat and cook till transparent.

2 Sprinkle in flour and stir into mixture. Mix stock cube into boiling water and pour over meat. Season with salt, pepper, marjoram, caraway seed, a pinch of sugar and paprika. Cover tightly and cook gently for 1¼ hours.

3 Peel and roughly chop the potatoes. Wash and deseed capsicums and slice. Blanch, peel and chop tomatoes. Add all to pan, cover and cook for a further 25 minutes. Add wine and check seasoning. Bring to simmering point, stir in soured cream, if using, or serve it separately.

Left: Goulash — world famous beef stew named after Hungarian cowherders who invented it

Above: Swiss-style beef casserole — complete with vegetables

Above: Beef ragoût — red and green capsicums add colour

Swiss-style beef casserole

Flavourful combination of wine, paprika, tomatoes, cloves and garlic

MAIN MEAL Serves 4

Overall timing $2\frac{1}{4}$ hours

Equipment Large flameproof casserole

Freezing Omit potatoes. Cook and leave to cool. Place meat and carrots in a deep foil container, and pour liquid over. Leave $\frac{3}{4}$ inch (2cm) headspace, cover, label and freeze. Freezer life: 4–6 months. To use: heat slowly but thoroughly, from frozen

INGREDIENTS

2lb	Blade-bone or skirt	900g
4 tbsp	Oil	4×15ml
3 tbsp	Plain flour	3×15ml
1 tbsp	Paprika	15ml
4	Large onions	4
2	Garlic cloves	2
2 tbsp	Tomato paste	2×15ml
$\frac{1}{4}$ pint	Red wine	150ml
12fl oz	Hot beef stock	350ml
	Salt and pepper	
	Pinch of sugar	
3	Bay leaves	3
4	Cloves	4
1lb	Small potatoes	450g
12oz	Young carrots	350g

METHOD

1 Wash and dry meat. Bash meat with a rolling-pin. Cut into cubes.

2 Heat the oil in the casserole. Add the cubed meat, brown for 10 minutes on all sides, then sprinkle with flour and paprika. Turn mixture over with wooden spoon.

3 Peel and chop onions, peel and crush garlic, and add both to the casserole.

4 Blend tomato paste with the red wine and stir into casserole. Cook for 5 minutes, uncovered, then add stock, salt, pepper, sugar, bay leaves and cloves. Cover, reduce heat and cook for 1 hour.

5 Peel and quarter potatoes and scrape carrots. Add both to the casserole, removing cloves, and cook for a further 30 minutes.

TO SERVE

Serve in the casserole or transfer to a warmed serving dish. Sprinkle with chopped chives or parsley. Serve with a chinese cabbage salad, capsicum salad, or broccoli.

Beef ragoût

This gently cooked stew is simple chuck steak enriched with the warm flavours of red wine and brandy

MAIN MEAL Serves 4–6

Overall timing 2 hours

Equipment Large flameproof casserole

Freezing Cool rapidly, then pack into a foil-lined rigid container. Cover, label and freeze. Freezer life: 3 months. To use: put into a saucepan and heat through gently

INGREDIENTS

$1\frac{3}{4}$lb	Chuck steak	750g
3oz	Piece of fatty bacon	75g
12oz	Onions	350g
2 tbsp	Oil	2×15ml
2	Tomatoes	2
1 tbsp	Tomato paste	15ml
$\frac{1}{2}$ teasp	Salt	2.5ml
2 tbsp	Plain flour	2×15ml
$\frac{1}{4}$ pint	Red wine	150ml
$\frac{1}{2}$ pint	Hot beef stock	300ml
1	Bay leaf	1
5	White peppercorns	5
4oz	Button mushrooms	125g
1	Green capsicum	1
1	Red capsicum	1
2 tbsp	Chopped parsley	2×15ml
2 tbsp	Brandy	2×15ml

METHOD

1 Wash and dry beef. Trim and cube. Cube bacon. Peel and chop onions.

2 Cook bacon in casserole until fat runs. Add beef and cook for 10 minutes over a high heat, turning contents over with a wooden spoon after 5 minutes.

3 Add onions and oil. Cook for a further 3 minutes. Scald tomatoes, remove skins and chop flesh finely. Stir into casserole with tomato paste and salt.

4 Sprinkle flour into casserole, stir in well and cook for 3 minutes. Add red wine, beef stock, bay leaf and peppercorns. Cover and simmer gently for about 50 minutes or until the meat is tender.

5 Wipe mushrooms; halve. Deseed capsicums and cut into strips. Add both to casserole and cook for 15 minutes more.

6 Add parsley and brandy, raise heat and cook for 10 minutes, uncovered. Leave to stand for 5 minutes before serving.

Braised beef à la provençale

Braised beef – browned first and then cooked very slowly on top of the stove or in the oven – is one of the tastiest dishes around. In this dish from the Provence region of France, tomatoes, garlic and black olives are used to enrich the wine sauce. For best results, make sure the lid of the casserole fits very tightly

MAIN MEAL Serves 6

Overall timing 3 hours

Equipment Flameproof casserole, small saucepan, frying pan

Freezing Omit pork fat and olives and use half the quantity of wine. Cook and cool completely. Pack into container, label and freeze, leaving $\frac{3}{4}$ inch (2cm) headspace. Cover, label and freeze. Freezer life: 3–4 months. To use: thaw for 4 hours, add rest of wine and heat gently but thoroughly. Add pork fat and olives and cook for 15 minutes more

INGREDIENTS

3	Onions	3
$2\frac{1}{4}$lb	Braising beef	1kg
1oz	Butter	25g
1 tbsp	Oil	15ml
1 teasp	Salt	5ml
	Black pepper	
2 tbsp	Plain flour	2×15ml
2	Tomatoes	2
2 teasp	Tomato paste	2×5ml
1 pint	Red wine	560ml
$\frac{1}{2}$ pint	Beef stock	300ml
1	Garlic clove	1
1	Bouquet garni	1
8oz	Mushrooms	225g
5oz	Pork fat	150g
4oz	Black olives	125g

METHOD

1 Peel and quarter onions. Cut the beef into 2 inch (5cm) cubes. Put onions and beef into a casserole, with the butter and oil, and cook until brown. Add the salt and pepper. Sprinkle on the flour, stir it in and leave it to colour over a strong heat.

2 Scald tomatoes, peel and quarter. Reduce heat and add tomato paste, tomatoes, red wine, beef stock (made with 1 stock cube if necessary), peeled and crushed garlic and bouquet garni to casserole. Cover and simmer for $2\frac{1}{4}$ hours over a gentle heat without stirring. If you prefer, it can be cooked in the oven at 325F (170C) Gas 3, for the same length of time.

3 Meanwhile, wipe and slice mushrooms or cut into quarters if large. Cut the pork fat into small pieces, place in a pan of cold water, bring to the boil, then immediately drain and wipe dry. Brown fat gently in a frying pan with a little oil and then set aside. At the end of cooking time, add the mushrooms, pork fat and olives to casserole and cook for a further 15 minutes.

TO SERVE

Serve with mashed potatoes or buttered noodles, and lightly dressed green salad.

money savers

When buying beef for your freezer, a hindquarter or forequarter can be cut as you want. A lot of the weight is taken up by bones and fat and as you pay for it in the overall price, put both to good use.

The hard, firm, dry fat can be made into suet (perfect for mincemeat and Christmas pudding). To use suet grate or scrape it – a little flour will prevent it sticking to the knife. Suet freezes well so store it in the freezer till needed.

To render fat down, place in roasting tin or casserole and cook gently on top of the stove or in the oven till dripping runs freely. It does take time! Strain it well through muslin.

All the bones from beef can be used to make stock or *bouillon*. Again, it is a long process but worth it when you taste the difference it makes.

The bones should be chopped into manageable pieces and "cracked" with a cleaver. Put them in a large pot with any attached meat, lots of cold water, a bouquet garni, large chunks of onions, carrots, parsnips and some whole peppercorns. Bring slowly to the boil, skim surface, then simmer on the lowest heat for 12 hours. Strain. Leave to cool, uncovered. Chill for 4 hours, then lift off the set fat. Freeze in ice-cube trays (freezer life, 3 months; ice compartment of fridge, 2 months).

Beef and onions

Chuck or blade-bone steak cut into thin strips, and finely sliced onions, make this a quickly cooked dish for four. Herbs and wine vinegar add a lovely aromatic flavour

MAIN MEAL Serves 4

Overall timing $1\frac{1}{2}$ hours

Equipment Frying pan with lid

Freezing Cool rapidly, skim off surplus fat. Pack in suitable container, cover, label and freeze. Freezer life: 3 months. To use: heat gently and bring to the boil. Continue to cook gently for 10 minutes till heated through

INGREDIENTS

$1\frac{1}{2}$lb	Chuck or blade-bone steak	700g
12oz	Onions	350g
1oz	Butter	25g
1 tbsp	Oil	15ml
1 tbsp	Plain flour	15ml
$\frac{1}{2}$ pint	Beef stock	300ml
1	Garlic clove	1
$\frac{1}{2}$ teasp	Cumin	2.5ml
	Pinch of dried marjoram	
2 tbsp	Wine vinegar	2×15ml
	Salt	
	Freshly-ground black pepper	

METHOD

1 Cut meat across the grain into thin fingerlength strips. Peel onions, slice crossways and separate rings.

2 Put the butter and oil into frying pan. Add the onion rings and cook, covered, over a low heat until transparent. Turn them over constantly so that they cook evenly but do not brown. Remove from pan.

3 Increase heat, put strips of meat into pan and brown them. Add onion rings. Sprinkle with flour and stir. When flour begins to colour, pour in stock (made up with 1 stock cube if necessary) and add peeled and crushed garlic, cumin, marjoram, wine vinegar, salt and pepper. Stir well, then cover and simmer for 1 hour over a moderate heat. Serve with potatoes or rice and a crisp mixed salad.

Right: Beef and onions – a flavoursome stew that goes well with a dish of plain boiled rice and a crisp mixed salad

Boeuf bourguignon

This dish comes from the Burgundy region of France, hence the use of red wine! The marination makes the meat especially tender and flavourful

MAIN MEAL Serves 6

Overall timing $2\frac{3}{4}$ hours plus marination

Equipment 1 large and 1 small bowl, frying pan with lid, flameproof casserole with lid

Freezing Cool, pour into foil-lined rigid container making sure meat is well covered by sauce. Cover, label and freeze. Freezer life: 4 months. To use: heat from frozen in moderate oven

INGREDIENTS

	Marinade	
1	Large onion	1
1	Carrot	1
1–2	Cloves	1–2
6	Peppercorns	6
3 tbsp	Oil	3×15ml
25fl oz	Bottle of red wine	700ml

	Other ingredients*	
$3\frac{1}{2}$lb	Braising beef	1.6kg
3oz	Pork fat	75g
2 tbsp	Brandy	2×15ml
8oz	Pickling onions	225g
4oz	Button mushrooms	125g
2oz	Butter	50g
1 tbsp	Oil	15ml
3 tbsp	Plain flour	3×15ml
1	Garlic clove	1
	Bouquet garni	
	Salt and pepper	

METHOD

1 Peel and chop onion. Scrape and slice carrot. Put both into a bowl with the rest of the marinade ingredients. Cut beef into 2 inch (5cm) cubes, add to marinade and leave in a cool place overnight or for at least 3 hours. Stir from time to time.

2 Pour boiling water over the pork fat in a bowl. Leave for 2–3 minutes, then drain and wipe fat dry. Cut into thin strips and put back into bowl. Sprinkle with brandy and place in fridge.

3 Peel pickling onions. Wipe mushrooms. Put into frying pan with the butter, half cover with lid and cook gently for about 10 minutes.

4 Lift meat cubes from marinade with draining spoon and wipe them dry. Heat oil in a casserole and, when fairly hot, add the meat and brown on all sides. Sprinkle with flour, mix in and brown over a strong heat.

5 Add peeled and crushed garlic, pork fat and the juice in which it has been soaked. Cook for 2 minutes then ignite.

6 Pour in reserved marinade, strained, and if necessary add a little water or stock so meat is covered. Add bouquet garni and salt and pepper. Cover tightly and simmer for 2 hours over a low heat (or cook in oven at 350F/180C/Gas 4). Add onions and mushrooms 15 minutes before end of cooking.

TO SERVE

Serve with a crisp green salad, and plain boiled rice.

*With a dish of this kind, it's worth cooking twice the amount – the cooking time and work involved will be the same. Freeze half or cover and keep in the fridge for 2–3 days.

Below: Boeuf bourguignon is one of the classics of French cooking and a dish in which cheaper cuts of beef can be used

Boeuf carbonade

A hearty dish typical of Belgian cuisine. Beef is braised in ale with brown sugar, onions and vinegar

MAIN MEAL Serves 4

Overall timing 2–2½ hours

Equipment Large saucepan or casserole with tight-fitting lid

Freezing Cool rapidly, skim off surplus fat, pack in container, seal, label and freeze. Freezer life: 3 months. To use: thaw over gentle heat and bring to boiling point, continue to cook for 20 minutes until heated through

Above: Boeuf carbonade – a famous dish from a country of beer drinkers. Any type of ale can be used in the cooking

INGREDIENTS

2¼lb	Braising beef	1kg
3oz	Butter	75g
8oz	Onions	225g
1 tbsp	Plain flour	15ml
1 tbsp	Brown sugar	15ml
1 tbsp	Wine vinegar	15ml
18fl oz	Ale	500ml
	Salt and pepper	
1	Bouquet garni	1

METHOD

1 Trim off any fat, then cut meat into large thin slices.

2 Melt 2oz (50g) of the butter in a pan or casserole. Add the meat and brown over a high heat. Remove beef from pan and put aside.

3 Peel and finely chop onions. Add onions to pan with remaining butter. Reduce heat, cover and cook for 10 minutes without burning.

4 Sprinkle flour into pan with the brown sugar and stir with a wooden spoon. Add vinegar, then the beer and stir until thick.

5 Replace beef in pan, season with salt and pepper and add bouquet garni. Cover and simmer for about 1½–2 hours over a low heat or cook in the oven at 350F (180C) Gas 4. Serve with mashed potatoes and endive salad.

Combine minced pork and bacon with egg, salt, pepper, allspice and juniper berries. Sprinkle with half the chopped parsley

Season flattened-out slices of meat with salt and pepper and put a fifth of the stuffing in the centre of each one

Fold the edges of the meat slices over the stuffing, overlapping them as necessary, and making each a well-wrapped parcel

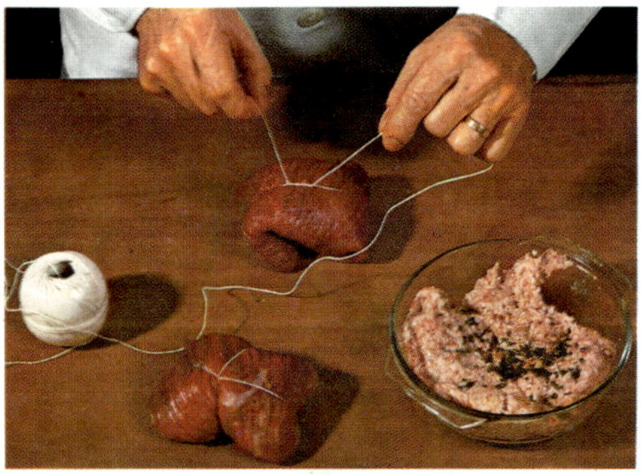

Using fine string, tie up the paupiettes securely – not too loosely or the stuffing will escape. Right: the finished dish

Beef olives

Beef olives – or paupiettes as they are sometimes called – are thin slices of meat stuffed and rolled, then cooked in very little liquid. They can make a simple dish – originally they used up leftovers – or quite a grand one, according to the kind of meat, stuffing and cooking liquid used – often wine or some kind of alcohol. This version from France has a distinctive flavour because of the gin and juniper berries

MAIN MEAL Serves 5

Overall timing 2½ hours

Equipment Mincer, bowl, string, casserole or frying pan with lid

Freezing Cool rapidly after 1 hour's cooking. Add the onions. Pack into suitable container, seal, label and freeze. Freezer life: 3 months. To use: thaw over gentle heat, bring to the boil, then simmer for 30 minutes. Or, place in a cold oven, set at 400F (200C) Gas 6, and allow to heat through for 1½ hours

INGREDIENTS

	Stuffing	
12oz	Lean pork	350g
4oz	Streaky bacon	125g
1	Egg	1
	Salt and pepper	
½ teasp	Allspice	2.5ml
4	Crushed juniper berries *or*	4
¼ teasp	Powdered juniper berries	1.25ml
3 tbsp	Chopped parsley	3×15ml
	Other ingredients	
5	Thin slices of rump steak	5
	Salt and pepper	
2oz	Butter	50g
20	Button onions	20
3 tbsp	Gin	3×15ml
1	Garlic clove	1
1 pint	Beer	560ml
2 tbsp	Tomato paste	2×15ml

METHOD

1 To make stuffing, finely mince the pork and bacon. Place in a bowl with the egg, salt, pepper, allspice and crushed or powdered juniper berries. Mix well. Sprinkle with half the chopped parsley.

2 Spread out the slices of meat; salt and pepper them lightly. Put some stuffing on each slice, and roll up (see step by step, far left). Tie securely with string.

3 Melt the butter in casserole or frying pan, add the peeled onions and cook until golden brown. Remove the onions and reserve. Add the rolls and brown over a medium heat, and then spoon over the gin. Allow the alcohol to warm for a moment before setting alight.

4 When flames die down, stir in peeled and crushed garlic, beer and tomato paste. Bring to the boil, reduce heat, cover and simmer for 1 hour.

5 Return the onions to the pan and simmer uncovered for a further 30 minutes.

6 Remove pan from heat and lift the rolls and onions on to a warmed serving dish. Remove string from olives, pour over the sauce and sprinkle with the remaining chopped parsley before serving.

VARIATION

As an inexpensive alternative, use pork sausagemeat instead of minced pork for the stuffing. Either of the stuffings could be varied by adding two dill gherkins, chopped – this is something they do in Germany where the combination of pork or sausage and gherkins is common. The gherkins add crunch and texture to the stuffing as well as extra flavour and sharpness. This dish may also be cooked in a moderate oven, 350F (180C) Gas 4, for 45 minutes or longer according to the thickness of the cut of meat.

cook's know-how

When buying meat for beef olives ask your butcher to suggest different cuts and compare prices. Sirloin and rump will often be dearer than "leg of mutton" cut or top rump/thick flank, both of which lend themselves well to cutting in thin slices which can be made even thinner with a meat bat.
Paupiettes can also be made from lamb, veal or pork slices cut from the leg which should also be well flattened.

Boeuf à la mode

This is a classic French, full of flavour, dish. It can be made well ahead of time as it reheats extremely well. The sauce can be made two ways – but if you intend freezing it, it's best not to add the cream and brandy

Above: Boeuf à la mode – tender, tasty meat served with button onions and sliced carrots

MAIN MEAL Serves 8–10

Overall timing 3 hours plus marination

Equipment Large bowl, large heavy-based flameproof casserole

Freezing Cool joint, wrap well. Put sauce in rigid container and cover. Freezer life: 2 months. To use: thaw for 24 hours in fridge, place meat and sauce in casserole. Cook for 1 hour in oven 400F (200C) Gas 6

INGREDIENTS

4lb	Braising beef	1.8kg
6oz	Pork fat with rind	175g
1	Large onion	1
½ pint	Red or white wine	300ml
3	Stalks of celery	3
3	Carrots	3
1	Garlic clove	1
	Fresh parsley	
2	Bay leaves	2
	Fresh thyme	
	Freshly-ground white pepper	
	Salt	
1oz	Butter	25g
2 tbsp	Oil	2×15ml
1	Pigs trotter	1
4fl oz	Water	120ml
1 tbsp	Tomato paste	15ml
2 tbsp	Cream (optional)	2×15ml
1 tbsp	Brandy (optional)	15ml
¾lb	Button onions	350g
1lb	Carrots	450g

1 Assemble all ingredients. A bouquet garni can be used instead of the fresh herbs

2 Rub beef with pepper and salt. Slice pork fat, secure around beef with string

3 Cover beef with chopped onion, celery, 3 carrots, crushed garlic, herbs, wine

4 After overnight marination, dry meat. Brown in casserole in hot butter/oil mixture

5 Add marinade, halved pigs trotter, water, paste. Cover and cook gently for 2½ hours

6 Remove beef from casserole. Discard trotter. Strain cooking juices, cool and skim

7 To thicken, either reduce juices, or whisk in beurre manié over gentle heat

8 Cream, brandy can be added to sauce with already-cooked onions and carrots (optional)

Summer casserole of lamb

A light casserole which makes the most of a cheap cut of lamb and fresh summer vegetables. Use newly picked herbs to make the bouquet garni for superb results. At other times of year, use frozen beans and peas but reduce the cooking time to 5 minutes after adding them

MAIN MEAL Serves 6

Overall timing 1 hour

Equipment Flameproof casserole

Freezing Make as Steps 1–3. Cool, pack into rigid container with the onions. Make sure meat is well covered with the sauce. Cover, label and freeze. Freezer life: 3 months. To use: reheat slowly from frozen, then complete as Step 4

INGREDIENTS

8oz	Button onions	225g
1oz	Butter	25g
1 tbsp	Oil	15ml
$2\frac{1}{2}$lb	Middle neck lamb chops	1.1kg
6	New carrots	6
2	Garlic cloves	2
1 tbsp	Plain flour	15ml
4	Tomatoes	4
2 tbsp	Tomato paste	2×15ml
$\frac{3}{4}$ pint	Stock	400ml
	Bouquet garni	
	Salt and pepper	
1lb	New potatoes	450g
2oz	Haricots verts	50g
2oz	Peas	50g

Above: Summer casserole of lamb – an appetizing and colourful meal

METHOD

1 Peel button onions. Heat butter and oil in casserole and fry onions for 5 minutes. Remove from pan and reserve. Add chops and brown on all sides over a high heat.

2 Scrape carrots, halve if liked. Add to pan with peeled and crushed garlic and cook for 5 minutes. Sprinkle flour over and cook, stirring, for 3 minutes.

3 Blanch, peel and chop tomatoes. Add to the pan with tomato paste, stock, bouquet garni, salt and pepper. Cover and simmer for 30 minutes.

4 Peel potatoes and add to the casserole. Cook for a further 10 minutes. Top and tail beans and cut into short lengths. Add to pan with peas and reserved onions. Cover and cook for a further 10 minutes. Taste and adjust seasoning if necessary. Discard bouquet garni and serve.

Turkish meatballs

Crisp on the outside, tender and moist on the inside, these lamb meatballs make a wholesome meal with rice or potatoes and a cool cucumber salad

MAIN MEAL Serves 6

Overall timing 50 minutes

Equipment 2 bowls, 2 large non-stick frying pans

Freezing Freeze at end of Step 4. Pack in rigid container, cover, seal and label. Freezer life: 2 months. To use: cook from frozen, completing Steps 5 and 6

INGREDIENTS

$1\frac{1}{2}$lb	Finely minced lamb	700g
1	Onion	1
2	Garlic cloves	2
3	Eggs	3
1 teasp	Olive oil	5ml
1 tbsp	Chopped parsley	15ml
1 teasp	Ground coriander	5ml
	Salt	
	Freshly-ground black pepper	
$\frac{1}{4}$ pint	Stock	150ml
4 tbsp	Plain flour	4×15ml
2oz	Butter	50g

METHOD

1 Put the minced lamb into a large bowl. Peel and finely chop the onion and add to the lamb with the peeled and crushed garlic.

2 Beat in 2 of the eggs, the oil, parsley, coriander and plenty of seasoning and mix to a stiff paste.

3 Shape into $1\frac{1}{2}$ inch (4cm) balls between wet hands and arrange in the frying pan. Gently add the stock (made with cubes if necessary) so that the meatballs are not broken and bring to the boil.

4 Cover the pan and simmer for about 20 minutes, shaking the pan occasionally to prevent the meatballs sticking. Lift the meatballs out with a draining spoon and allow to cool.

5 Beat the remaining egg in a bowl and coat the meatballs in the egg, then in the flour, shaking off any excess.

6 Heat the butter in another frying pan, add the meatballs and fry over a high heat, turning them frequently till crisp and brown. Serve with a cucumber, yogurt and mint salad and boiled rice or potatoes.

Below: Turkish meatballs, made with finely minced lamb

Westmorland lamb pie

Westmorland in the north of England is famous for its sheep – as well as several delicious ways of cooking them

LUNCH OR SUPPER Serves 4

Overall timing $1\frac{1}{4}$ hours

Equipment Bowl, saucepan, deep pie dish

Freezing Make pie in foil dish, cool, wrap, label and freeze. Freezer life: 2 months. To use: thaw for 4 hours at room temperature, then cover with foil and reheat in oven at 350F (180C) Gas 4 for about 40 minutes. If browning too quickly, cover with foil

INGREDIENTS

13oz	Packet of frozen puff pastry	375g
12oz	Minced lamb	350g
3oz	Butter	75g
8oz	Apples	225g
2oz	Almonds	50g
3 tbsp	Orange juice	3×15ml
2 tbsp	Lemon juice	2×15ml
1oz	Sultanas	25g
1oz	Candied peel	25g
3 tbsp	Rum	3×15ml
$\frac{1}{4}$ teasp	Ground cinnamon	1.25ml
$\frac{1}{4}$ teasp	Grated nutmeg	1.25ml
	Salt	
	Freshly-ground black pepper	
1	Egg	1

METHOD

1 Thaw pastry. Preheat oven to 425F (220C) Gas 7.

2 Place meat in a bowl. Melt butter. Peel, core and grate apples. Blanch, peel and chop almonds. Add to meat with orange and lemon juices, sultanas, candied peel, rum, cinnamon, nutmeg, salt and pepper. Mix well.

3 Roll out two-thirds of the pastry and use to line the pie dish. Roll out remaining pastry to cover the top.

4 Spoon the meat mixture into the pie dish. Moisten the edges of the pastry and place pastry lid on top of filling, pressing edges together. Knock up and crimp the edges.

5 Decorate top of pie with pastry trimmings. Beat egg and glaze pie.

6 Bake near the top of the oven for 15 minutes, reduce heat to 350F (180C) Gas 4 and cook for a further 40 minutes until well risen and golden. Serve hot with creamed potatoes.

Above: Moussaka – a rich mixture of aubergines, lamb and cheese sauce

Moussaka

Best-known of the Balkan dishes – particularly to holidaymakers in Greece. It's best of all made with lamb

MAIN MEAL Serves 6

Overall timing $2\frac{1}{4}$ hours

Equipment 2 saucepans, large casserole, frying pan, roasting tin

Freezing Foil-line casserole, add aubergines and lamb mixture as Step 4. Cover well with foil and freeze. When frozen, ease foil out of dish, overwrap in polythene, seal and label. Freezer life: 3 months. To use: remove wrapping and return moussaka to original dish. Defrost in fridge for 8 hours or place frozen on baking tray and cook at 375F (190C) Gas 5 for $1\frac{1}{2}$ hours. Pour cheese sauce over. Cook, uncovered, for 30 minutes to 1 hour

INGREDIENTS

1lb	Onions	450g
4	Sprigs of parsley	4
4	Garlic cloves	4
1 tbsp	Oil	15ml
2lb	Boned shoulder of lamb, minced	900g
4	Tomatoes	4
2 tbsp	Tomato paste	2×15ml
	Salt and pepper	
$\frac{1}{4}$ pint	Dry white wine or stock	150ml
2oz	Fresh white breadcrumbs	50g
2lb	Aubergines	900g
	Plain flour	
$\frac{1}{4}$ pint	Oil	150ml
1oz	Butter	25g
1oz	Plain flour	25g
$\frac{3}{4}$ pint	Milk	400ml
2	Egg yolks	2
4oz	Strong cheese	125g

METHOD

1 Chop the onions and parsley and peel and crush the garlic. Heat oil in a deep saucepan and add onion, parsley, garlic and lamb. Brown lightly, stirring occasionally. Add a little water if necessary to prevent burning.

2 Blanch, peel and cut tomatoes into quarters and add to pan with the tomato paste. Season well then pour in the wine or stock (made with a cube if necessary). Stir to blend, then cover and simmer gently for 45 minutes. Remove from heat and stir in breadcrumbs.

3 Remove stalks then wipe aubergines and slice diagonally to $\frac{1}{4}$ inch (6mm) thickness. Dust lightly with flour. Heat oil in frying pan and brown aubergines over a medium heat. Remove from pan with draining spoon; drain carefully on kitchen paper.

4 Grease casserole. Arrange two-thirds of the aubergines to cover the bottom and the sides. Add the meat mixture and then top with the remaining aubergines. Leave to stand. Preheat oven to 350F (180C) Gas 4.

5 To make the sauce, melt the butter in a small saucepan, stir in the flour and cook for 1–2 minutes (it mustn't brown). Remove from heat and gradually stir in the milk. Return to the heat and cook, stirring constantly, until thickened. Remove from heat, cool just a little then stir in the beaten egg yolks and half the cheese, grated. Taste, and adjust seasoning, if necessary.

6 Pour sauce over aubergines and lamb mixture in casserole. Cover with the rest of the grated cheese.

7 Stand casserole in a roasting tin containing a little water. Cook in the oven for 1 hour. Cover with aluminium foil after about 20 minutes if top shows signs of browning too quickly.

cook's know-how

When making the cheese sauce, there is a danger of the mixture curdling when the egg yolks are added. It doesn't lessen the taste but it does alter the look, so to prevent it happening stand the saucepan containing the sauce in a bowl of cold water for a few minutes before stirring in beaten yolks and cheese.

Spread pâté on chops, roll out pastry and cut it into four equal strips

Brush strips with egg and wind each around a chop, overlapping the turns

Alternatively, spread the chops with mint jelly and cut out pastry into triangles

Place each chop across a triangle, bring pastry ends over to wrap around meat

Lamb cutlets in pastry

Lamb can be stuffed with pâté or spread with mint jelly and then wrapped in strips of puff pastry or enveloped in a shortcrust pastry case

MAIN MEAL Serves 4

Overall timing $1\frac{1}{4}$ hours

Equipment Bowl, frying pan, rolling pin, pastry brush, baking tray

Freezing Allow the final egg glaze to dry, wrap cutlets in foil, padding bone ends well, and pack in polythene bag. Seal, label and freeze. Freezer life: 3 months. To use: unwrap and thaw at room temperature for about 3–4 hours. Complete Step 6

INGREDIENTS

4	Large lamb cutlets	4
1 tbsp	Oil	15ml
2oz	Liver pâté	50g
	Salt	
	Freshly-ground black pepper	
$7\frac{1}{2}$oz	Packet of frozen puff pastry	212g
1	Egg	1

Below: Lamb chops with two different coverings

METHOD

1 Preheat oven to 425F (220C) Gas 7. Wipe and trim the cutlets, cleaning 1 inch (2.5cm) down from the tip of the bone end and removing excess fat.

2 Heat the oil in a frying pan and fry the cutlets quickly for about 2 minutes on each side to sear them. Remove, drain on kitchen paper and cool.

3 In a small bowl beat the pâté till soft and creamy, adding salt and pepper. Spread the pâté over 1 side of each cutlet.

4 On a well-floured surface roll out pastry to an oblong, 6 inches × 20 inches (15cm×50cm). Cut into 4 equal strips and brush lightly with beaten egg.

5 Wind each pastry strip, egg side outside, around a cutlet, starting at the thin end and overlapping each previous "turn"; pinch to seal.

6 Brush again with beaten egg and place on a greased baking tray. Bake for about 30 minutes until golden.

VARIATION

For minty lamb cutlets en croûte, season fried cutlets with salt and pepper. Thaw and roll out 12oz (350g) packet frozen shortcrust pastry to an oblong 16 inches × 8 inches (40cm×20cm). Cut in 4 equal triangles, large enough to enclose the cutlets completely. Place 1 cutlet with the thick end in the right angle on each triangle, spread with 1 teasp (5ml) mint jelly. Brush pastry edges with beaten egg, fold pastry over cutlet to make a diagonal seam. Seal edges. Brush with beaten egg, and bake for 30 minutes in preheated oven at 400F (200C) Gas 6.

Above: Curried lamb served with créole rice – rice cooked with tomatoes and red capsicum

Curried lamb

For a true Indian flavour, serve this dish with mango chutney, lime pickle and chapattis

SUPPER Serves 4

Overall timing 1¾ hours

Equipment Flameproof casserole

Freezing Cool, pack in rigid container, leaving ¾ inch (2cm) headspace. Cover, seal, label and freeze. Freezer life: 3 months. To use: reheat slowly from frozen

INGREDIENTS

2½lb	Middle neck stewing lamb	1.1kg
2	Onions	2
3oz	Clarified butter	75g
2 tbsp	Plain flour	2×15ml
1 tbsp	Curry powder	15ml
1 pint	Stock	560ml
2oz	Desiccated coconut	50g
	Salt and pepper	

METHOD

1 Trim and chop lamb into smallish pieces. Peel and finely slice the onions.
2 Heat the butter in a flameproof casserole. Add the lamb and brown on all sides. Add the onions and fry until transparent. Sprinkle in the flour and the curry powder and cook for about 3 minutes, stirring all the time.
3 Gradually stir in the stock (made with cubes if necessary). Bring to the boil, stirring. Add the coconut and seasoning.
4 Reduce heat, cover and cook for 1 hour or until meat is tender. Adjust seasoning. Serve with créole or plain boiled rice.

VARIATION

You can vary the taste of this dish by using different curry powder mixtures.

Heat the butter in a flameproof casserole or frying pan. Add the pieces of lamb and brown them on all sides

Add the sliced onions to the meat in the pan and cook until transparent, stirring frequently with a wooden spoon

Sprinkle in the flour and the curry powder and cook over a low heat for about 3 minutes, stirring all the time

After sauce has boiled and thickened add desiccated coconut and seasoning, then continue cooking till the meat is tender

Paupiettes d'agneau

Escalopes rolled round a mixture of sausagemeat and capsicum and served in onion and tomato sauce

MAIN MEAL Serves 4

Overall timing $1\frac{1}{4}$ hours

Equipment Frying pan, flameproof casserole, string

Freezing Cook, pack into rigid container, seal, label and freeze. Freezer life: 3 months. To use: thaw overnight in fridge, then reheat in oven

INGREDIENTS

1	Green capsicum	1
3oz	Butter	75g
8oz	Sausagemeat	225g
2oz	Fresh breadcrumbs	50g
	Salt	
	Freshly-ground black pepper	
4	Lamb escalopes cut from the leg	4
2	Onions	2
2	Tomatoes	2
1	Garlic clove	1
	Bouquet garni	
	Strip of lemon rind	
3fl oz	Dry white wine	90ml

METHOD

1 Wash, deseed and finely chop capsicum. Heat 1oz (25g) of the butter in frying pan, add sausagemeat and capsicum and cook over high heat for 5 minutes, stirring. Remove from heat, stir in breadcrumbs and season. Place a quarter of the mixture on each slice of lamb, roll into a small parcel, turning in sides to cover stuffing. Tie with string.

2 Preheat oven to 400F (200C) Gas 6. Peel and chop onions. Heat remaining butter in flameproof casserole and brown paupiettes on all sides with the peeled and chopped onions.

3 Blanch, peel and chop tomatoes. Peel and crush garlic. Add to casserole with salt, pepper, bouquet garni and lemon rind. Cook, covered, in the oven for 30 minutes.

4 Remove paupiettes from casserole and discard strings. Place on warmed serving dish and keep hot. Add wine to casserole and boil rapidly until mixture is thick and reduced. Remove bouquet garni and lemon rind, taste and adjust seasoning. Spoon sauce over meat and garnish with parsley and lemon wedges. Serve immediately.

Italian lamb casserole

The marinade of red wine is reserved and used in cooking the lamb – the traditional Veronese dish uses Recioto amarone, a local full-bodied wine

MAIN MEAL Serves 4

Overall timing $2\frac{1}{2}$ hours plus overnight marination

Equipment Large bowl, large saucepan or flameproof casserole

Freezing Reduce the cooking time to $1\frac{1}{2}$ hours. Cool completely and pack into rigid container leaving 1 inch (2.5cm) headspace. Cover, label and freeze. Freezer life: 4 months. To use: place block in saucepan, heat gently till thawed. Bring to the boil and simmer for 30 minutes

INGREDIENTS

2lb	Lean lamb	900g
1	Stalk of celery	1
1 pint	Red wine	560ml
3	Onions	3
3 tbsp	Oil	3×15ml
14oz	Can of tomatoes	397g
	Salt	
	Freshly-ground black pepper	

METHOD

1 Wipe and trim the meat and cut into neat pieces. Wash, trim and thinly slice the celery. Put meat and celery into a large bowl and add the wine. Cover and place in the bottom of the fridge and leave to marinate for 24 hours. Turn the meat from time to time.

2 Peel and slice the onions. Heat the oil in the saucepan or casserole and fry the onions till transparent. Drain the meat and reserve the marinade. Add the meat to the pan and fry till browned on all sides.

3 Add the tomatoes and juice, the marinade and seasoning. Bring to the boil, cover and simmer for about 2 hours till the meat is tender.

4 Taste and adjust the seasoning and serve immediately with creamed potatoes or buttered pasta.

Minted lamb braise

The redcurrant jelly provides added flavour. If made the night before, surface fat can be skimmed off

MAIN MEAL Serves 4–6

Overall timing $2\frac{1}{2}$ hours

Equipment Flameproof casserole

Freezing Reduce cooking time to $1\frac{1}{2}$ hours and omit the mint garnish. Pour into rigid container, leaving $\frac{3}{4}$ inch (2cm) headspace. Cover, label and freeze. Freezer life: 4 months. To use: thaw overnight in fridge, transfer to casserole and reheat at 350F (180C) Gas 4 for about 45 minutes

INGREDIENTS

3lb	Neck of lamb chops	1.4kg
2 tbsp	Oil	2×15ml
2	Onions	2
2	Carrots	2
3 tbsp	Redcurrant jelly	3×15ml
2 tbsp	Chopped mint	2×15ml
	Salt	
	Freshly-ground black pepper	
8oz	Can of tomatoes	227g
$\frac{1}{2}$ pint	Stock	300ml

METHOD

1 Preheat the oven to 350F (180C) Gas 4. Wipe and trim the lamb chops.

2 Heat the oil in the casserole and fry the chops, a few at a time, till browned on both sides. Remove from pan and reserve.

3 Peel and slice the onions, scrape and slice the carrot. Add to the casserole, cover and leave to sweat for 5 minutes. Stir in the redcurrant jelly and half the chopped mint.

4 Arrange the chops on the vegetables, season and pour in the canned tomatoes and their juice and the stock (made with cubes if necessary).

5 Cover tightly and cook in the centre of the oven for 2 hours till the lamb is tender and falling off the bones. Adjust the seasoning, mix well and stir in the remaining mint. Serve with new potatoes and curly kale.

nutrition know-how

Liver, one of the best sources of iron, is essential to a balanced diet as it replenishes and keeps healthy the haemoglobin, the red cells in the blood, which carry oxygen round the body. As a lack of iron can cause general tiredness and disability and even one type of anaemia, liver should be eaten once a week. Liver is especially important to pregnant women (to guard against anaemia and to provide a healthy blood supply for the unborn child), growing children and old people (who are also prone to anaemia). And, as iron needs vitamin C to encourage absorption, drink orange juice the same day or add it to the dish.

Liver casserole

This is a Burgundy-style dish, cooked with red wine

LUNCH OR SUPPER Serves 4

Overall timing 20 minutes

Equipment Frying pan

Freezing Cool, pack into rigid container, leaving $\frac{3}{4}$ inch (2cm) headspace. Cover, label and freeze. Freezer life: 2 months. To use: reheat gently from frozen

INGREDIENTS

1lb	Calves or lambs liver	450g
	Salt and pepper	
3 tbsp	Plain flour	3×15ml
3oz	Butter	75g
1	Onion	1
	Sprig of thyme	
1	Bay leaf	1
$\frac{1}{2}$ pint	Red wine	300ml
	Chopped parsley	

METHOD

1 Wipe, trim and slice liver. Toss in seasoned flour till well coated. Heat 1oz (25g) of the butter, add liver slices and fry for 3–4 minutes on each side. Remove from pan, place on serving plate and keep hot.

2 Peel and chop onion. Heat another 1oz (25g) of the butter in the pan, add onion, thyme and bay leaf and fry till onion is golden. Add wine, bring to the boil and simmer for 5 minutes. Remove thyme and bay leaf.

3 Mix remaining butter with 1 teasp (5ml) of leftover seasoned flour and blend into sauce with a wooden spoon. Bring to the boil, stirring constantly, and cook for 2 minutes. Pour sauce over liver and garnish with chopped parsley. Served with boiled rice or steamed new potatoes and cauliflower.

Liver in onion sauce

Use fresh or frozen liver and a sauce from the freezer to make this traditional dish

MAIN MEAL Serves 4

Overall timing 45 minutes

Equipment 3 saucepans, sieve, bowl, frying pan

Freezing Prepare sauce to Step 4. Cool, pour into rigid container, cover, label and freeze. Freezer life: 2 months.
To use: thaw liver in refrigerator. Reheat sauce very gently from frozen in double saucepan. Complete as Steps 5 and 6

INGREDIENTS

$1\frac{1}{2}$	Onions	$1\frac{1}{2}$
$\frac{1}{2}$	Carrot	$\frac{1}{2}$
$\frac{1}{2}$	Stalk celery	$\frac{1}{2}$
1	Bay leaf	1
1 pint	Milk	560ml
4oz	Butter	100g
3oz	Flour	75g
	Salt and pepper	
	Nutmeg	
$\frac{1}{2}$ teasp	Sugar	2.5ml
1lb	Calves or lambs liver	450g

METHOD

1 Peel and chop half an onion and the carrot; chop the celery. Put them in a saucepan with the bay leaf, add the milk and bring to the boil. Remove from the heat and leave for 15 minutes.

2 In another pan, melt 2oz (50g) butter without browning, stir in 2oz (50g) flour and cook for 1 minute to make a roux.

3 Strain the milk and gradually stir it into roux. Bring to the boil, then simmer for 3 minutes, stirring. Season lightly with salt and pepper.

4 Peel and chop the remaining onion and blanch it in boiling water for 1 minute. Drain thoroughly. Put it into a saucepan with 1oz (25g) butter, cover and sweat for 10 minutes without browning. Add to the basic sauce and cook for 5 minutes, stirring. Remove from the heat and rub the sauce through a sieve. Add a pinch of grated nutmeg and the sugar.

5 Wipe, trim and slice the liver. Toss it in the remaining 1oz (25g) flour till well coated. Heat 1oz (25g) butter, add the liver slices and fry for 3–4 minutes on each side. Remove from pan, place on serving plate and keep hot.

6 Reheat onion sauce gently, adjust seasoning and pour over liver. Serve with creamed potatoes and brussels sprouts or peas.

Peel and chop 1 large onion, blanch in boiling water for 1 minute. Drain thoroughly. Put into pan with 1oz (25g) butter, cover and sweat for 10 minutes without browning. Add to basic sauce, cook for 5 minutes

Remove from heat and rub the sauce through a sieve. Reheat gently. Add a pinch of freshly-grated nutmeg and $\frac{1}{2}$ teasp (2.5ml) sugar, then taste and adjust seasoning

Sauté kidneys with parsley

Use frozen kidneys and fresh parsley for this quick dish

LUNCH OR SUPPER Serves 4

Overall timing 20 minutes

Equipment Frying pan

Freezing Not recommended for the finished dish

INGREDIENTS

1lb	Frozen calf kidneys	450g
1	Onion	1
2oz	Butter	50g
2 tbsp	Chopped parsley	2×15ml
1 tbsp	Wine vinegar	15ml
	Salt and pepper	

METHOD

1 Thaw the kidneys. Dry on kitchen paper, then slice very thinly. Peel and finely chop onion.

2 Heat butter in frying pan and cook the onion and parsley for 5 minutes. Add the kidneys and cook for a further 5–10 minutes, stirring occasionally.

3 Stir in the vinegar, bring to the boil, then remove from heat immediately. Add salt and pepper to taste and serve with creamed potatoes.

Below: Sauté kidneys with parsley – the chopped parsley adds freshness and colour to this Italian dish which can be served with either rice or creamed potatoes

Add kidney slices to fried chopped onion and parsley and cook for 5–10 minutes

Gradually add 1 tbsp (15ml) of vinegar, bring to the boil, then remove from heat

Beef heart ragoût

Ragoût, from the French verb ragoûter (to revive the taste), is a dish made from meat, poultry or fish cut into small pieces, which are briefly fried and then cooked slowly with stock and seasoning

MAIN MEAL Serves 6–8

Overall timing 2½ hours

Equipment Frying pan, casserole

Freezing Cool, turn into rigid container, cover, label and freeze. Freezer life: 2 months. To use: reheat slowly from frozen

INGREDIENTS

3lb	Beef heart	1.4kg
4 tbsp	Plain flour	4×15ml
	Salt and pepper	
3 tbsp	Oil	3×15ml
2	Large onions	2
2 tbsp	Tomato paste	2×15ml
½ pint	Beef stock	300ml
14oz	Can of tomatoes	397g
	Bouquet garni	
2 teasp	Sugar	2×5ml

METHOD

1 Trim the heart of gristle and fat, and cut into ½ inch (12.5mm) thick slices. Wash well and dry with kitchen paper. Preheat oven to 325F (170C) Gas 3.

2 Coat heart slices with seasoned flour. Heat oil in a frying pan and brown slices quickly on both sides. Transfer to casserole.

3 Peel, slice and fry the onions until golden. Add any remaining seasoned flour and the tomato paste. Gradually stir in the stock (made with stock cube if necessary), bring to the boil and simmer for 2 minutes.

4 Add the canned tomatoes, bouquet garni, sugar and seasoning. Pour sauce into casserole, cover and bake on the centre shelf of the oven for 2 hours until tender.

5 Discard bouquet garni and adjust seasoning. Serve with baked jacket potatoes and a green vegetable.

Oxtail and chestnut hot-pot

Although oxtail is widely used to flavour soup or stock, it can also be braised as an inexpensive meat dish. The chestnuts add extra flavour as well as contrasting texture

MAIN MEAL Serves 6

Overall timing 3¾ hours plus overnight chilling

Equipment Large flameproof casserole

Freezing Cool, place in foil container, cover, label and freeze. Freezer life: 4 months. To use: thaw overnight in fridge, then reheat gently in saucepan

INGREDIENTS

3	Large onions	3
3 tbsp	Oil	3×15ml
3–4lb	Chopped oxtails	1.4–1.8kg
4	Carrots	4
2	White turnips	2
1	Garlic clove	1
	Salt and pepper	
1½ pints	Beef stock	850ml
2 tbsp	Tomato paste	2×15ml
	Bouquet garni	
8oz	Chestnuts	225g
¼ pint	Red wine	150ml
2 tbsp	Cornflour	2×15ml
4 tbsp	Water	4×15ml
2 tbsp	Chopped parsley	2×15ml

METHOD

1 Preheat oven to 350F (180C) Gas 4. Peel and slice the onions. Heat oil in casserole, add onions and oxtail and fry quickly till oxtail is browned on all sides.

2 Prepare and chop the other vegetables and add to casserole. Fry till vegetables are golden brown, then season with salt and pepper.

3 Pour in stock (made up with 3 cubes if necessary), stir in tomato paste and add bouquet garni. Bake in oven, uncovered, for 2 hours. Cool, then leave overnight in fridge.

4 The next day, skim cold fat from the surface of the casserole. Blanch and skin chestnuts. Add to casserole with the red wine and bake for a further 1 hour.

5 Discard bouquet garni. Blend cornflour with the water and stir into casserole. Return to the oven for 30 minutes. Sprinkle with chopped parsley and serve with jacket potatoes.

Italian-style tongue

Tongue slices in a piquant sauce

MAIN MEAL Serves 4–6

Overall timing 2½ hours

Equipment Saucepan, flameproof casserole, blender

Freezing Arrange sliced tongue in foil dish and cover with sauce. Cool, cover, label and freeze. Freezer life: 3 months. To use: thaw overnight in fridge, then reheat thoroughly in oven

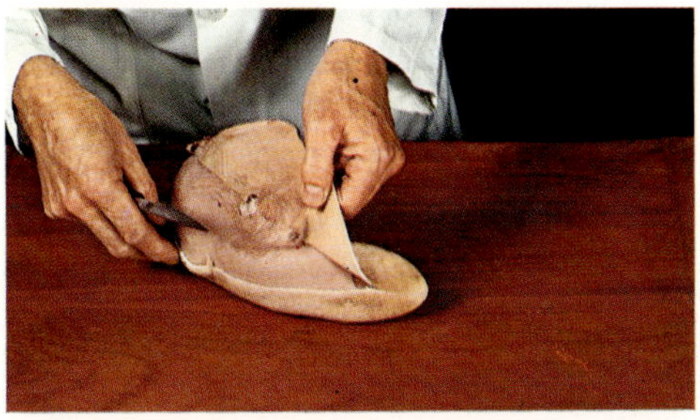

Remove the skin from the cooked tongue by slicing along the length and pulling away

Hold skinned tongue firmly and cut into thick but even slices with a sharp knife

Below: Italian-style tongue – cut generous slices and arrange decoratively in the dish

INGREDIENTS

2lb	Calves tongue	900g
	Salt and pepper	
3	Medium-size carrots	3
2	Medium-size onions	2
3oz	Butter	75g
¼ pint	Dry white wine	150ml
14oz	Can of tomatoes	397g
2 tbsp	Tomato paste	2×15ml
4	Sprigs of thyme	4
4	Large gherkins	4
2 teasp	Oregano	2×5ml

METHOD

1 Trim and rinse the tongue and put into a large saucepan. Cover with lightly salted cold water and bring to the boil. Cover and simmer for 20 minutes. Drain the tongue and plunge it into cold water. Drain, then remove the skin, and any bones from the root.

2 Scrape and chop the carrots, peel and finely chop the onions. Heat the butter in the casserole, add the carrots and onions and fry gently for 5 minutes.

3 Place the tongue on top of the vegetables and add the wine, ¼ pint (150ml) water, the canned tomatoes and juice, tomato paste, thyme and seasoning. Bring to the boil, cover tightly and simmer for 1–1½ hours till the tongue is tender.

4 Lift out the tongue and slice thickly. Arrange on a serving dish and keep hot.

5 Discard the thyme, pour the sauce into a blender. Add the roughly chopped gherkins and the oregano and blend.

6 Reheat the sauce and adjust the seasoning to taste. Pour round the tongue and serve immediately with creamed potatoes and brussels sprouts.

POULTRY

Remember to thaw frozen poultry completely before cooking, and to cook it thoroughly. It is a good idea to test the internal temperature of the cooked bird with a meat thermometer – it should read 190F (88C) in the thickest part of the meat

Chicken Kiev

Originally a Russian speciality, the success of the dish lies in having the chicken breasts very cold and the flavoured butter frozen hard so it doesn't ooze out during the frying. But warn guests to cut into the chicken carefully so hot butter doesn't spurt out everywhere

MAIN MEAL　　Serves 4

Overall timing $1\frac{1}{2}$ hours

Equipment Bowl, wooden cocktail sticks, deep-fryer

Freezing Complete to Step 4. Place sheet of greaseproof paper between each chicken roll, then wrap in foil. Put in plastic bag, seal, label, freeze. Freezer life: 1 month. To use: thaw overnight in fridge, then complete as from Step 5

INGREDIENTS

4oz	Softened butter	125g
2 tbsp	Lemon juice	2×15ml
1	Garlic clove	1
1 tbsp	Chopped parsley	15ml
	Salt and pepper	
4	Boneless chicken breasts	4
	Oil for frying	
3 tbsp	Plain flour	3×15ml
1	Beaten egg	1
3 tbsp	Fresh white breadcrumbs	3×15ml

METHOD

1 In a bowl, work together the butter and lemon juice until smooth. Peel and crush the garlic and add to the bowl with the parsley, salt and pepper. Stir well. Shape into a cylinder, wrap in foil and place in freezer or freezing compartment of fridge for 1 hour to firm.

2 Place the chicken breasts between 2 pieces dampened greaseproof paper on a flat surface and beat flat with a heavy knife or wooden mallet until thin.

3 Heat the oil in the deep-fryer to 340F (170C).

4 Place a piece of butter on each chicken breast. Roll chicken round butter and secure with a cocktail stick.

5 Coat each piece of chicken all over with the flour, then dip in the beaten egg to cover and finally in the breadcrumbs, pressing them on well. Fry for 12–15 minutes until golden brown.

6 Drain on kitchen paper, remove cocktail sticks and serve immediately with lemon wedges and a green salad.

Left: Chicken Kiev – boned chicken breasts stuffed with a garlicky butter and deep fried

Left: Coq au vin, garnished and ready to be served with boiled potatoes or rice

Coq au vin

Chicken in wine is a classic French dish and the colour and richness of the sauce comes from the wine in which the chicken is first marinated, then cooked. The small measure of brandy adds that "little extra something" to the final taste

MAIN MEAL Serves 6–8

Overall timing $2\frac{1}{2}$ hours plus 8 hours marination

Equipment Large bowl, large casserole, small saucepan, metal ladle

Freezing After cooking, allow dish to cool quickly. *Do not* reduce the sauce. Skim any fat from surface. Pack into a foil container, cover, label and freeze. Freezer life: 3 months. To use: thaw overnight, then thoroughly heat through (about 30 minutes). Carry out Steps 8 and 9, right, and garnish – see To serve

INGREDIENTS

	Marinade	
1	Onion	1
1	Shallot	1
1	Large carrot	1
2	Garlic cloves	2
3 tbsp	Olive oil	3×15ml
18fl oz	Full-bodied red wine	500ml
3	Cloves	3
	Black pepper	
	Bouquet garni	
	Other ingredients	
$3–3\frac{1}{2}$lb	Chicken joints	1.5kg
5oz	Streaky bacon	150g
2 tbsp	Plain flour	2×15ml
2 tbsp	Brandy	2×15ml
$\frac{1}{4}$ pint	Water	150ml
2 tbsp	Tomato paste	2×15ml
	Salt	
	Black pepper	
24	Button onions	24
2oz	Butter	50g
8oz	Button mushrooms	225g
2	Slices of white bread	2
	Fresh parsley	

METHOD

1 Peel and coarsely chop onion and shallot; scrape and slice carrot; peel and crush garlic. Place in large polythene bag with oil, wine, cloves, black pepper, bouquet garni and wiped and dried chicken joints. Place the bag in a large bowl for support and tie the end of the bag well. Leave in a cool place (*not* the fridge) for at least 8 hours, turning bag over from time to time.

2 Remove rind and cut bacon into small strips. Put in base of a large flameproof casserole and cook over a gentle heat for about 10 minutes until the fat starts to run.

3 Remove chicken joints from marinade and dry well. Add to casserole and cook until golden brown on all sides. Sprinkle with the flour and cook over a high heat until brown.

4 Remove casserole from heat. In a ladle, heat brandy and set light to it. Pour it flaming over the chicken joints. When the flames have died down, return the casserole to heat.

5 Add marinade, water and tomato paste. Cook for 3 minutes, stirring. Season well. Cover and simmer very gently for 30 minutes.

6 While it's cooking, blanch and peel button onions. If button onions are not available, use the bulbs of spring onions instead. Melt 1 oz (25g) of the butter in a saucepan and cook onions for a few minutes until they are golden brown. Drain well and add to casserole. Continue cooking for 45 minutes more.

7 Wipe the button mushrooms and fry them for 5 minutes in the butter in which the onions were cooked. Add more butter if necessary. Drain well, then add to the casserole. Continue cooking for a further 15 minutes.

8 Remove chicken and vegetables from liquid and arrange in a warm serving dish. Cover and keep warm.

9 Discard bouquet garni. Put liquid from casserole into a saucepan and boil rapidly until reduced by half. Pour the sauce over chicken.

TO SERVE

Toast slices of bread and cut into triangles. Dip ends of triangles first in the sauce then into chopped parsley and arrange on top of the Coq au vin. As this dish is rich, it is best accompanied by small boiled potatoes or rice, and a crisp green salad.

Chicken with wine and mushroom sauce

The chicken in this dish is roasted, cut into portions and served in a winey sauce. To achieve the smooth, shiny look, remove the skin

Below: Chicken with wine and mushroom sauce – rich treatment for simple roast chicken

Heat the butter in a frying pan, add the sliced mushrooms and fry for 2 minutes

Add the wine and stock to the roux to make the sauce, bring to the boil and cook

Add the drained mushrooms, beaten egg yolk, lemon juice plus seasoning to taste

Cut the hot roast chicken into four or six portions, using poultry shears, then remove the skin for a smooth finish, if liked

Place the chicken portions in a warmed serving dish and spoon the sauce and mushrooms evenly over the surface

MAIN MEAL Serves 4–6

Overall timing $1\frac{1}{2}$ hours

Equipment Roasting tin, frying pan, 2 saucepans

Freezing Cool, then pack in rigid container leaving $\frac{3}{4}$ inch (2cm) headspace. Cover, label and freeze. Freezer life: 4 months. To use: thaw for 4 hours, then turn into casserole, cover and cook in oven preheated to 350F (180C) Gas 4 for 45 minutes

INGREDIENTS

3lb	Ovenready chicken	1.4kg
$1\frac{1}{2}$ teasp	Salt	7.5ml
2oz	Butter	50g
8oz	Button mushrooms	225g
	Sauce	
$1\frac{1}{2}$oz	Butter	40g
$1\frac{1}{2}$oz	Plain flour	40g
$\frac{1}{2}$ pint	Dry white wine	300ml
$\frac{1}{2}$ pint	Chicken stock	300ml
1	Egg yolk	1
1 tbsp	Lemon juice	15ml
	Salt	
	Freshly-ground white pepper	

METHOD

1 Preheat the oven to 400F (200C) Gas 6. Wash and dry the chicken, then rub with 1 teasp (5ml) of the salt and dot with half the butter. Place in a roasting tin and cook for $1\frac{1}{4}$ hours, basting occasionally.

2 Meanwhile, wipe and trim mushrooms and slice thinly. Heat remaining butter in a frying pan till frothy, add mushrooms, sprinkle with remaining salt and stir-fry for 2 minutes. Remove from heat.

3 To make the sauce, heat butter in a saucepan, stir in flour and cook for 1 minute without burning. Gradually add wine and stock (made with chicken giblets or cubes if necessary). Bring to the boil, stirring, then cook gently for 5 minutes, stirring occasionally.

4 Add drained mushrooms, beaten egg yolk, lemon juice, and salt and pepper to taste. Return to gentle heat and cook, stirring till sauce is smooth and of coating consistency. Place in larger pan of simmering water to keep hot.

5 Remove chicken from oven and cut into portions, removing skin if liked. Place in warmed serving dish, cover with the sauce and serve immediately with roast potatoes, baked tomatoes and broccoli spears.

Chicken with basil butter

MAIN MEAL Serves 6

Overall timing $1\frac{1}{4}$ hours

Equipment Casserole with lid, heavy-based frying pan

Freezing Cool, pack chicken into a foil-lined container, then spoon sauce over, seal, label and freeze. Freezer life: 4 months. To use: cook from frozen in a moderate oven

INGREDIENTS

$3\frac{1}{2}$lb	Chicken	1.6kg
	Salt and pepper	
3oz	Plain flour	75g
4 tbsp	Butter	4×15ml
4 tbsp	Oil	4×15ml
3 tbsp	Chopped shallots	3×15ml
4fl oz	White wine	120ml
8fl oz	Chicken stock	220ml
14oz	Can of tomatoes	397g
1 tbsp	Chopped parsley	15ml
2 tbsp	Lemon juice	2×15ml
1 teasp	Cornflour	5ml
	Basil butter	
4oz	Butter	100g
$\frac{1}{2}$ tbsp	Olive oil	7.5ml
3 tbsp	Chopped fresh basil	3×15ml
1	Garlic clove	1

METHOD

1 Prepare and make basil butter. In a bowl, combine the butter, oil, finely chopped basil and peeled and crushed garlic. Mash well with a fork till the mixture is blended and smooth. Shape into a roll, wrap in greaseproof paper and put in fridge till wanted.

2 Preheat the oven to 325F (170C) Gas 3. Grease a casserole dish and set aside.

3 Joint the chicken into 8 or 10 pieces. Place in a plastic bag with well-seasoned flour and toss well so chicken is coated.

4 Melt half the butter and oil in the frying pan and when hot, brown the chicken pieces on all sides. Place in casserole.

5 Add chopped shallots to frying pan and cook for a few seconds – they should be transparent, not brown. Add the wine and bring to the boil. Raise heat to allow the liquid in the frying pan to reduce slightly.

6 Add the chicken stock and use a wooden spoon to scrape the bottom of the pan well. Pour sauce over chicken, cover casserole and bake in oven for 45 minutes.

7 While the chicken is cooking, prepare the garnish. Heat remaining butter and oil in the frying pan. Add drained tomatoes, reserving liquid. Heat through for 2–3 minutes then sprinkle with parsley.

8 When the chicken is done, lift out the pieces and place on a warmed serving dish. Sprinkle with lemon juice and surround with the tomatoes.

9 Pour the sauce from casserole into the frying pan. Add the cornflour, mixed with a little tomato liquid, and cook till sauce thickens. Remove pan from heat, add the basil butter and whisk sauce until butter melts. Spoon the sauce over the chicken and tomatoes. Serve with plain boiled or mashed potatoes, parsleyed carrots, broccoli or petits pois.

how to joint chicken

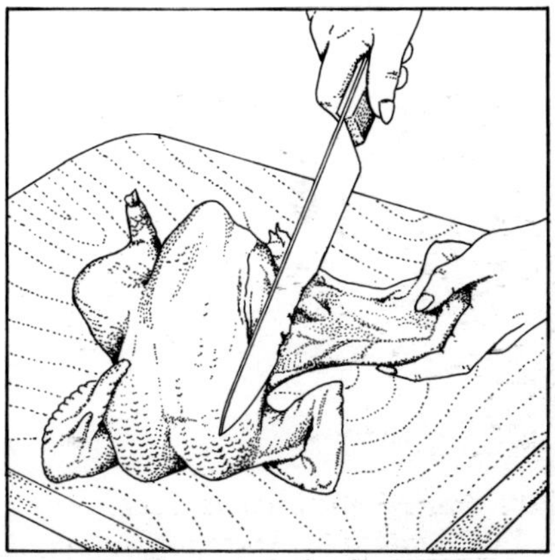

Place chicken breast-side up on board. Pull leg outwards. Cut skin between body and thigh, then cut through exposed ball and socket joint. To separate drumstick, cut centre joint of leg

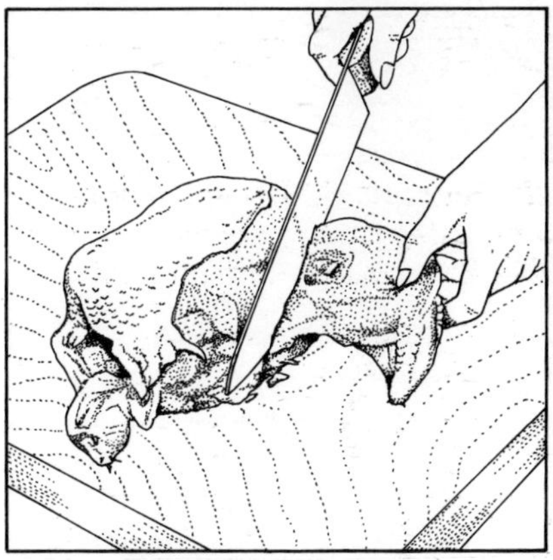

To remove wing, slice into breast above shoulder joint. To give a better portion, take in a good chunk of white breast meat. Pull wing away to expose joint, then cut through

Spiced chicken

The good thing about mace is that it adds a hint of heat to a dish without being fiery. Used here in conjunction with a little curry powder, the overall effect is mild yet the spiciness is there to be appreciated. The chicken is cooked in a mixture of stock and coconut milk which is then reduced by boiling before the cream is stirred in. Serve with a variety of side dishes for an Indian-style meal

1 When the chicken is cooked till tender, remove and then strain stock if liked

2 Reduce the stock by half by fast boiling, then spoon in cream and stir until smooth

Below: Spiced chicken – an Indian-style dish that's mild rather than hot

MAIN MEAL Serves 4–6

Overall timing $1\frac{1}{2}$ hours

Equipment Large saucepan with tight-fitting lid

Freezing Reduce sauce but do not add cream. Cool, pack in rigid container, leaving $\frac{3}{4}$ inch (2cm) headspace. Cover, seal, label and freeze. Freezer life: 3 months. To use: thaw for 3 hours, then reheat slowly but thoroughly, adding cream just before serving

INGREDIENTS

3lb	Chicken portions	1.4kg
2	Medium onions	2
4 tbsp	Oil	4×15ml
2 teasp	Curry powder	2×5ml
1 teasp	Ground mace	5ml
1 pint	Chicken stock	560ml
1 pint	Coconut milk (see opposite)	560ml
	Bouquet garni	
3 tbsp	Single cream	3×15ml
	Salt	
	Freshly-ground black pepper	

METHOD

1 Wipe chicken portions and cut into small pieces. Peel and finely chop onions.

2 Heat oil in saucepan, add onions and cook over low heat till transparent. Add curry powder and mace and cook, stirring, for 2 minutes. Add chicken pieces and stir-fry over high heat for 10–15 minutes till golden on all sides.

3 Reduce heat and stir in stock (made with cubes if necessary), coconut milk and bouquet garni. Cover and cook over medium heat for 45 minutes, stirring occasionally.

4 Remove chicken pieces with a draining spoon, place on a warmed serving dish and keep hot. Remove bouquet garni and discard.

5 Reduce sauce by half by cooking over high heat. Remove from heat and strain sauce through a sieve if liked. Return to pan and stir in cream. Stir over gentle heat till sauce is smooth and heated through. Taste and adjust seasoning. Either pour sauce over chicken or serve separately in a sauce boat. Serve immediately with plain boiled rice and curry side dishes.

Indian-style chicken

A flavourful mild curry – serve it with crunchy apple and cucumber

MAIN MEAL Serves 4

Overall timing 1 hour

Equipment Large flameproof casserole

Freezing Make up to Step 2, turn into rigid container, leaving $\frac{3}{4}$ inch (2cm) headspace, cool, seal, label and freeze. Freezer life: 3 months. To use: reheat gently from frozen in saucepan or flameproof casserole, stirring from time to time. Complete Step 3

INGREDIENTS

1	Onion	1
1oz	Butter	25g
1 tbsp	Oil	15ml
3lb	Chicken portions	1.4kg
2 tbsp	Mild curry powder	2×15ml
$\frac{1}{2}$ pint	Chicken stock	300ml
1	Garlic clove	1
2 tbsp	Lemon juice	2×15ml
	Salt	
	Cayenne pepper	
2 tbsp	*Coconut milk or single cream	2×15ml

METHOD

1 Peel and chop onion. Heat butter and oil in a casserole and cook onions till transparent. Add chicken portions, a few at a time, and brown on all sides.

2 Sprinkle chicken with curry powder and pour in stock (made up with 1 stock cube if necessary). Add peeled and crushed garlic, lemon juice and a pinch each of salt and cayenne pepper. Cover and simmer for 35 minutes over a low heat.

3 Add coconut milk or cream and cook gently for 10 minutes. Do not boil.

TO SERVE

Serve straight from casserole with plain boiled rice and side dishes of apple slices, cucumber sprinkled with sea-salt and grated fresh coconut, if liked.

*Coconut milk is not in fact the clear liquid found inside a coconut but a creamy liquid made by steeping grated fresh or desiccated coconut in hot water for about 20 minutes and straining. To 4oz (125g) coconut, add about $\frac{1}{4}$ pint (150ml) hot water for a thick coconut milk, or $\frac{3}{4}$ pint (400ml) water for a thin milk.

Right: Indian-style chicken, served with boiled rice, grated coconut and apple slices

Cold chicken fricassée

A fricassée is slowly-cooked meat served in a thickened sauce. Although this chicken dish can be eaten hot, with rice, chilling improves its flavour

LUNCH OR SUPPER — Serves 4

Overall timing 2 hours plus overnight chilling

Equipment 2 saucepans, measuring jug, flameproof casserole

Freezing Make up to Step 4 and discard bouquet garni. Turn into rigid container, leaving $\frac{3}{4}$ inch (2cm) headspace, cool, seal, label and freeze. Freezer life: 4 months. To use: reheat gently from frozen in saucepan or casserole, then complete as from Step 5

INGREDIENTS

1	Onion	1
3	Cloves	3
$1\frac{1}{2}$ pints	Water	850ml
1	Pigs trotter or calves foot	1
1	Stock cube	1
	Salt and pepper	
4oz	Button mushrooms	125g
2 tbsp	Lemon juice	2×15ml
3lb	Chicken portions	1.4kg
2 tbsp	Plain flour	2×15ml
2oz	Butter	50g
	Bouquet garni	
2	Egg yolks	2
3 tbsp	Double cream	3×15ml

METHOD

1 To make stock, peel onion and spike with cloves. Put into a saucepan with the water, the pigs trotter or calves foot (cut in half), stock cube, salt and pepper. Bring to the boil, remove any scum, then simmer gently for $1\frac{1}{2}$ hours. Alternatively, use a pressure cooker to make the stock. Put the bones into open cooker with 1 pint (560ml) water. Bring to boil, then skim. Add vegetables, then more water – don't fill pan more than half full. Bring to pressure and cook for 45 minutes. Reduce pressure, cool, remove fat.

2 Wipe mushrooms and cook for 3 minutes over a low heat in $\frac{1}{4}$ pint (150ml) of stock and lemon juice.

3 Dry chicken portions and coat with seasoned flour. Heat butter in casserole and brown chicken on all sides, a few pieces at a time.

4 Strain stock and pour over chicken. Add bouquet garni, simmer for 20 minutes, then add the mushrooms and their cooking liquor.

5 Remove chicken from casserole with a draining spoon and place on serving dish. Garnish with the drained mushrooms. Discard the bouquet garni and reserve the stock.

6 Mix egg yolks and cream in a saucepan. Gradually stir in 1 pint (560ml) of the stock and stir vigorously over a low heat until sauce thickens. Do not allow sauce to boil. Remove from heat, adjust seasoning and pour over chicken. Allow to cool, then place in fridge overnight. Serve garnished with sprigs of parsley, and with a crisp green salad.

Below: Old German casserole, a combination of three meats with crisp fried potatoes

Old German casserole

No stock is used for this filling three-meat casserole. Gentle cooking draws out the rich, natural juices

MAIN MEAL — Serves 4

Overall timing $1\frac{1}{4}$ hours

Equipment Heavy-based flameproof casserole, saucepan, large frying pan

Freezing Make, omitting the potatoes. Cool, pack in foil container, seal, label and freeze. Freezer life: 3 months. To use: place, covered, in oven at 375F (190C) Gas 5 for 45 minutes, then add hot fried potatoes

INGREDIENTS

4	Chicken legs	4
	Salt and pepper	
4	Onions	4
4oz	Streaky bacon rashers	125g
2oz	Margarine	50g
$1\frac{1}{2}$lb	Potatoes	700g
4 tbsp	Oil	4×15ml
8oz	Button mushrooms	225g
8oz	Pigs liver	225g
	Plain flour	
12oz	Pork tenderloin	350g
	Fresh parsley	

METHOD

1 Wash and dry chicken legs. Sprinkle with salt and pepper. Peel and slice onions. Cut off rind and chop bacon into 2 inch (5cm) pieces.

2 Heat margarine in a heavy-based casserole and fry bacon for a few minutes. Add onions and cook till golden. Add chicken and brown on all sides. Cover and cook gently for 30 minutes.

3 Meanwhile, peel potatoes and cut into 1 inch (2.5cm) cubes. Cook for 5 minutes in boiling salted water. Drain and dry well.

4 Heat oil in frying pan, add potatoes and cook till crisp and golden brown all over. Remove from pan with a draining spoon. Dry on kitchen paper and sprinkle with salt.

5 Wipe and slice mushrooms. Fry for 2 minutes, then remove from pan.

6 Slice liver thinly and coat with seasoned flour. Cut pork into 4 pieces and sprinkle with salt and pepper. Add both to frying pan and cook gently for about 5 minutes on each side.

7 Add pork, liver, mushrooms and potatoes to chicken mixture in casserole. Cook, uncovered, for a further 15 minutes. Garnish with parsley.

Mandarin chicken

A fruity-flavoured dish, with sultanas soaked in Madeira, and canned mandarin oranges – they're sweeter and juicier than fresh ones. A little cream and flaked almonds, browned in butter, finish the dish

MAIN MEAL Serves 4

Overall timing 1 hour

Equipment Bowl, large heavy-based frying pan, measuring jug, small saucepan

Freezing Make up to Step 4. Transfer to a rigid container, leaving $\frac{3}{4}$ inch (2cm) headspace, and cool. Seal, label and freeze. Freezer life: 4 months. To use: reheat from frozen in saucepan, then complete as from Step 5

Below: Mandarin chicken in a fruity sauce, with hot spicy flavours added for contrast

INGREDIENTS

2oz	Sultanas	50g
$\frac{1}{4}$ pint	Madeira	150ml
3lb	Chicken portions	1.4kg
1 teasp	Salt	5ml
1 teasp	White pepper	5ml
2 teasp	Paprika	2×5ml
5 tbsp	Oil	5×15ml
10oz	Can of mandarin oranges	312g
1	Garlic clove	1
4fl oz	Chicken stock	120ml
1 tbsp	Cornflour	15ml
2 tbsp	Soy sauce	2×15ml
$\frac{1}{2}$ teasp	Ground ginger	2.5ml
4fl oz	Carton of double cream	113ml
1oz	Butter	25g
2oz	Flaked almonds	50g

METHOD

1 Put sultanas in a bowl with Madeira. Wash chicken portions and dry on kitchen paper. Mix together salt, pepper and paprika and pat on to the chicken pieces.

2 Heat oil in a large frying pan, add chicken, a few pieces at a time, and cook for 10 minutes till brown all over.

3 Drain oranges, measure out 4fl oz (120ml) of the juice and pour it into the pan. Peel and chop the garlic and add to the chicken.

4 Pour the stock (made up with 1 stock cube if necessary) into the pan, bring to the boil, cover and simmer for 30 minutes. Add sultanas and the Madeira in which they have been soaking, and simmer for a further 10 minutes.

5 Remove chicken portions from pan with a draining spoon. Put into serving dish and keep warm. Mix cornflour with a little warm water in a cup. Stir into pan juices and bring to boil. Add soy sauce, ginger and most of the mandarin oranges (reserve a few for garnish). Stir the cream into the sauce and heat gently for a few minutes but do not let it boil.

6 Heat butter in a small pan, add the almonds and cook till brown all over, turning them frequently with an egg slice or spatula.

TO SERVE

Pour sauce over chicken and sprinkle with almonds and reserved oranges. Serve with a green salad and a dish of plain boiled rice.

Above: Chicken parcels – pastry casings for a succulent creamy filling

Chicken parcels

An interesting alternative to a pie – individual parcels made with puff pastry and cooked chicken

SUPPER OR STARTER Serves 6

Overall timing 35 minutes

Equipment Saucepan, 2 bowls, pastry brush, baking tray

Freezing Open freeze unbaked parcels. Wrap individually in foil, seal and label. Freezer life: 2 months. To use: unwrap, then proceed as Step 7, increasing baking time by 10–20 minutes

INGREDIENTS

13oz	Packet of frozen puff pastry	375g
1	Medium-size onion	1
1oz	Butter	25g
10oz	Cooked boneless chicken	275g
3 tbsp	Chopped parsley	3×15ml
4 tbsp	Double cream	4×15ml
	Salt and pepper	
3	Slices of ham	3
1	Egg yolk	1
6	Lettuce leaves	6

METHOD

1 Thaw pastry. Preheat oven to 400F (200C) Gas 6.

2 Peel and chop onion and lightly fry in the butter till transparent.

3 Set aside 6 fairly large pieces of chicken and finely chop the rest. Put chopped chicken into a bowl with the chopped parsley and fried onion.

4 In another bowl, lightly beat the cream, then stir into the chicken and parsley. Season with salt and pepper.

5 Roll out pastry on a lightly-floured surface. Cut out six 5 inch (12.5cm) squares.

6 Cut ham slices in half. Place 1 piece in centre of each pastry square. Top with a reserved piece of chicken, then cover with chopped chicken mixture. Dampen pastry edges with cold water. Fold corners to centre to cover the filling, pinching the edges together, but leaving a small hole in the top.

7 Beat the egg yolk with a pinch of salt and brush over pastry. Place parcels on a greased baking tray and bake in the centre of the oven for 25 minutes or until well risen and golden-brown. Remove from oven.

TO SERVE

Place each chicken parcel on a lettuce leaf and serve with a tomato and onion salad and mashed potatoes.

Chicken croquettes

Leftover chicken is used to form croquettes which are then deep fried. They can be shallow fried if preferred

LIGHT LUNCH OR SUPPER Serves 4–6

Overall timing 30 minutes

Equipment Saucepan, deep-fryer, bowl, 3 shallow dishes

Freezing Cool completely, then open freeze until hard, put in polythene bag or rigid container, seal, label and return to freezer. Freezer life: 1 month. To use: thaw overnight in fridge. Reheat in moderately hot oven 375F (190C) Gas 5 for about 20 minutes or deep fry for 5–10 minutes (don't overbrown)

INGREDIENTS

12oz	Cooked boneless chicken	350g
3oz	Butter	75g
3oz	Plain flour	75g
½ pint	Cold milk	300ml
	Salt and pepper	
	Grated nutmeg	
2	Egg yolks	2
1 tbsp	Grated Gruyère	15ml
1 tbsp	Chopped parsley	15ml
	Oil for frying	
2 tbsp	Plain flour	2×15ml
1	Egg	1
4oz	Dried breadcrumbs	125g
	Fresh parsley	
1	Lemon	1

METHOD

1 Finely chop or mince chicken.

2 To make sauce, melt the butter in a pan over a low heat and stir in the flour. When the mixture begins to froth, add the cold milk, salt, pepper and a pinch of nutmeg. Whisk till sauce thickens.

3 Remove from heat and stir in egg yolks and Gruyère. Turn into a bowl and mix in chicken and parsley. Cool.

4 Heat oil for frying to 340F (170C) or till bread cube browns in 1 minute.

5 Using your hands, shape chicken mixture into small cylindrical croquettes. Roll them in the flour, then in the lightly beaten egg to coat them completely and finally in the breadcrumbs, pressing them on well with a palette knife or spatula.

6 Fry the croquettes, 4 or 5 at a time, in the hot oil until golden brown. Drain on kitchen paper and keep in a warm oven until all are fried. Arrange on a hot serving plate, garnish with parsley and serve with lemon wedges.

Fry chopped onion and chopped capsicum in butter, then stir in the flour and cold milk

Warm the milk then add to the mixture. Cook gently for 15 minutes till thick

Chop the cooked chicken into small chunks and add the pieces to the sauce

Add the sherry to the sauce, then simmer gently for about 5 minutes

Above: Chicken à la king – a creamy mix surrounded by a garnish of sliced capsicum

Chicken à la king

Chefs like to invest their culinary inventions with a touch of glamour by christening them with exotic names – a favourite ploy being to toss in a few French words. This North American chicken recipe is a classic example of this but it is also an excellent, and simple, way of using up leftover chicken

MAIN MEAL Serves 4

Overall timing 35 minutes

Equipment Flameproof casserole

Freezing Place in rigid container, cover, lable and freeze. Freezer life: 2 months. To use: thaw overnight in fridge, then reheat gently

INGREDIENTS

1lb	Cooked boneless chicken	450g
1	Onion	1
1	Large green capsicum	1
2oz	Butter	50g
2oz	Plain flour	50g
2 tbsp	Cold milk	2×15ml
½ pint	Warm milk	300ml
	Salt and pepper	
	Grated nutmeg	
2 tbsp	Sherry	2×15ml

METHOD

1 Cut chicken into small pieces. Peel and finely chop onion. Deseed capsicum and finely chop half of it. Heat the butter in the casserole and gently fry onion and capsicum till onion is transparent.

2 Stir in the flour with a wooden spoon, then the cold milk. Remove from heat then gradually add the warm milk. Bring to the boil. Season with salt, pepper and a pinch of nutmeg. Reduce heat and simmer gently for 15 minutes.

3 Add chicken and sherry and cook for 5 minutes more or until chicken is well heated through. Stir frequently during this time to prevent mixture sticking.

TO SERVE

Place chicken and sauce on warmed serving plate and surround with slices of remaining capsicum which have been blanched in boiling water for 5 minutes. Serve with boiled rice or noodles.

VARIATION

Fry 4oz (125g) wiped sliced button mushrooms with the onion and capsicum. At Step 3, stir chicken pieces into the sauce, then blend 1 egg yolk with 4fl oz (120ml) soured or double cream and the sherry, stir into chicken mixture and heat through but do not allow to boil. Turn into a hot, precooked vol au vent case and serve with a salad.

Catalan chicken

A substantial chicken casserole with the delicious taste of Spain

MAIN MEAL Serves 4

Overall timing $1\frac{1}{2}$ hours

Equipment 2 bowls, flameproof casserole

Freezing Cool, pack in rigid container, seal, label and freeze. Freezer life: 3 months. To use: reheat slowly from frozen in oven at 350F (180C) Gas 4

INGREDIENTS

8	Chicken legs and wings	8
2	Red capsicums	2
8oz	Onions	225g
1lb	Tomatoes	450g
2	Aubergines	2
	Salt	
2 tbsp	Oil	2×15ml
2oz	Butter	50g
1	Garlic clove	1
	Paprika	
4fl oz	Dry white wine	120ml

METHOD

1 Wash chicken and dry well. Wash, deseed and cut capsicums into strips. Peel and chop onions. Blanch, peel and quarter tomatoes. Wash aubergines and cut into thick strips. Put aubergines in a bowl, sprinkle with salt and leave for 20 minutes.

2 Heat oil and butter in a casserole. Add chicken and cook till golden on all sides. Remove from pan.

3 Add capsicums and onions to casserole. Cook till onions are transparent, then add tomatoes and cook for 5 minutes. Transfer mixture to a bowl and keep warm.

4 Rinse aubergines under cold water, then dry on kitchen paper. Add to casserole and cook for 10 minutes. Remove from pan.

5 Return chicken to casserole. Cover with tomato mixture and aubergines, peeled and crushed garlic, salt and a pinch of paprika. Pour in wine, cover and cook for 45 minutes. Serve with boiled rice.

Above: Catalan chicken – a Spanish way of making cheaper cuts of chicken into a tasty meal

Fry the chicken pieces in a mixture of oil and butter (butter alone will burn too quickly). Turn the pieces until they are golden on all sides. Remove from pan

The sliced capsicums, chopped onions and chopped tomatoes are cooked separately, then removed so that the aubergines can be fried and cooked for 10 minutes

cook's know-how

There are certain rules to remember when freezing chicken. Chicken dishes which have enough sauce to cover the meat adequately can be frozen for up to 4 months. If garlic or strong herbs are included these can affect the flavour, causing a "musty" taste, so freeze for less time or not at all. Never refreeze made-up dishes once thawed, and always reheat thoroughly, boiling for at least 15 minutes to eliminate any harmful bacteria present, stirring occasionally to prevent sticking.

Return chicken and tomato mixture to the pan and add fried aubergines, paprika and garlic. Add white wine and cook for a further 45 minutes

Chicken in Muscadet

Muscadet is a light, very dry white wine from Brittany which goes well with chicken, fish and shellfish – but any dry white wine can be used as a substitute if necessary

MAIN MEAL Serves 4

Overall timing 1¾ hours

Equipment Flameproof casserole, small bowl, frying pan

Freezing Make to end of Step 4, then cool. Joint chicken and pack into rigid container. Pour sauce over, leave ¾ inch (2cm) headspace, then cover, label and freeze. Freezer life: 4 months. To use: thaw for 4 hours, then reheat thoroughly before carrying out Steps 5 to 8

INGREDIENTS

2oz	Butter	50g
1 tbsp	Oil	15ml
4lb	Ovenready chicken	1.8kg
1	Large onion	1
12oz	Carrots	350g
	Dried thyme	
½ teasp	Salt	2.5ml
	Pepper	
1	Bay leaf	1
½ pint	Muscadet	300ml
½ pint	Stock	300ml
12oz	Button mushrooms	350g
3	Egg yolks	3
	Grated nutmeg	

METHOD

1 Heat half the butter and all the oil in a casserole. Add chicken and cook gently for few minutes, just to firm the skin.
2 Peel onion and carrots and slice into thick slices. Remove chicken from casserole. Place half of the prepared vegetables in the bottom of the casserole and put chicken, breast side up, on top. Cover with remaining vegetables.
3 Add a pinch of thyme, the salt, pepper and bay leaf. Pour in wine and enough stock (made up with 1 cube if necessary) to half cover. Bring to boil, uncovered; cover and simmer for 40 minutes.
4 Wipe mushrooms and add a quarter of them to the casserole. Turn chicken over making sure there is still an even layer of vegetables underneath. Simmer for a further 20 minutes.
5 Remove chicken and place on serving dish. Lift out vegetables with a draining spoon and arrange around chicken. Keep warm.
6 Reduce cooking liquor in casserole by boiling fast, uncovered, for 5–8 minutes.
7 Beat egg yolks with 2 or 3 pinches of nutmeg in a bowl. Mix in a little of the cooking liquor. Stir this into casserole and remove immediately from heat. Leave to thicken without stirring, but rotate pan once or twice to ensure that sauce is smooth.
8 Melt remaining butter in a frying pan and lightly fry remaining mushrooms. Garnish chicken with mushrooms. Pour some of the sauce over and place rest in a sauce boat. Serve with potatoes and brussels sprouts or broccoli.

Fricassée de poulet à l'ancienne

A classic French method of cooking chicken with button onions and mushrooms. Just before serving the cooking liquor is thickened with egg yolks and cream

MAIN MEAL Serves 4

Overall timing 1¾ hours

Equipment Flameproof dish, saucepan

Freezing Make up to end of Step 4. Cool, remove fat from surface, turn into rigid container, cover, label and freeze. Freezer life: 4 months. To use: reheat gently from frozen. Complete Step 5

INGREDIENTS

3oz	Butter	75g
1 tbsp	Oil	15ml
3lb	Chicken portions	1.4kg
1oz	Plain flour	25g
1 pint	Hot chicken stock	560ml
1	Carrot	1
1	Stalk of celery	1
	Parsley sprigs	15ml
	Salt and pepper	
6oz	Button mushrooms	175g
6oz	Button onions	175g
2 tbsp	Lemon juice	2×15ml
2	Egg yolks	2
4fl oz	Carton of single cream	113ml

METHOD

1 Heat 2oz (50g) of the butter and oil. Add the wiped chicken portions and cook quickly on all sides till golden. Sprinkle with the flour, then add the stock gradually, stirring constantly.
2 Add the scraped carrot, washed celery and parsley and season well with salt and pepper. Cover pan and cook gently for 45 minutes.
3 Meanwhile, wipe the mushrooms and place in a small saucepan with the peeled button onions. Cover with salted water and add a little pepper, remaining butter and the lemon juice. Simmer for 10 minutes. Leave to cool.
4 Remove carrot, celery and parsley from the flameproof pan and replace them with the drained mushrooms and onions. Reserve their cooking liquor. Cook for 5 minutes, then add cooking liquor and cook for a further 5 minutes.
5 Remove pan from heat. Beat the egg yolks with the cream in a bowl, then pour into the hot but not boiling chicken mixture, stirring all the time until the cooking liquid thickens. Serve immediately with plain boiled rice and a green vegetable such as spinach or broccoli.

The chicken pieces are lightly fried until golden brown and firm, then the button onions and mushrooms are added

The creamy sauce is spooned into the pan and cooked just long enough for the mixture to coat the chicken pieces

Chicken chasseur

Tarragon, a herb well suited to chicken, is a good complement to a chasseur sauce: double the quantity if using fresh instead of dried herbs

MAIN MEAL Serves 4

Overall timing $1\frac{1}{2}$ hours

Equipment Flameproof casserole

Freezing Make as Steps 1–3. Cool, pack into rigid container, cover, label and freeze. Freezer life: 4 months. To use: thaw for 3 hours then heat slowly but thoroughly

INGREDIENTS

8oz	Mushrooms	225g
4	Shallots	4
1oz	Butter	25g
1 tbsp	Oil	15ml
$2\frac{1}{2}$lb	Chicken portions	1.1kg
2 tbsp	Plain flour	2×15ml
8fl oz	Dry white wine	220ml
$\frac{1}{4}$ pint	Chicken stock	150ml
1 tbsp	Dried tarragon	15ml
1 tbsp	Tomato paste	15ml
	Bouquet garni	
	Salt and pepper	

METHOD

1 Wipe and slice mushrooms. Peel and slice the shallots.

2 Heat the butter and oil in the casserole and cook mushrooms and shallots over a high heat. Add the chicken portions and brown on all sides. Sprinkle with flour. Cook for 1–2 minutes, stirring all the time, till flour colours.

3 Add the wine and the stock (made up with 1 cube if necessary) half the tarragon, the tomato paste, bouquet garni, salt and pepper. Bring to the boil, stirring. Cover and simmer slowly for about 1 hour.

4 Place on a hot serving dish and sprinkle with remaining tarragon. Serve with boiled or sauté potatoes.

cook's know-how

The chasseur sauce – the name literally means the huntsman – is a classic French garnish for chicken and other meats, or even eggs. It contains mushrooms (which the hunter picked on the way home), wine, shallots and chopped gherkins as well as tomato paste to improve the colour.

Italian-style chicken

Basil and sage, both widely used in cooking by Italians, give a flavourful cold chicken – ideal for picnics or a light meal

LUNCH Serves 4

Overall timing $1\frac{3}{4}$ hours plus overnight standing time

Equipment Heavy-based casserole with tight-fitting lid, bowl

Freezing Double wrap chicken in freezer foil, place in plastic bag, seal, label and freeze. Freezer life: 2 weeks. To use: thaw overnight in fridge. Serve cold

INGREDIENTS

1	Large onion	1
1	Carrot	1
1	Stalk of celery	1
1	Sprig of parsley	1
3lb	Ovenready chicken	1.4kg
	Salt and pepper	
4oz	Basil leaves	125g
1oz	Sage leaves	25g

METHOD

1 Cut onion in half. Scrape carrot. Wash celery and parsley. Put them all into the casserole with the chicken. Cover with water and season. Bring to the boil and simmer for about $1\frac{1}{2}$ hours or until chicken is tender.

2 Remove chicken from casserole and pour stock into a bowl.* Put a layer of basil and sage leaves in the bottom of the casserole and place the chicken on top. Cover with remaining herbs and put on lid. Leave overnight in a cool place (not the fridge), so the flavour of the herbs can penetrate the flesh of the chicken. Serve cold.

*When cool, skim to remove fat. Keep in fridge or freezer till needed to make soup or sauce, or a colourful rice salad to accompany the cold chicken. Cook 3oz (75g) rice in 6fl oz (170ml) chicken stock until all the stock has been absorbed – about 10 minutes. Cool rice in a bowl, then add 2 deseeded, chopped green peppers, 3 peeled, chopped tomatoes, some pine nuts and seasoning to taste. Chill and serve, garnished with parsley.

Roast chicken with tarragon

A classic way of roasting a chicken. The gravy is made from the tarragon-flavoured pan juices

MAIN MEAL Serves 4

Overall timing $1\frac{1}{4}$ hours

Equipment Roasting tin

Freezing Freeze sauce separately in rigid container. Double wrap chicken in thick foil, place in plastic bag, seal, label and freeze. Freezer life: 2 weeks.
To use: thaw overnight in fridge and serve cold

INGREDIENTS

$3\frac{1}{2}$lb	Ovenready chicken	1.6kg
	Salt and pepper	
2oz	Butter	50g
4 tbsp	Chopped fresh tarragon *or*	4×15ml
1 tbsp	Dried tarragon	15ml
	Watercress	

METHOD

1 Preheat oven to 425F (220C) Gas 7.

2 Wipe chicken and season inside and out. Put 1oz (25g) of the butter and the fresh or dried tarragon inside bird.

3 Place chicken on its side in the roasting tin and coat with remaining butter. Cook on the middle shelf of the oven for 15 minutes, then turn the chicken on to its other side. Cook for 15 minutes, then turn chicken on its back and continue cooking for 35 minutes.

4 Remove chicken from roasting tin and place on serving dish. Stir a little wine, water or chicken stock into the pan juices in the tin, bring to the boil and cook for 1 minute.

TO SERVE

Pour gravy into gravy boat. Garnish chicken with watercress.

Roman-style turkey drumsticks

Turkey drumsticks are especially good value because they're meaty, tender and full of flavour. The boning's not difficult but you do need a sharp knife to scrape the flesh towards the knobbly end. When the bones are out, fill, close the openings and spike skin with herbs

MAIN MEAL Serves 4

Overall timing 2 hours

Equipment Skewers, flameproof casserole

Freezing Not recommended for finished dish

INGREDIENTS

2×1lb	Frozen turkey drumsticks	2×450g
	Salt	
	Freshly-ground black pepper	
4oz	Thinly sliced smoked bacon rashers	125g
	Fresh rosemary leaves	
2oz	Butter	50g
2 teasp	Plain flour	2×5ml
$\frac{1}{4}$ pint	Chicken stock	150ml
4 tbsp	Dry white vermouth	4×15ml
	Lettuce leaves	

METHOD

1 Thaw drumsticks. Preheat the oven to 375F (190C) Gas 5.

2 Wipe the drumsticks. Using a sharp knife scrape the flesh away from the bone without cutting through the skin. When the bone is fully revealed, cut through the skin still attached to remove the bone and leave a tube of meat.

3 Return the drumsticks to their original shape, then season. Derind and chop the bacon and stuff into the cavities. Close the openings with skewers. Pierce the skin in several places and insert the rosemary leaves.

4 Rub the butter over the drumsticks and place in the casserole. Cover and bake in the centre of the oven for about $1\frac{1}{4}$ hours till the juices run clear when the thickest part of the flesh is pierced with a fine skewer.

5 Lift out the drumsticks and remove the skewers. Cut into thick slices, arrange on a serving dish and keep hot.

6 Add the flour to the casserole and stir over a low heat for 1 minute. Gradually add the stock (made with a cube if necessary) and vermouth and bring to the boil, stirring. Simmer for 2 minutes then adjust the seasoning to taste.

7 Pour sauce over the turkey. Garnish with lettuce leaves and serve immediately with roast potatoes and brussels sprouts purée (recipe below).

Below: Roman-style turkey drumsticks – superbly enhanced by rosemary and vermouth

cook's know-how

To make brussels sprouts purée, trim 2lb (900g) sprouts and cook in boiling salted water for 10 minutes. Drain, rinse under cold water and drain again. Heat 1oz (25g) butter in a large pan, add sprouts and cook for 30 minutes over low heat, shaking gently from time to time. Meanwhile wash 9oz (250g) potatoes and cook in their skins for 30 minutes. Peel potatoes and mash with the sprouts. Return purée to pan, add 2oz (50g) butter and $\frac{1}{2}$ teasp (2.5ml) grated nutmeg and season to taste with salt and pepper.

Turkey and mace pie

It's rare that the whole turkey is ever finished on Christmas day and this dish takes advantage of the situation. Using ingredients mostly from the storecupboard, the pie can be eaten during the holiday period or frozen and served up when the festivities are over

LUNCH OR SUPPER Serves 6

Overall timing $1\frac{1}{4}$ hours

Equipment 2 saucepans, 2 pint (1.1 litre) pie dish

Freezing Cool, wrap in foil, seal, label and freeze. Freezer life: 1 month.
To use: thaw in wrappings in fridge overnight. Remove wrappings, cover top with foil and reheat in oven at 350F (180C) Gas 4 for 35–40 minutes

INGREDIENTS

$7\frac{1}{2}$oz	Packet of frozen puff pastry	212g
1 pint	Chicken stock	560ml
2oz	Pasta shells	50g
1lb	Cooked turkey	450g
1oz	Butter	25g
2 tbsp	Plain flour	2×15ml
1 teasp	Ground mace	5ml
$\frac{1}{4}$ pint	Milk	150ml
1 tbsp	Chopped parsley	15ml
	Salt and pepper	
1	Egg	1

METHOD

1 Thaw pastry. Put stock (made with cubes if necessary) in a saucepan and bring to the boil. Add the pasta and cook till al dente. Drain, reserving the stock.

2 Preheat oven to 425F (220C) Gas 7. Grease pie dish. Dice the turkey.

3 Melt the butter in a saucepan, add the flour and mace and cook for 2 minutes. Gradually stir in $\frac{1}{4}$ pint (150ml) reserved stock and the milk and bring to the boil, stirring constantly. Reduce heat and cook for 3 minutes. Add the pasta, turkey and parsley and mix well. Taste and adjust seasoning. Pour into the pie dish.

4 Roll out pastry on a lightly floured surface to $\frac{1}{4}$ inch (6mm) thickness and use to cover the pie, lightly pressing down the edges. Glaze surface with lightly beaten egg. Bake for 15 minutes, reduce the temperature to 350F (180C) Gas 4 and cook for a further 20 minutes. Serve hot with wedges of buttered cabbage, or brussels sprouts.

Sweet and sour turkey

The combination of so many flavours – some sweet, some spicy, some hot and some cool – gives this dish its memorable taste. Serve with chutney

MAIN MEAL Serves 4–6

Overall timing 45 minutes plus marination

Equipment Bowl, 2 saucepans, frying pan

Freezing Prepare to end of Step 3. Place turkey in foil dish and strain sauce over; cool, cover, label and freeze. Freezer life: 3 months. To use: thaw overnight in fridge then turn into saucepan and complete as Steps 5 and 6

INGREDIENTS

1½lb	Turkey breasts	700g
2 tbsp	Oil	2×15ml
1 teasp	Salt	5ml
¼ teasp	Finely-ground white pepper	1.25ml
	Tabasco sauce	
4oz	Butter	125g
8oz	Onions	225g
1 tbsp	Curry powder	15ml
1 teasp	Sugar	5ml
2	Dessert apples	2
1	Garlic clove	1
¾ pint	Stock	400ml
3 tbsp	Lemon juice	3×15ml
1 inch	Piece of fresh ginger	2.5cm
¼ pint	Carton of single cream	150ml
1	Banana	1
	Plain boiled rice	

METHOD

1 Slice the turkey breasts and cut into 1×2 inch (2.5×5cm) strips. Place in a bowl with the oil, salt, pepper and a few drops of Tabasco sauce. Turn till coated and marinate for 15 minutes.

2 Heat half the butter in pan, add turkey and marinating juices and cook over high heat till brown. Remove from heat and cover.

3 Peel and chop the onions. Heat 1½oz (40g) of butter in a saucepan and fry the onions. Sprinkle in the curry powder and sugar and fry till the onions are transparent. Peel and finely chop 1 apple and add to the onions with the peeled whole garlic clove and salt. Add the stock (made with a cube if necessary) and bring to the boil. Simmer uncovered for 20 minutes.

4 Strain the sauce and pour over turkey. Add lemon juice, grated ginger and cream. Cook for 10 minutes till heated through but not boiling.

5 Meanwhile peel the banana and finely slice diagonally. Peel remaining apple and cut lengthways into fine slices. Lightly fry apple and banana in remaining butter till hot. Pour turkey and sauce over a bed of rice and garnish with the banana and apple.

Spice coated duck

A dish from Malaysia. If liked, use two ducklings and grill or barbecue

MAIN MEAL Serves 4

Overall timing 1¾ hours

Equipment Poultry shears, rolling-pin, skewer, blender, wire rack, roasting tin

Freezing Not recommended for finished dish

INGREDIENTS

4lb	Frozen ovenready duck	1.8kg
2	Medium-size onions	2
½ inch	Piece of green ginger	12.5mm
1	Garlic clove	1
2	Fresh chillies	2
1 tbsp	Ground coriander	15ml
½ teasp	Ground fennel seeds	2.5ml
1 teasp	Ground cumin	5ml
½ teasp	Ground turmeric	2.5ml
½ teasp	Freshly-grated nutmeg	2.5ml
½ teasp	Freshly-ground black pepper	2.5ml
¼ pint	Tamarind water	150ml
2oz	Coconut cream	50g

METHOD

1 Thaw duck completely. Preheat the oven to 350F (180C) Gas 4.

2 Wipe the duck and cut right through the breast with poultry shears. Pull the duck open and flatten by pressing with a rolling-pin to break the rib bones. Push a skewer through one leg, then through the body and the other leg to keep duck flat during cooking. Prick through skin several times with a fork.

3 Peel and chop the onions, peel and chop the ginger. Peel garlic and deseed the chillies. Put into a blender with the spices, tamarind water and coconut cream. Blend to a smooth paste.

4 Place duck, skin side up, on a wire rack in a roasting tin. Brush half the spice paste over. Bake in the centre of the oven for 20 minutes.

5 Turn duck over and brush with remaining paste. Cook for a further 20 minutes.

6 Turn duck again and baste with the cooking liquor. Cook for a further 40 minutes, basting frequently till the juices run clear when the thickest part of the meat is pierced with a skewer.

7 Cut through duck along each side of the back-bone with poultry shears. Remove and discard back-bone. Cut across each half of the duck diagonally and arrange pieces on a warmed serving dish. Serve immediately with boiled rice.

Duck with cider

The acidity of cider takes the edge off the natural fattiness of the duck and also helps to tenderize the flesh. But the cooking juices are too oily to use in making the sauce and must, therefore, be discarded. A light sprinkling of pepper over the duck helps to dry and crisp the skin during cooking

MAIN MEAL Serves 4

Overall timing 1¼ hours

Equipment Large heavy-based saucepan or flameproof casserole, kitchen scissors

Freezing Cool duck and sauce separately. Slice flesh and layer in foil container pouring a little sauce between each one and ending with sauce. Cover, label and freeze. Freezer life: 4 months. To use: remove lid, reheat from frozen in moderate oven 350F (180C) Gas 4

INGREDIENTS

3¾lb	Ovenready duck	1.7kg
	Salt	
	Freshly-ground black pepper	
2oz	Butter	50g
1 tbsp	Oil	15ml
4 tbsp	Boiling water	4×15ml
18fl oz	Dry cider	500ml
	Sauce	
4oz	Shallots or button onions	125g
2 tbsp	Cornflour	2×15ml
¼ pint	Single cream	150ml
	Mustard and cress	

METHOD

1 Remove fat glands in tail of duck with scissors. Wash duck and dry well with kitchen paper. Prick thighs and back with a fork to help release fat during cooking. Sprinkle inside the duck with

salt and pepper and rub extra pepper over surface of skin.

2 Heat half the butter and all of the oil in the pan. Put in the duck and brown it all over – about 12–15 minutes. Remove excess fat, then add the boiling water and 2 tbsp (2×15ml) of the cider. Cover and cook for 40–45 minutes over moderate heat. When the juices from the thigh run clear, not pink, when the flesh is pierced with a skewer, the duck is cooked.
3 Remove duck from pan. Keep warm by wrapping in foil. Discard cooking liquor from pan.
4 To make the sauce: wash and peel the shallots or button onions, slice thinly and add to pan with remaining butter. Cook gently for 2 minutes, without letting them brown.
5 Pour in remaining cider, bring to the boil and boil, uncovered, until the liquid is reduced by one third. Season with salt and pepper to taste.
6 Blend the cornflour with the cream in a bowl, then stir into sauce and cook for a few minutes, stirring all the time until thickened. Pour into a warm sauce boat.

TO SERVE
Carve the duck into slices and arrange on a warm serving dish. Garnish with cress. Serve the sauce separately. Serve duck with boiled potatoes and a dish of braised red cabbage.

cook's know-how

If you can't obtain fresh or frozen duck portions, you can cut them yourself. You'll need game scissors or sharp kitchen scissors. Split the duck in half along the breast bone, then cut out and discard the backbone. Divide each side of the duck into three pieces – a leg joint, wing joint and a portion of breast. Trim off the fat, wing pinions and leg ends. Remove skin, using a sharp knife, if the recipe requires. Cutting a cooked duck into portions is best done in the kitchen so the pieces can be served at the same temperature as the accompaniments.

Above: Salmis de canard – duck braised with mushrooms in a creamy sauce

Salmis de canard

Part roasted duck is cut up, braised in a sauce and served with toast

MAIN MEAL Serves 4

Overall timing 2¼ hours

Equipment Roasting tin and wire rack, large saucepan

Freezing Make omitting cream. Cool, pack in rigid container, cover, label and freeze. Freezer life: 3 months. To use: reheat gently from frozen, then stir in cream

INGREDIENTS

3½lb	Ovenready duck	1.6kg
	Salt and pepper	
4oz	Celery	125g
1	Onion	1
2oz	Butter	50g
½ pint	Chicken stock	300ml
½ pint	Dry white wine	300ml
4oz	Button mushrooms	125g
2oz	Plain flour	50g
2 tbsp	Single cream	2×15ml
2 tbsp	Brandy	2×15ml
	Parsley	

METHOD
1 Preheat the oven to 400F (200C) Gas 6. Wipe the duck and season inside and out with salt and pepper. Prick all over with a fork. Place duck on wire rack in roasting tin and cook in the centre of the oven for an hour.
2 Drain duck. Remove all the meat from the carcass. Chop into bite-size pieces.
3 Wash and chop celery. Peel and chop the onion. Heat 1oz (25g) of the butter in a saucepan and gently fry the celery and onion for 10 minutes.
4 Break up the duck carcass and add to the pan. Pour in the stock (made up with 1 stock cube if necessary) and wine. Bring to the boil, cover and simmer for 30 minutes. Strain and reserve stock.
5 Heat remaining butter in a saucepan and add the wiped whole mushrooms. Cook for 5 minutes, then stir in the flour and cook gently for 2 minutes. Gradually stir in the reserved stock, bring to the boil, stirring, and simmer for 3 minutes. Taste for seasoning.
6 Add cream, brandy, then chopped meat. Cook 10 minutes more without boiling.

TO SERVE
Transfer duck and sauce to warmed serving dish. Garnish with parsley. Serve with toast, beans and fondant potatoes.

FAMILY MEALS

A supply of simple dishes in the freezer will stand you in good stead as family meals on days when you are too busy to cook. They are also an important part of the routine for a working mum

Quick carrot and mince fry-up

An ideal budget dish with minced beef – just the thing for hearty appetites. Leeks add extra flavour

Above: Quick carrot and mince fry-up – good for a family meal

MAIN MEAL Serves 4

Overall timing 45 minutes

Equipment 2 frying pans or saucepan and frying pan, bowl

Freezing Cool, pack in polythene bag, seal, label and freeze. Freezer life: 2 months. To use: thaw overnight in fridge or for 2–4 hours at room temperature, then heat thoroughly

INGREDIENTS

1lb	Carrots	450g
8oz	Leeks	225g
2oz	Butter	50g
9fl oz	White wine	250ml
	Salt and pepper	
1lb	Minced beef	450g
$\frac{1}{2}$ teasp	Worcestershire sauce	2.5ml

METHOD

1 Scrape and wash carrots. Chop into 1 inch (2.5cm) pieces. Trim, wash and chop leeks into $\frac{1}{2}$ inch (12.5mm) slices.

2 Gently heat half the butter in frying pan or saucepan and fry chopped carrots for 3 minutes. Pour in white wine, cover and cook over a low heat for 20 minutes.

3 Add the leeks, season with salt and pepper and cook for a further 15 minutes, or until tender.

4 Meanwhile, put mince in bowl, mix in salt and pepper with a fork. Roughly shape mince into 1 inch (2.5cm) pieces. Gently heat remaining butter in another frying pan and fry meat for about 15 minutes until lightly browned and no longer pink in the middle. Stir from time to time.

5 Reduce any excess liquid in vegetable pan by boiling rapidly for a minute or two. Add meat and sprinkle with Worcestershire sauce. Serve from the pan, and serve creamy mashed potatoes and also a green vegetable, if liked, separately.

VARIATIONS

Instead of wine use beef stock (made with cubes if necessary) or a light, dry cider. Other vegetables may be added, such as celery, mushrooms or chopped onions.

Above: Steak and kidney pie — a tasty old English favourite

Steak and kidney pie

This is typical old English fare, made with steak and kidney and a packet of frozen puff pastry

MAIN MEAL Serves 6

Overall timing 3¼ hours

Equipment Flameproof casserole, deep pie dish, baking tray

Freezing After Step 6, let egg glaze dry, then wrap in cling film or foil, label and freeze. Freezer life: 3 months. To use: remove wrappings and bake from frozen in hot oven 425F (220C) Gas 7 for 30 minutes, then reduce temperature to 350F (180C) Gas 4 and bake for a further 30 minutes till hot through

INGREDIENTS

1½lb	Chuck or blade steak	750g
8oz	Ox kidney	225g
4 tbsp	Plain flour	4×15ml
	Salt	
	Freshly-ground black pepper	
2	Large onions	2
2oz	Dripping or lard	50g
¼ pint	Beef stock	150ml
¼ pint	Red wine	150ml
3 tbsp	Tomato paste	3×15ml
9oz	Frozen puff pastry	250g
1	Egg yolk	1

METHOD

1 Preheat the oven to 325F (170C) Gas 3. Wipe the steak and kidney, trim and cut into large chunks. Spread the flour on a plate and season well. Toss the beef and kidney in the flour, a few pieces at a time, until evenly coated.

2 Peel and slice the onions. Heat the dripping or lard in a casserole and fry onions for 3–5 minutes until golden. Remove from pan and reserve.

3 Add the meat and kidney to the pan, a few pieces at a time, and fry quickly till brown on all sides.

4 Return onions and all the meat and kidney to the casserole. Add a little of the stock (made up with 1 stock cube if necessary) and scrape base of pan with a wooden spoon to release sediment. Gradually stir in remaining stock and wine and bring to the boil, stirring. Add tomato paste and season.

5 Cover and cook in the centre of the oven for about 2 hours or until the meat is tender. Transfer to pie dish, piling up the meat to give a domed surface. Meanwhile, thaw pastry.

6 Turn oven up to 425F (220C) Gas 7. Roll out pastry on a lightly floured surface to a round 1 inch (2.5cm) larger than the dish. Moisten edges of pie dish. Lift pastry with the aid of the rolling-pin and place on top of pie. Knock up, then crimp edges. Brush with beaten egg yolk.

7 Place on baking tray and cook in the centre of the oven for 20 minutes. Reduce heat to 350F (180C) Gas 4 and cook for a further 15 minutes or until the pastry is well risen and golden.

Cornish pasties

With a savoury filling of potatoes, onions and meat, these hearty pastry parcels were traditionally the Cornishman's lunch, taken in the back pocket to the harvest fields or to the tin mines

LIGHT LUNCH OR SUPPER Makes 4 or 8

Overall timing 1 hour

Equipment Bowl, baking tray

Freezing Cool pasties. Pack in rigid container, seal, label and freeze. Freezer life: 3–4 months. To use: thaw and then reheat in a hot oven for 10–15 minutes

INGREDIENTS

1lb	Shortcrust pastry	450g
2	Uncooked potatoes	2
4oz	Kidney	125g
1	Onion	1
8oz	Minced beef	225g
	Salt and pepper	
1	Small egg *or* a little milk	1

METHOD

1 Preheat the oven to 450F (230C) Gas 8. Roll out pastry thinly and cut out circles using saucer or plate as guide. Peel and chop potatoes into small pieces. Chop kidney. Peel and finely chop onion.

2 Put potatoes, minced beef, kidney, salt, pepper and onion into a bowl and mix.

3 Place mixture in centre of circles, dampen edges and pinch together.

4 Place pasties on baking tray and brush with beaten egg or milk. Bake for 10 minutes then reduce the heat to 400F (200C) Gas 6 and cook for a further 30–35 minutes.

Cottage pie

Vary this family dish as you wish – add crushed garlic, fresh or dried herbs, green beans or corn kernels

LUNCH OR SUPPER Serves 6

Overall timing 1¼ hours

Equipment Saucepan, flameproof casserole

Freezing Make in a foil container, cover with foil and overwrap in a plastic bag. Seal, label and freeze. Freezer life: 2 months. To use: unwrap, bake from frozen at 425F (220C) Gas 7 for 1 hour

INGREDIENTS

2lb	Floury potatoes	900g
	Salt	
2	Large onions	2
1oz	Beef dripping	25g
2lb	Minced beef	900g
2 tbsp	Plain flour	2×15ml
½ pint	Strong beef stock	300ml
14oz	Can of tomatoes	397g
	Freshly-ground black pepper	
8oz	Frozen vegetables	225g
¼ pint	Milk	150ml
2oz	Butter	50g

METHOD

1 Peel and quarter the potatoes, cover with cold salted water and bring to the boil. Simmer for 15 minutes till tender.

2 Meanwhile, preheat the oven to 375F (190C) Gas 5. Peel and thinly slice the onions. Heat the dripping in the casserole and fry the onion till transparent. Add the minced beef and fry, stirring frequently, for 5–10 minutes till browned all over.

3 Sprinkle in the flour and cook, stirring for 1 minute. Gradually add the stock (made with a cube if necessary) and bring to the boil, stirring constantly. Add the canned tomatoes and juice and salt and pepper and bring to the boil. Stir in the frozen vegetables and simmer for 5 minutes.

4 Drain the potatoes. Add the milk and butter to the potato pan and heat till just below boiling point. Return the potatoes to the pan and mash well.

5 Pipe or spread the potato over the minced beef mixture, and smooth the top. Bake near the top of the oven for about 30 minutes till the potato is golden. Serve immediately.

Above: Ham and vegetable bake – an all-in-one meal that is simple to prepare

Ham and vegetable bake

A substantial and nutritious dish that can be made as a freezer standby. If you have any leftover mashed potatoes, combine them with the celeriac

LUNCH OR SUPPER Serves 4

Overall timing 1 hour 10 minutes

Equipment 2 saucepans, potato masher or vegetable mill, ovenproof dish, bowl

Freezing Arrange in foil container, but don't top with egg or cook. Wrap, seal, label and freeze. Freezer life: 1 month. To use: cook in the covered foil container at 350F (180C) Gas 4 for 1¼ hours, then complete Step 6

INGREDIENTS

8oz	Frozen spinach	225g
1lb	Celeriac	450g
2lb	Potatoes	900g
	Salt and pepper	
2½oz	Butter	65g
3 tbsp	Single cream	3×15ml
3fl oz	Hot milk	90ml
	Pepper	
1	Small celery stick	1
8oz	Sliced ham	225g
4oz	Grated cheese	125g
2	Eggs	2

METHOD

1 Place spinach in a sieve to thaw. Peel celeriac and potatoes and cut into small chunks. Put prepared vegetable chunks into a saucepan of cold salted water and bring to the boil. Cook for 20 minutes until tender.

2 Drain well and mash or purée chunks with 2oz (50g) of the butter, cream and enough milk to give a creamy purée. Season to taste.

3 Preheat oven to 400F (200C) Gas 6.

4 Wash and top and tail celery and blanch stalks in boiling water for 5 minutes. Drain well and cut into pieces.

5 Grease ovenproof dish with remaining butter. Spread the well-drained spinach over, arrange the chopped celery on top, and cover with ham slices. Sprinkle over half the cheese and cover with purée. Bake on centre shelf of oven for 15 minutes.

6 In a bowl, lightly beat the eggs with salt and pepper. Pour over the purée, top with remaining cheese and return to oven for another 15 minutes until golden. Serve immediately.

Quick chilli con carne

Famous Tex-Mex dish to make in double-quick time

MAIN MEAL Serves 4

Overall timing 40 minutes

Equipment Flameproof casserole

Freezing Cool, pour into a rigid container, leaving 1 inch (2.5cm) headspace. Cover, label and freeze. Freezer life: 3 months. To use: place block in pan, heat gently till thawed, then simmer for 5 minutes

INGREDIENTS

2	Large onions	2
2 tbsp	Oil	2×15ml
1lb	Minced beef	450g
1 tbsp	Plain flour	15ml
½ pint	Strong beef stock	300ml
14oz	Can of tomatoes	397g
1 teasp	Tabasco	5ml
	Salt	
	Freshly-ground black pepper	
14oz	Can of red kidney beans	397g

METHOD

1 Peel and chop the onions. Heat the oil in the casserole, add the onions and fry till golden. Add the minced beef and fry, stirring to break up any lumps, till browned all over.

2 Sprinkle in the flour and cook for 1 minute. Gradually add the stock (made with a cube if necessary) and bring to the boil, stirring constantly.

3 Add the canned tomatoes and juice, the Tabasco and seasoning. Cover and simmer for 10 minutes.

4 Drain the beans in a sieve and rinse under cold water. Drain thoroughly and add to the pan. Cover and simmer for a further 10 minutes.

5 Adjust the seasoning and serve immediately with boiled rice and a tossed green or mixed salad.

Mexican mince

There are probably two hundred different types of chilli and more than a hundred of them are found in Mexico – no wonder they are the favourite flavour of Mexican food

MAIN MEAL Serves 4

Overall timing 50 minutes

Equipment Saucepan or flameproof casserole

Freezing Cool, put in rigid container, cover, label and freeze. Freezer life: 3 months. To use: reheat gently from frozen in saucepan or casserole, stirring from time to time

INGREDIENTS

1	Medium-size onion	1
1½lb	Minced beef	700g
¾ pint	Stock	400ml
1 tbsp	Tomato paste	15ml
2 teasp	Curry powder	2×5ml
½ teasp	Chilli powder	2.5ml
1 tbsp	Chopped parsley	15ml
	Salt and pepper	
11½oz	Can of sweetcorn kernels	326g

METHOD

1 Peel and chop onion and place in saucepan or casserole with remaining ingredients (make stock with 1 or 2 stock cubes if necessary), except the corn kernels.

2 Bring quickly to the boil, then reduce heat, cover with tight-fitting lid and simmer for 40 minutes. Add drained corn for last 5 minutes of cooking time. Serve with mashed potatoes or plain boiled rice.

Bolognese sauce

Known correctly as *ragù* and usually served with lasagne verdi, this is the classic Italian mince sauce

SAUCE Serves 8–10

Overall timing 1 hour

Equipment Saucepan

Freezing Make a large quantity, divide into meal-size portions and place in rigid containers, leaving 1½ inch (4cm) headspace. Cover, label and freeze. Freezer life: 2 months. To use: heat block in saucepan till thawed. Heat through, stirring

INGREDIENTS

2	Onions	2
1	Carrot	1
1	Small stalk of celery	1
2	Bacon rashers	2
8oz	Chicken livers	225g
1oz	Butter	25g
3 tbsp	Oil	3×15ml
2lb	Minced beef	900g
1 tbsp	Plain flour	15ml
½ pint	Stock	300ml
¼ pint	Dry white wine	150ml
2×14oz	Cans of tomatoes	2×397g
2 tbsp	Tomato paste	2×15ml
	Salt	
	Freshly-ground black pepper	
	Grated nutmeg	

METHOD

1 Peel and finely chop onions. Wash and finely chop the carrot and celery. Derind and finely chop the bacon. Wash and finely chop chicken livers.

2 Heat the butter and oil in a large saucepan and fry the prepared vegetables and bacon till lightly browned. Add the meat and chicken livers and fry over high heat, stirring, till browned.

3 Add the flour and cook for 1 minute. Gradually add the stock (made with cubes if necessary) and the wine, and bring to the boil, stirring. Add the tomatoes and their juice, tomato paste, salt and pepper to taste, and a pinch of nutmeg. Break up tomatoes with a wooden spoon.

4 Reduce heat so mixture simmers and cook, uncovered, for about 45 minutes till the sauce is reduced and thick. Serve very hot with pasta and a side dish of grated Parmesan.

Left: Bolognese sauce – Italy's famous traditional meaty accompaniment to pasta

Above: Hamburgers with eggs – a satisfying meal that takes only minutes to prepare

Hamburgers

Though widely thought of as an American invention, hamburgers were first made by immigrants travelling by sea to America from Hamburg. During the voyage, they used the famous salted Hamburg beef to make minced patties, and took the recipe with them to their new homeland

LUNCH OR SUPPER Serves 4

Overall timing 10 minutes

Equipment Heavy-based frying pan or griddle

Freezing Wrap each uncooked hamburger in cling film, pack into polythene bags, label and freeze. Freezer life: 3 months. To use: thaw and cook as recipe

INGREDIENTS

1lb	Finely minced beef	450g
1	Onion	1
	Salt	
	Freshly-ground black pepper	
2 teasp	Oil	2×5ml

METHOD

1 Put the mince into a large bowl. Peel and finely chop the onion and add to the beef with plenty of seasoning. Mix.

2 Divide into 4 portions and shape each into a thick burger.

3 Preheat the frying pan or griddle and brush lightly with oil. Fry the burgers for about 5 minutes, then turn carefully and cook for a further 3–5 minutes.

HAMBURGERS WITH EGGS

Called *Oeufs à cheval* in France, this makes a quick and satisfying meal. While the hamburgers are cooking, fry 2 onions cut into rings, in butter in another frying pan till crisp. (If preferred, they can be coated in milk and flour and deep fried.) Remove from pan, add extra butter and fry 4 eggs. Arrange on top of hamburgers. Serve with watercress lightly fried in butter, and grilled whole tomatoes.

HAMBURGERS WITH ROLLS

While the hamburgers are cooking, peel and slice another onion into rings. Heat 2 tbsp (2×15ml) oil in another frying pan and cook the onion till golden. Meanwhile, lightly toast 4 whole rolls, halve and spread cut sides with 2oz (50g) butter mixed with 1 tbsp (15ml) French mustard. Place a hamburger in each roll, top with fried onions. Serve immediately.

Danish-style burgers

Most countries have their own version of the hamburger. Called *hakkebøf*, these can be made with veal or beef and use the world-famous Danish bacon to add extra flavour

MAIN MEAL Serves 4

Overall timing 25 minutes

Equipment Mincer, bowl, frying pan

Freezing Allow to cool. Interleave burgers with foil and pack in polythene bag. Seal, label and freeze. Freezer life: 2 months. To use: shallow fry from frozen

INGREDIENTS

8oz	Veal or beef	225g
8oz	Lean bacon	225g
	Salt	
	Freshly-ground black pepper	
½ teasp	Worcestershire sauce	2.5ml
2 teasp	Oil	2×5ml

METHOD

1. Wipe and trim meat and derind the bacon. Mince the meat and bacon into a bowl and add salt, pepper and Worcestershire sauce.
2. Mix well with a wooden spoon and divide into four portions. Shape into 4 thick burgers.
3. Preheat the frying pan and brush lightly with oil. Fry the burgers for 3–5 minutes each side according to taste. Serve with fried onions.

VARIATION

A good accompaniment is a lettuce, tomato and cucumber salad. Alternatively, lightly toast 4 slices of bread and put a lettuce leaf on each, followed by a slice of tomato and then the burgers.

A creamy sauce is often served with the burgers in Denmark. Blend 1 tbsp (15ml) cornflour with 2 tbsp (2×15ml) cold water and stir into ¾ pint (400ml) hot beef stock (made with cubes if necessary). Bring to boil, stirring, and cook for 1 minute. Remove from heat and stir in 3 tbsp (3×15ml) single cream and 2 tbsp (2×15ml) chopped parsley. Season to taste.

Below: Hamburgers with rolls – the succulent meat patties are flavoured with mustard here, but you can also serve them with a variety of pickles and relishes

cook's know-how

When you buy commercial hamburgers there's usually only one question to answer – "with or without", usually referring to onions! Hamburgers, however, can be made even more nutritious and filling by adding extra protein in the form of sliced or grated cheese or egg (see left). In Australia, the meat is topped with shredded lettuce, beetroot and tomato slices plus a dollop of mayonnaise or tomato sauce, to give a wonderful combination of hot and cold.

Thin pineapple rings, or soured cream with chopped gherkins make a splendid difference, as does coleslaw which has the dressing mixed in. Piquancy can be added with mustard (see Hamburgers with rolls, left), or the meat can be sprinkled with a few drops of Worcestershire sauce. Don't toast the rolls too far ahead – and only toast them lightly on the cut sides to make them crisp and warm. There's no need to butter them, but if you do, spread it just before you add the meat pattie so the rolls don't become soggy.

Above: Raised chicken and ham pie – chicken in a jellied sauce to be eaten cold either at home or at a picnic

Raised chicken and ham pie

The raised pie, a British contribution to international cooking, is one of the earliest forms of pastry case. The sides are raised up – originally round wooden moulds – to support a lid

LUNCH OR SUPPER Serves 6

Overall timing $2\frac{3}{4}$ hours plus cooling

Equipment Saucepan, 2 bowls, 6 inch (15cm) loose-bottomed cake tin

Freezing When cold and set, wrap pie in foil, seal, label and freeze. Freezer life: 2 months. To use: thaw in wrappings in fridge overnight

INGREDIENTS

	Hot water crust	
4oz	Lard	125g
$\frac{1}{4}$ pint	Water	150ml
12oz	Plain flour	350g
	Pinch of salt	
1	Egg yolk	1
	Filling	
$1\frac{1}{2}$lb	Boneless chicken	700g
1 teasp	Grated lemon rind	5ml
$\frac{1}{4}$ teasp	Dried sage	1.25ml
4oz	Sliced ham	125g
	Salt and pepper	
1 teasp	Powdered gelatine	5ml
6 tbsp	Chicken stock	6×15ml
	Glaze	
1	Egg	1

METHOD

1 To make the hot water crust, put lard and water into a saucepan and heat until fat has melted.

2 Sift flour and salt into a bowl and add melted lard and water. Knead lightly and add egg yolk. Keep dough warm or it will harden and become difficult to work.

3 Roll out dough on a lightly-floured surface and cut out 2 circles the same size as the base of the pie tin. Grease tin and put a circle of dough in the bottom. Keep other circle of dough warm.

4 Roll remaining dough into a band to fit round the sides of the tin. Moisten edges of dough base with water and fit sides of pie into tin. Preheat oven to 375F (190C) Gas 5.

5 Finely dice chicken, keeping breast and dark meat separate. Season both well and add lemon rind and sage. Dice ham. Cover dough base with half the breast meat, then with half the dark meat. Spread all the ham on top, then repeat layering of dark and breast meats.

6 Moisten dough edges and place lid in position. Press down firmly to seal. Make a small hole in the centre and decorate top with leaves made from dough trimmings. Crimp edges of dough together and glaze surface with lightly beaten egg.

7 Bake for 1 hour, then reduce oven temperature to 350F (180C) Gas 4 and bake for a further $1–1\frac{1}{4}$ hours. Remove pie from oven, cool for about 30 minutes then remove from tin and leave to get quite cold.

8 Meanwhile, soften the gelatine in the cold stock (made up with half a chicken stock cube if necessary) in a small pan for about 5 minutes. Then heat gently till gelatine dissolves, but do not allow to boil. Leave to cool.

9 When the jelly mixture begins to set, put a funnel or cone of foil or greaseproof paper into the centre hole in the pie. Pour in jelly and leave pie in fridge till set. Serve cold with salad.

Chicory and ham in cheese sauce

This dish is browned under the grill, but if you prefer it can be put in a hot oven for 10 minutes instead

LUNCH OR SUPPER Serves 4–6

Overall timing 1¼ hours

Equipment Heavy-based casserole, saucepan, ovenproof dish

Freezing Assemble chicory, ham and sauce in foil container but do not bake. Cool, cover, label and freeze. Freezer life: 3 months. To use: uncover, dot with butter, place in cold oven set to 350F (180C) Gas 4. Cook for 1 hour. Increase heat to 450F (230C) Gas 8 for extra 10 minutes

INGREDIENTS

8	Large heads of chicory	8
2oz	Butter	50g
2 tbsp	Lemon juice	2×15ml
1 teasp	Sugar	5ml
	Salt	
	White pepper	
2oz	Butter	50g
1oz	Plain flour	25g
½ pint	Milk	300ml
	Nutmeg	
2	Egg yolks	2
2oz	Grated Parmesan	50g
8	Thin slices of ham	8

METHOD

1 Prepare chicory. Melt butter in casserole. Add the chicory, lemon juice, sugar, salt and pepper. Cover and cook gently for about 30 minutes, turning the chicory occasionally.

2 Meanwhile, make the sauce. Melt half the butter in a saucepan over a low heat, and stir in the flour with a wooden spoon. Remove from heat and add milk gradually. Return to heat and stir till sauce reaches boiling point. Add pinch of nutmeg and cook over lowered heat, stirring constantly. Remove from heat, stir in egg yolks and Parmesan.

3 Preheat the grill. Grease dish.

4 Lift out chicory with draining spoon. Reserve cooking liquor. Wrap each chicory head in a slice of ham and arrange in the baking dish. Add reserved liquor to sauce, beat well, then pour over chicory. Dot with the rest of the butter and grill until golden on top – it will take 5 to 10 minutes. Serve immediately.

1 Cook chicory very gently in a covered pan, with butter, sugar, salt, pepper and lemon – which keeps the chicory white

2 Stir flour into melted butter, add milk gradually and nutmeg. Heat till nearly boiling. Take off heat, add egg yolks and Parmesan

3 Drain chicory heads, reserving liquor. Wrap each in ham, arrange in baking dish, join underneath. Add reserved liquor to sauce

4 Beat sauce well, pour over chicory and ham. Dot with butter, then grill until golden Below: Chicory and ham in cheese sauce

Leek pie

Sliced leeks, bacon and single cream baked in a shortcrust case

MAIN MEAL Serves 4

Overall timing 1 hour

Equipment 2 frying pans, shallow pie dish, bowl

Freezing Open freeze baked pie. Wrap well, put in polythene bag, seal and label. Freezer life: 3 months. To use: thaw for 3 hours at room temperature then reheat in oven at 350F (180C) Gas 4 for 30 minutes

INGREDIENTS

$1\frac{1}{2}$lb	Leeks	700g
2	Onions	2
2oz	Butter	50g
	Salt	
	Freshly-ground white pepper	
8oz	Streaky bacon rashers	225g
12oz	Shortcrust pastry	350g
1 tbsp	Cornflour	15ml
$\frac{1}{4}$ pint	Carton of single cream	150ml
1	Egg	1

METHOD

1 Preheat the oven to 400F (200C) Gas 6. Wash, trim and slice leeks. Peel and slice onions.

2 Melt butter in a frying pan and fry onions till golden. Add sliced leeks, salt and pepper and cook gently for 5 minutes.

3 Meanwhile, derind and lightly fry bacon rashers in another pan.

4 Roll out two-thirds of the pastry and line base and sides of the pie dish. Cover with leek mixture and arrange bacon rashers on top. Mix cornflour with the cream and pour over.

5 Roll out remaining pastry and cover filling. Seal and crimp edges, using any pastry trimmings to decorate top. Glaze with beaten egg. Bake for 45 minutes until golden brown.

Fry sliced onions in butter until golden, then add the sliced leeks, salt and pepper and cook gently for a further 5 minutes

Spread leek mixture in a pastry-lined dish and arrange derinded and fried bacon on top

Left: Leek pie – a dish featured in several regional cuisines. Wales, Cornwall and Brittany, for example, all have their own special versions

Raised veal and pork pie

Use the hot water crust from page 112 to make this classic raised pie

MAIN MEAL Cuts into 8

Overall timing $3\frac{1}{2}$ hours plus marination

Equipment 3 bowls, saucepan, baking tray

Freezing Wrap in foil, seal, label and freeze. Freezer life: 2 months. To use: thaw in fridge overnight in wrappings

INGREDIENTS

1lb	Lean pie veal	450g
1lb	Minced pork	450g
8oz	Pork sausagemeat	225g
2	Shallots	2
1 tbsp	Chopped parsley	15ml
$\frac{1}{4}$ teasp	Dried thyme	1.25ml
$\frac{1}{4}$ pint	White wine	150ml
2 tbsp	Cognac	2×15ml
	Salt and pepper	
12oz	Hot water crust (see page 112)	350g
1	Egg	1
$\frac{1}{4}$ pint	Jellied stock	150ml

METHOD

1 Wipe and trim the veal and cut into small cubes. Place in a large bowl, add the minced pork and sausagemeat and mix well. Peel and chop the shallots and add to bowl with the herbs, wine, Cognac and seasoning. Cover and marinate for 3 hours, turning mixture occasionally.

2 Make the hot water paste according to instructions, then cut off a third of the pastry, wrap and keep warm. Roll out remaining dough on a floured surface to a rectangle about 12×9 inches (30×23cm) and place on greased baking tray.

3 Preheat the oven to 375F (190C) Gas 5.

4 Put the meat stuffing along the centre of the pastry and raise the 4 sides of the pastry around the filling, pinching the corners together to make a rectangular box. Trim joins, if necessary, with a sharp knife. Brush the top edges with water.
5 Roll out remaining pastry and make 2 small holes about 2 inches (5cm) apart in the centre. Place over the pie, sealing and crimping the pastry edges. Lightly beat the egg and brush over the top and sides of the pie.
6 Using a sharp knife, score the top decoratively, then bake in the centre of the oven for 1 hour.
7 Cover the pie loosely with foil when the pastry is lightly browned, reduce the temperature to 350F (180C) Gas 4 and cook for a further $1\frac{1}{2}$ hours.
8 Remove from the oven and leave to cool completely on a rack. Meanwhile, make the jellied stock using a packet of bought aspic which is flavoured and is added to water, or use gelatine and chicken stock (made with a cube if necessary). Leave till syrupy, then use a potato piping nozzle set in one of the holes in the top of the pastry to direct the stock into the cooled pie. Leave to cool, then chill till set. Serve cold, cut into thick slices, with salad.

1 Roll out two-thirds of pastry (wrap rest and keep warm) and put filling along centre

2 Bring sides of pastry up round filling and pinch corners together to make a box

3 Trim off any excess pastry at the joins and brush the top edges lightly with water

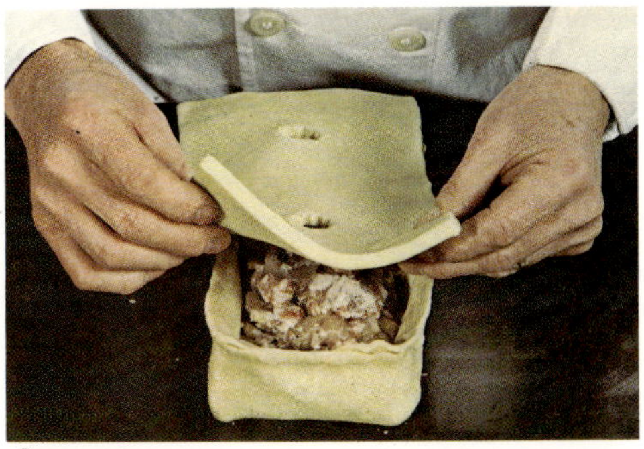

4 Unwrap reserved pastry, roll out and make two holes in top before placing over pie

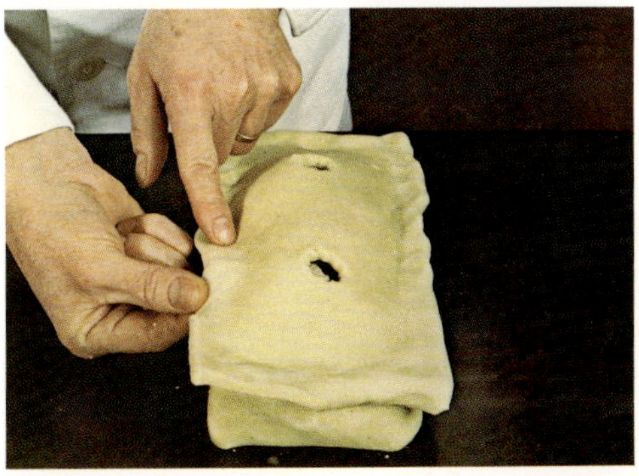

5 Press the top firmly on to sides, then seal and crimp the pastry edges together

6 After glazing with egg, score the top of the pie decoratively with a sharp knife

pastry know-how

A pie funnel may be used to help hold up the upper crust, but the pastry should not be pierced and the funnel revealed till the steam has raised it to a slight dome. If not using a funnel, after 15–20 minutes slip a knife under the edge of the pastry to allow the steam to escape and prevent the pastry being soggy inside.

Right: Raised veal and pork pie — a traditional pie with a flavoursome filling that's perfect for a picnic or cold buffet

Swiss flan

Two of Switzerland's favourite cheeses are combined in this flan

LIGHT LUNCH Serves 4–6

Overall timing 1½ hours

Equipment Saucepan, mixing bowl, 2 bowls, 9 inch (23cm) flan tin

Freezing Cook flan in foil dish. Cool, open freeze, then wrap in polythene, seal and label. Freezer life: 3 months. To use: thaw for 4 hours, then refresh in a hot oven for 10–15 minutes

INGREDIENTS

4oz	Margarine	125g
3 tbsp	Water	3×15ml
¼ teasp	Salt	1.25ml
8oz	Self-raising flour	225g
2	Medium-size onions	2
1oz	Margarine	25g
1 tbsp	Plain flour	15ml
4fl oz	Milk	120ml
4fl oz	Water	120ml
3	Eggs	3
	Salt and pepper	
¼ teasp	Grated nutmeg	1.25ml
	Cayenne pepper	
4oz	Emmenthal	125g
4oz	Gruyère	125g

METHOD

1 To make pastry, melt the margarine in a saucepan over a gentle heat. Allow to cool slightly, then stir in water and salt. Put flour into a bowl. Slowly add contents of saucepan and mix until smooth. Cover and place in the fridge for 30 minutes. Grease flan tin. Preheat the oven to 350F (180C) Gas 4.

2 To make filling, peel and chop onions. Melt margarine in a saucepan and fry onions for 10 minutes until soft, but not coloured. Leave to cool.

3 Mix flour and a little of the milk in a bowl, then add the rest of the milk and the water. Separate the eggs. Mix the yolks into the flour and milk mixture. Season with salt, pepper, nutmeg and a pinch of cayenne. Beat egg whites in another bowl till stiff, then fold into yolk mixture.

4 Remove dough from fridge. Roll it out on a lightly-floured surface and line the tin.

5 Spread onions over bottom of flan, then grate both sorts of cheese on top. Cover with egg and milk mixture. Bake just below centre of the oven for 15 minutes. Reduce heat to 325F (170C) Gas 3 and cook for a further 45 minutes. Serve hot with a green salad into which radishes and parsley have been mixed.

Below: Swiss flan – Emmenthal and Gruyère are both included in the filling

Onion flan

A yeast-based pastry topped with onion rings, Cheddar and bacon

LIGHT LUNCH OR SUPPER Serves 4–6

Overall timing 2¼ hours

Equipment Small bowl, mixing bowl, 10 inch (25cm) loose-bottomed flan tin, frying pan

Freezing Cool, then open freeze. Overwrap, seal and label. Freezer life: 2 months. To use: unwrap and reheat from frozen at 350F (180C) Gas 4 for about 20 minutes.

INGREDIENTS

	Pastry	
½oz	Fresh yeast *or*	15g
1 teasp	Dried yeast	5ml
	Pinch of sugar	
4fl oz	Lukewarm water	120ml
8oz	Plain flour	225g
1 teasp	Salt	5ml
1	Egg	1
	Filling	
5oz	Bacon rashers	150g
6oz	Onions*	175g
1oz	Margarine	25g
5oz	Cheddar*	150g

Above: Onion flan – delicious mixture of tastes, simple to prepare and present

METHOD

1 Crumble fresh yeast into a small bowl, add sugar and 1 tbsp (15ml) of the lukewarm water and mix well. If using dried yeast, add sugar, mix with most of the water and leave for 15 minutes in a warm place till frothy.
2 Sift flour and salt into bowl, make a well in the centre and add yeast mixture, any remaining water and egg. Mix well to a dough, then turn on to floured surface and knead for 5 minutes, stretching and pushing with the heel of the hand until smooth and elastic.
3 Place dough in a clean bowl, cover with a damp cloth and leave to rise in a warm place for 45 minutes–1 hour, until doubled in size.
4 Preheat oven to 400F (200C) Gas 6. Grease flan tin. Roll out dough on a floured surface, then line tin. Leave for 15 minutes.
5 Finely chop bacon. Peel onions and cut into rings. Heat margarine in a pan and fry onions for 5 minutes till golden. Slice the cheese.
6 Cover flan base with onion and bacon and arrange cheese slices on top. Bake in oven for 30–35 minutes. Remove from tin and serve hot with salad.

*Both these can be as strong or as mild-flavoured as you like.

Quiche Lorraine

This dish from the Alsace-Lorraine region is a firm favourite for family meals. The rich filling provides a good contrast to the shortcrust pastry

LIGHT LUNCH OR SUPPER Serves 4–6

Overall timing $1\frac{1}{2}$ hours

Equipment 2 bowls, 8 inch (20cm) pie plate or flan dish, frying pan

Freezing Cook in foil dish, cool, open freeze, wrap in polythene and label. Freezer life: 3 months. To use: thaw for 4 hours then reheat in a hot oven

INGREDIENTS

8oz	Plain flour	225g
	Pinch of salt	
	Freshly-ground black pepper	
4oz	Butter	125g
2 tbsp	Water	2×15ml
2	Throughcut bacon rashers	2
1oz	Butter	25g
3oz	Gruyère	75g
2	Eggs	2
1 teasp	Salt	5ml
	Pepper	
$\frac{1}{2}$ pint	Milk or single cream	300ml

METHOD

1 Put the flour, salt and pepper into a bowl. Rub in the butter till mixture resembles breadcrumbs. Gradually add the water and knead to a ball. Roll out pastry. Line a greased pie plate or flan dish and leave to stand for 30 minutes.
2 Preheat the oven to 400F (200C) Gas 6. Remove rind and dice the bacon. Sauté lightly in butter.
3 Grate or finely slice the cheese. Sprinkle bacon and cheese over the flan case.
4 Beat together the eggs, salt and pepper in a bowl. Add milk or single cream. Pour mixture into flan. Do not overfill.
5 Bake for 15 minutes then reduce heat to 325F (170C) Gas 3 and cook for further 25–30 minutes. Serve hot or cold with salad and potatoes.

Below: Quiche Lorraine – so often the perfect answer for a quick lunch or supper dish

Parsleyed fish cakes

The simplest method of making fish cakes, with mashed potatoes for bulk and parsley for extra flavour

SUPPER Serves 4

Overall timing 1 hour plus chilling

Equipment 2 saucepans, large plate, bowl, frying pan

Freezing Make as Steps 1–4. Open freeze till firm, then wrap and label. Freezer life: 1 month. To use: fry from frozen

INGREDIENTS

1lb	Potatoes	450g
	Salt	
1oz	Butter	25g
1lb	Fish fillets	450g
$\frac{1}{2}$ pint	Milk	300ml
2 tbsp	Chopped parsley	2×15ml
	Pepper	
2	Eggs	2
2 tbsp	Plain flour	2×15ml
2oz	Dried breadcrumbs	50g
$\frac{1}{4}$ pint	Oil	150ml

METHOD

1 Peel potatoes and put into a pan of salted water. Bring to the boil and cook for 20–25 minutes until tender. Drain and mash with the butter.

2 Put fish and milk into another pan. Cover and poach for 10 minutes or till tender. Drain, reserving poaching liquor, and mash fish.

3 Mix fish with potatoes. Add poaching liquor, parsley, salt and pepper and one of the eggs. Mix together well, then spread out mixture on a large plate and chill for 30 minutes.

4 Divide fish mixture into eight equal portions, and shape each piece into a flat cake. Coat lightly with flour. Beat remaining egg. Dip fish patties into egg, then coat with breadcrumbs.

5 Heat the oil in a large frying pan, add fish cakes and cook till golden brown and crisp on both sides. Remove from pan with a draining spoon and drain on kitchen paper. Serve with tartare sauce or a tomato sauce.

VARIATIONS

Add 2oz (50g) chopped and fried bacon, 2oz (50g) blue cheese, a little chopped gherkin, $\frac{1}{2}$ teasp (2.5ml) dried dill or 2 tbsp (2×15ml) anchovy essence to the basic mix. You can also alter the taste by the type of fish you use – for example, use half white and half smoked fish.

Finnish fish cakes

Instead of potatoes for bulk, this recipe has extra fish – canned sardines – and fresh breadcrumbs. Scandinavian dishes often feature dill, and here the herb's feathery green leaves are used to good advantage both in the fish cake mixture and for the garnish

LUNCH OR SUPPER Makes 8

Overall timing 45 minutes

Equipment Saucepan, bowl, large frying pan

Freezing Make as Steps 1–3. Leave to dry, then open freeze till firm. Wrap and label. Freezer life: 1 month. To use: shallow fry straight from frozen

INGREDIENTS

1	Large onion	1
$1\frac{1}{2}$lb	Fish fillets	700g
6 tbsp	Milk	6×15ml
1oz	Butter	25g
1 tbsp	Lemon juice	15ml
$4\frac{1}{4}$oz	Can of sardines in oil	120g
4oz	Fresh breadcrumbs	125g
1 tbsp	Chopped parsley	15ml
1 tbsp	Chopped dill	15ml
	Salt and pepper	
3	Eggs	3
4 tbsp	Dried breadcrumbs	4×15ml
$\frac{1}{4}$ pint	Oil	150ml
	Garnish	
1	Lemon	1
	Fresh dill	

METHOD

1 Peel and finely chop the onion. Chop fish. Put both into a pan with the milk, butter and lemon juice and poach for 10 minutes.

2 Drain, saving cooking liquor, and put into a bowl. Drain sardines and add to bowl with fresh breadcrumbs, chopped parsley and dill, salt and pepper. Mash well, then add 2 of the eggs, lightly beaten, and enough of the reserved cooking liquor to bind the mixture together.

3 Shape the mixture into 8 flat cakes. Lightly beat the remaining egg. Dip fish cakes first in flour, then in egg, coat with dry breadcrumbs.

4 Heat the oil in a large frying pan and fry the fish cakes on both sides till crisp and golden. Serve with lemon wedges, sprigs of dill and dill sauce or with mayonnaise.

Corned beef patties

The soft texture of corned beef lends itself to moulding and shaping as in these patties. Instead of egging and crumbing, they could be coated in fritter batter and deep fried

MAIN MEAL Serves 4

Overall timing 30 minutes

Equipment 3 bowls, large frying pan

Freezing Do not cook. Arrange in layers, interleaved with foil, in a rigid container. Cover, label and freeze. Freezer life: 1 month. To use: cook very gently from frozen in oil and butter

INGREDIENTS

12 tbsp	Breadcrumbs	12×15ml
3 tbsp	Warm milk	3×15ml
1lb	Corned beef	450g
2	Eggs	2
2 tbsp	Grated Parmesan	2×15ml
	Grated rind of $\frac{1}{2}$ a lemon	
	Flour	
2oz	Butter	50g
1 tbsp	Oil	15ml
	Lemon wedges	
	Parsley	

METHOD

1 Soak 4 tbsp (4×15ml) breadcrumbs in a bowl with the milk.

2 Cut off any excess fat from the edge of the corned beef and discard. Mash beef in a bowl with a fork, then add squeezed-out breadcrumbs, 1 egg, grated cheese and lemon rind. Mix well.

3 With well floured hands, make patties from the mixture, then coat with flour.

4 Lightly beat remaining egg. Using 2 forks, dip the patties first into beaten egg, then into remaining breadcrumbs (see step-by-step pictures, right).

5 Heat butter and oil in a large frying pan. Add the patties and cook over a moderate heat till brown on both sides. Remove from pan and drain on kitchen paper. Garnish with lemon wedges and parsley. Serve with hot broad beans or a salad.

Add egg, cheese and lemon rind to squeezed-out breadcrumbs and mashed corned beef

After flouring hands well, shape corned beef mixture into patties. Coat with flour

Egg and crumb patties, then fry till brown. Above (large picture): Corned beef patties

Tomato and marjoram pizza

An easy-to-make pizza with a base made with a packet of bread mix to save you going through the full process of making a yeast dough

LUNCH OR SUPPER Serves 4

Overall timing 1½ hours

Equipment Saucepan, bowl, 10 inch (25cm) pizza pan or flan tin

Freezing Prepare pizza to end of Step 5, then wrap in foil, seal, label and freeze. Freezer life: 2 months. To use: remove foil, place pizza in oven; then turn on to 450F (230C) Gas 8. Cook for 35 minutes till well-risen and golden.

Below: Tomato and marjoram prize – a superbly flavoured pizza. Cut into wedges and serve with mixed green salad or coleslaw

INGREDIENTS

	Topping	
1½lb	Ripe tomatoes	700g
1	Large onion	1
4 tbsp	Oil	4×15ml
2	Garlic cloves	2
2 teasp	Dried marjoram	2×5ml
1 teasp	Sugar	5ml
	Salt	
	Freshly-ground black pepper	
	Fresh marjoram leaves (optional)	
	Base	
10oz	Packet of bread mix	283g
4oz	Grated cheese	125g
¼ teasp	Powdered mustard	1.25ml
	Hot water	

METHOD

1 Blanch, peel and roughly chop the tomatoes. Peel and finely chop the onion. Heat 3 tbsp (3×15ml) of the oil in a saucepan and fry the onion till transparent.

2 Add the tomatoes, peeled and crushed garlic, 1 teasp (5ml) of the dried marjoram, sugar and seasoning. Bring to the boil, stirring. Cover and simmer for 15 minutes.

3 Empty the bread mix into a large bowl and stir in the grated cheese and powdered mustard. Add hot water (according to packet instructions) and mix to a soft, but not sticky dough.

4 Knead for 5 minutes, then roll out on a floured surface to a circle 10 inches (25cm) in diameter. Lift dough on to rolling pin and place in the greased pizza pan or flan tin. Pinch up the edges to make a slight lip.
5 Spread the tomato mixture over the pizza and sprinkle with the remaining dried marjoram and the fresh leaves if using.
6 Preheat the oven to 425F (220C) Gas 7.
7 Put pizza in a warm place for about 30 minutes till base has risen to double its size.
8 Sprinkle the remaining oil over the pizza and bake near the top of the oven for 25 minutes. Serve hot with green salad or coleslaw.

Storecupboard pizza

As a standby for lunch or supper, this pizza takes some beating. It also freezes well, so make it for a time when you may not feel like cooking

LIGHT LUNCH OR SUPPER Serves 4–6

Overall timing 1 hour 10 minutes

Equipment 2 mixing bowls, baking tray or flat ovenproof dish

Freezing When baked, cool and open freeze. Wrap in foil and then place in a polythene bag. Label and freeze. Freezer life: 3 months. To use: either thaw for 2 hours at room temperature and heat for 15 minutes at 400F (200C) Gas 6 or heat from frozen at same temperature for about 40 minutes

INGREDIENTS

	Topping	
14oz	Can of tomatoes	396g
2	Garlic cloves	2
1	Small onion	1
½ teasp	Dried basil *or*	2.5ml
½ teasp	Sweet mixed herbs	2.5ml
	Worcestershire sauce	
	Salt and pepper	
4oz	Can of sardines*	125g
	Base	
8oz	Self-raising flour	225g
	Pinch of salt	
3 tbsp	Oil	3×15ml
	Water to mix	
	Garnish	
6oz	Cheddar	175g
1	Small can of anchovy fillets	1
12	Small black olives	12
2 tbsp	Parmesan	2×15ml

*alternatives: 4oz (125g) of diced pork ring or salami; chopped streaky bacon

METHOD

1 To make topping, put mashed tomatoes and juice, crushed garlic, finely-chopped onion, herbs, a dash of Worcestershire sauce, seasonings and drained and chopped sardines into a bowl and mix lightly together. Leave for 15 minutes. Preheat oven to 450F (230C) Gas 8.
2 Meanwhile, make base: in another bowl place sieved flour and salt. Stir in oil and sufficient water to mix to a soft but not sticky dough.
3 Lightly oil a flat baking tray or ovenproof dish. Roll out dough to a large circle or rectangle as thick as you like. Pinch up the edge to make a ridge. Brush with oil.
4 Spread topping on to base. Cover with grated or sliced Cheddar and arrange anchovy fillets in a lattice shape on top. Garnish with olives and sprinkle with Parmesan.
5 Cook near top of oven for 15 minutes. Reduce heat to 375F (190C) Gas 5 and cook for a further 20–25 minutes. Serve for lunch or supper with mixed green salad.

Left: Storecupboard pizza – super standby

VEGETABLES

Lots of tasty vegetable dishes can be frozen, but if you have a glut in summer it is quicker to freeze the vegetables plain (see pages 20–21) and add a savoury sauce later when you cook them

Braised artichokes

Jerusalem artichokes have become popular all over the world. In this dish from Denmark, they are cooked gently in a stock made piquant with lemon juice. The reduction of the juices concentrates the flavour

VEGETABLE Serves 4–6

Overall timing 50 minutes

Equipment Saucepan or flameproof casserole

Freezing Prepare to the end of Step 3. Cool, pack in foil container, cover, label and freeze. Freezer life: 3 months. To use: reheat slowly from frozen

INGREDIENTS

1	Large onion	1
2lb	Jerusalem artichokes	900g
2oz	Unsalted butter	50g
1 tbsp	Oil	15ml
½ pint	Chicken stock	300ml
1 tbsp	Lemon juice	15ml
	Salt	
	Freshly-ground black pepper	
2 tbsp	Chopped parsley	2×15ml

METHOD

1 Peel and finely chop the onion. Peel artichokes but leave whole.
2 Heat the butter and oil in a saucepan or casserole and fry the onion until transparent. Add the artichokes and cook gently, stirring, for 5 minutes.
3 Add the chicken stock (made with cubes if necessary), lemon juice and seasoning. Cover and cook for about 30 minutes until tender.
4 Lift artichokes out of liquid, place in a warm serving dish and keep hot. Boil the cooking liquor till reduced by half. Taste and adjust seasoning. Stir in parsley, pour over artichokes and serve.

cook's know-how

Jerusalem artichokes were given the misleading name "artichoke" by French explorers in America in the 17th century, who discovered them in Massachussetts being grown by Indian tribes. The reason was probably that the flavour of this rather ugly, knobbly root – belonging to the sunflower family – reminded the French of their native globe artichoke. There is some controversy over how it acquired the prefix "jerusalem" The Italians called it sunflower artichoke – and, as sunflower in Italian is *girasole*, it is assumed that this word was eventually corrupted to jerusalem.

Left: Braised artichokes cooked in a tasty stock on top of the stove. Cover well to ensure that all the flavours remain in the vegetables

French bean purée

An unusual vegetable dish that's almost a meal in itself

VEGETABLE Serves 6

Overall timing 40 minutes

Equipment 2 saucepans, blender or vegetable mill

Freezing Pack in rigid container. Cover, seal, label and freeze. Freezer life: 3 months. To use: put block into saucepan and heat through gently. Adjust seasoning

INGREDIENTS

1lb	Potatoes	450g
	Salt	
2 tbsp	Single cream (optional)	2×15ml
1lb	French beans	450g
2oz	Butter	50g
3 tbsp	Grated Parmesan or Gruyère	3×15ml
	Freshly-ground black pepper	

METHOD

1 Peel potatoes and cook in boiling salted water until tender. Drain well and mash adding cream if liked.

2 Wash and top and tail beans and, if necessary, remove strings. Cook in boiling salted water for 10 minutes. Drain well.

3 Purée beans in a blender or vegetable mill. Pour purée into a saucepan and blend in the mashed potatoes.

4 Add butter and Parmesan or Gruyère and heat through, stirring gently. Add salt and pepper to taste and serve immediately with grilled meats.

Add butter to vegetable mixture, then stir in grated cheese and heat through gently

Stuffed cucumbers

An Austrian way of eating stuffed cucumbers in a creamy paprika sauce

LUNCH OR SUPPER Serves 6

Overall timing 1 hour

Equipment Bowl, flameproof casserole

Freezing Pack in rigid container, cover, label and freeze. Freezer life: 2 months. To use: reheat gently from frozen

INGREDIENTS

3	Large cucumbers	3
2oz	Ham	50g
4oz	Minced beef	125g
2 tbsp	Fresh breadcrumbs	2×15ml
1 tbsp	Chopped parsley	15ml
3 tbsp	Milk	3×15ml
1	Egg	1
	Salt and pepper	
	Sauce	
1	Onion	1
1	Leek	1
2oz	Butter	50g
1oz	Plain flour	25g
½ pint	Stock	300ml
1 tbsp	Chopped parsley	15ml
	Paprika	
	Salt	
1 tbsp	Vinegar	15ml
4fl oz	Carton of single cream	113ml

METHOD

1 Trim ends and cut cucumbers into 2 equal lengths or thirds. Peel and remove seeds from centre (a grapefruit knife makes this easy).

2 Finely chop or mince them. Put into a bowl with the minced beef, breadcrumbs, parsley, milk and egg and mix together well. Season generously. Stuff cucumbers with the mixture.

3 To make sauce, peel and finely chop onion. Wash, trim and finely chop leek. Heat the butter in a casserole and fry the onion and leek till golden.

4 Sprinkle flour into casserole and cook for 1 minute, stirring. Gradually stir in the stock (made with 1 stock cube if necessary), then add parsley, a pinch each of paprika and salt and the vinegar. Bring to the boil, stirring constantly.

5 Arrange cucumbers on top of sauce and surround with any leftover stuffing. Reduce heat, cover and cook gently for 30 minutes. Turn cucumbers over halfway through cooking time.

6 Stir cream into sauce, heat through uncovered for 2 minutes, then serve.

Below: Stuffed cucumbers – filled with a tasty beef and ham mixture

Broad beans and fennel

A vegetable dish with broad beans, flavoured by the celery-like stalks and frond-like leaves of Florence fennel. When fresh beans are not available, used canned or frozen

STARTER OR VEGETABLE Serves 4

Overall timing 1½ hours

Equipment 4 saucepans, sieve

Freezing Cool, then pack into rigid container. Freezer life: 6 months. To use: thaw for 4 hours, then heat gently

INGREDIENTS

	Béchamel sauce	
½	Small onion	½
½	Carrot	½
½	Stalk of celery	½
1	Bay leaf	1
½ pint	Milk	300ml
1oz	Butter	25g
1oz	Plain flour	25g
	Salt and pepper	
	Grated nutmeg	
	Other ingredients	
1¼lb	Shelled broad beans	600g
1	Large onion	1
3 tbsp	Oil	3×15ml
3 tbsp	Chopped parsley	3×15ml
2oz	Chopped fennel tops	50g

METHOD

1 Peel onion, peel and chop carrot. Wash and chop celery. Place in saucepan with bay leaf and milk and bring to boil. Remove from heat and leave to infuse for 15 minutes. Strain and discard flavourings.

2 Melt butter in another saucepan. Stir in flour and cook for 1 minute, stirring with a wooden spoon. Remove from heat and gradually stir in strained milk to give a smooth mixture.

3 Return pan to heat and bring to boil, stirring continuously. Reduce heat and cook sauce for 3 minutes. Add salt, pepper and nutmeg to taste.

4 Wash the beans and blanch for 5 minutes in lightly salted boiling water. Drain.

5 Peel and slice onion. Heat oil in a pan, add onion and cook till golden brown. Add beans, chopped parsley, chopped fennel tops, and Béchamel sauce. Mix well. Taste and add salt if necessary. Bring to boil and simmer gently for 30 minutes. Serve immediately.

Provençal-style lettuce

Because of its high water content, lettuce does not freeze well except in soups, purées or pulped mixtures – as here. It's certainly worthwhile making up a double quantity of this tomato and garlic flavoured dish and freezing half for later

STARTER OR VEGETABLE Serves 4–6

Overall timing 50 minutes

Equipment Large saucepan or flameproof casserole

Freezing Allow to cool, pack into rigid container, leaving 1 inch (2.5cm) headspace. Cover, seal, label and freeze. Freezer life: 3 months. To use: thaw in fridge if serving cold. To serve hot, reheat gently from frozen in a pan, stirring occasionally

INGREDIENTS

2	Lettuces	2
2	Large onions	2
4 tbsp	Oil	4×15ml
2	Garlic cloves	2
14oz	Can of tomatoes	397g
2 tbsp	Tomato paste	2×15ml
2 teasp	Sugar	2×5ml
	Salt	
	Freshly-ground black pepper	
2 tbsp	Chopped parsley	2×15ml

METHOD

1 Trim, wash and coarsely shred lettuces. Peel and slice onions. Heat oil in pan or casserole and fry onions and peeled and crushed garlic for 10 minutes.

2 Add the shredded lettuces and fry for 5 minutes. Add the tomatoes and their juice, tomato paste, sugar and plenty of seasoning. Bring to the boil, cover and simmer gently for about 30 minutes.

3 Just before the end of cooking time, stir in the chopped parsley. Taste and adjust seasoning. Serve hot topped with grated Parmesan, as a vegetable accompaniment with grilled meat. Alternatively, it can be chilled, then garnished with black olives and served as a starter with plenty of crunchy French bread.

Roman broccoli

This way of cooking broccoli in white wine and stock until these are all absorbed is really delicious. For the last 10 minutes of the cooking time it's important to shake the pan frequently to prevent the broccoli sticking.
If you prefer to use frozen broccoli instead of fresh when making this dish, there's no need for the first 20 minutes cooking in Step 2. Combine all ingredients and cook as Steps 3 and 4

VEGETABLE Serves 6

Overall timing 45 minutes

Equipment Saucepan

Freezing Pack in polythene bags and freeze. Freezer life: 4 months. To use: Cook gently in butter till soft

INGREDIENTS

1½lb	Broccoli	700g
4fl oz	Oil	120ml
1	Garlic clove	1
	Salt and pepper	
2 tbsp	Beef stock or water	2×15ml
8fl oz	Dry white wine	220ml

METHOD

1 Trim broccoli, then wash and drain well.

2 Heat the oil in a saucepan. Peel and crush the garlic. Add to the oil and lightly brown. Add the broccoli, salt and pepper. Cover and cook for 20 minutes over a low heat, stirring gently from time to time.

3 Add stock, which can be made from a cube, or water, and wine, cover and simmer for a further 10 minutes.

4 Remove the lid and, stirring all the time, cook over a fairly high heat for about 10 minutes till all the liquid has been absorbed and the broccoli is tender. Serve immediately.

cook's know-how

If you like your broccoli green, choose calabrese. And to keep it green during cooking, either wrap it in foil and cook in boiling water, or steam it, for about 15 minutes. Broccoli is a good source of vitamin C, and both these methods of cooking are best for retaining about 80 per cent of it.

Braised fennel

Fennel is cooked slowly to let the bacon and bouquet garni flavour it

VEGETABLE Serves 6

Overall timing 1 hour

Equipment Saucepan, flameproof casserole

Freezing Cool, pour into rigid container, cover, label and freeze. Freezer life: 2 months. To use: reheat gently from frozen

INGREDIENTS

5	Bulbs of fennel	5
	Salt	
4oz	Streaky bacon	125g
1	Onion	1
2oz	Butter	50g
½ pint	Chicken stock	300ml
	Bouquet garni	
	Freshly-ground black pepper	
	Fresh parsley	

METHOD

1 Trim and wash fennel. Cut each bulb in half and blanch for 10 minutes in boiling salted water. Drain.
2 Derind and chop bacon finely. Peel and chop onion. Heat butter in casserole and sauté bacon for 5 minutes.
3 Arrange onion and fennel pieces on top. Cover with stock (made with ½ a stock cube if necessary), add bouquet garni and season. Cover and simmer for about 45 minutes until tender.

TO SERVE

Remove bouquet garni. If liked, sprinkle fennel with grated Parmesan. Garnish with parsley and serve with chicken or a bacon joint.

Braised carrots with cream

A tasty way of dressing up carrots as an accompanying vegetable

VEGETABLE Serves 4

Overall timing 1¼ hours

Equipment Flameproof dish with tight-fitting lid

Freezing Do not add cream. Place in rigid container, cover, label and freeze. Freezer life: 3 months. To use: thaw, then heat in covered pan. Stir in cream and cook uncovered for 2–3 minutes

INGREDIENTS

2lb	Carrots	900g
4	Small onions	4
1	Clove	1
1	Garlic clove	1
2oz	Butter	50g
	Bouquet garni	
	Salt and pepper	
2 tbsp	Single cream	2×15ml

METHOD

1 Scrape, wash and thinly slice the carrots. Peel and quarter the onions. Stick a clove in one of the quarters. Peel and crush the garlic.
2 Melt butter in the flameproof dish over low heat and add carrots, onions, garlic, bouquet garni, salt and pepper. Cover and cook for 1 hour over low heat. Remove clove and bouquet garni.
3 Stir in cream, bring to boil and simmer, uncovered, for 2–3 minutes. Serve.

Below: Braised fennel – to accompany roast or grilled meats

Spanish stuffed capsicums

The smoked bacon in the filling adds special flavour to this dish

STARTER OR LUNCH Serves 8 or 4

Overall timing 1 hour

Equipment Saucepan, ovenproof dish

Freezing Freeze after filling peppers with stuffing, but without cooking. Place in rigid container, cover, label and freeze. Freezer life: 3 months. To use: part thaw at room temperature for about 1 hour, place in dish with oil and tomato sauce, and bake for 1 hour

INGREDIENTS

8	Firm green capsicums	8
14oz	Smoked bacon	400g
4oz	Fresh breadcrumbs	125g
	Pepper	
$\frac{1}{4}$ pint	Olive oil	150ml
$\frac{1}{2}$ pint	Tomato sauce (following recipe)	300ml

METHOD

1 Cut off the stalk end, then deseed the capsicums. Put them in a saucepan of lightly salted, boiling water for 5 minutes, then drain.
2 Preheat oven to 400F (200C) Gas 6.
3 To make stuffing, very finely chop or mince bacon, then mix into breadcrumbs with a fork. Season with pepper.
4 Pour 1 teasp (5ml) of the oil into each capsicum, then fill with stuffing. Pour remaining oil into ovenproof dish. Place capsicums in dish with tomato sauce between them. Cover with foil and cook in oven for 45 minutes, basting several times. Serve hot or cold.

Tomato sauce

A deliciously flavoured dressing for cold vegetables, or to serve hot with fish, chicken, steak, chops or pasta. Made from basil and fresh or canned tomatoes, Method 1 is for a mild tasting sauce, Method 2 a stronger one

SAUCE Makes 18fl oz (500ml)

Overall timing 15 minutes

Equipment Blender, sieve

Freezing Make sauce but omit Step 3. Pack, label and freeze. Freezer life: 6 months. To use: thaw overnight in fridge or for 3 hours at room temperature. If using hot, cook the sauce slowly from frozen. Stir in olive oil just before serving

INGREDIENTS

$1\frac{1}{4}$lb	Italian plum tomatoes	600g
1	Garlic clove (method 2)	1
	Freshly-ground salt and pepper	
12	Fresh basil leaves *or*	12
$\frac{1}{2}$ teasp	Dried basil	2.5ml
5 tbsp	Olive oil	5×15ml
1 tbsp	Tomato paste (method 1)	15ml

Left: Spanish capsicums with bacon stuffing

METHOD 1

1 If using fresh tomatoes, blanch them, then remove skins.
2 Put tomatoes into a blender and liquidize for a few seconds. Push purée through sieve to remove seeds. Season with salt and pepper, then add basil. Leave for at least 10 minutes, then remove leaves if using fresh basil.
3 Just before serving, stir in the olive oil and tomato paste and mix together until well blended.

METHOD 2

1 If using fresh tomatoes, blanch them, then remove skins.
2 Put tomatoes into a blender with the peeled garlic clove and liquidize for a few seconds. Push purée through sieve to remove seeds. Season with salt and pepper, then add basil. Leave for at least 10 minutes.
3 Just before serving, stir in the olive oil and mix well.

Fresh tomatoes need skins removed, but place contents of can straight in blender

Depending on which method used, the basil leaves can be left in or taken out of purée

Quiche aux champignons

A shallow quiche that's almost like a pastry-based pizza. It's just as good hot or cold which makes it useful for parties or summer picnics. From France, it uses the tiny *champignons* enjoyed in every region

LUNCH OR SUPPER Serves 6–8

Overall timing 50 minutes

Equipment 10 inch (25cm) loose-bottom flan tin, saucepan, bowl

Freezing Open freeze till firm, then wrap in double thickness of foil, seal and label. Freezer life: 2 months. To use: thaw at room temperature for 3–4 hours and serve cold, or reheat from frozen at 350F (180C) Gas 4 for 20 minutes

Below: Quiche aux champignons – mushroom packed. Cut into generous wedges to serve

INGREDIENTS

13oz	Packet of frozen puff pastry	375g
12oz	Small button mushrooms	350g
1oz	Butter	25g
	Salt	
	Freshly-ground white pepper	
3	Large eggs	3
¼ pint	Carton of single cream	150ml
¼ pint	Milk	150ml
¼ teasp	Grated nutmeg	1.25ml

METHOD

1 Thaw pastry. Preheat the oven to 425F (220C) Gas 7.

2 Roll out pastry on floured surface and line flan tin. Prick base with fork. Wipe and trim the mushrooms.

3 Heat butter in saucepan, add mushrooms and fry for 5 minutes. Remove from heat and add plenty of seasoning. Leave to cool slightly.

4 Break the eggs into bowl and using a fork mix in the cream, milk, salt, pepper and grated nutmeg. Spread mushrooms over flan base, then pour in the egg mixture.

5 Bake in the centre of the oven for 15 minutes, then reduce heat to 350F (180C) Gas 4 and cook for further 15 minutes till the filling is set and the top golden. Serve hot or cold with a mixed salad. Or cut into bite-size squares for finger food at parties.

Chive crêpes with mushroom filling

A distinctive flavour is given to these crêpes by making the batter with chives and the milk and lemon juice used to boil the mushroom filling

LUNCH OR SUPPER Serves 4–6

Overall timing $1\frac{1}{4}$ hours

Equipment Saucepan, mixing bowl, crêpe, heavy-based or non-stick frying pan, greaseproof paper, ovenproof dish

Freezing At Step 7 arrange filled crêpes and sauce in foil container, then leave till cool. Cover, label and freeze. Freezer life: 2 months. To use: thaw in fridge overnight, then cook, uncovered, in oven preheated to 350F (180C) Gas 4 for about 20 minutes

Below: Chive crêpes with mushroom filling – filled crêpes ready for baking in a sauce

INGREDIENTS

	Filling	
1lb	Button mushrooms	450g
1oz	Butter	25g
$\frac{1}{2}$ pint	Milk	300ml
	Salt	
	Freshly-ground black pepper	
$\frac{1}{4}$ teasp	Grated nutmeg	1.25ml
$1\frac{1}{2}$ tbsp	Lemon juice	22.5ml
	Crêpes	
5oz	Plain flour	150g
$\frac{1}{4}$ teasp	Salt	1.25ml
2	Eggs	2
2 tbsp	Chopped chives	2×15ml
	Sauce	
$\frac{1}{2}$ pint	Béchamel sauce (recipe page 26) or Tomato sauce (recipe page 126)	300ml

METHOD

1 Wipe and trim the mushrooms and chop finely. Heat the butter in a saucepan and fry the mushrooms for 3 minutes, stirring constantly. Add the milk, seasoning, nutmeg and lemon juice. Bring to the boil and simmer, uncovered, for 10 minutes.

2 Strain the mixture, reserving the milk for the crêpes.

3 To make the crêpes, sift the flour and salt into a mixing bowl. Make a well in the centre and add the eggs, drawing in the flour. Whisk, gradually adding the reserved milk to make a smooth batter, then stir in the chives. Preheat the oven to 350F (180C) Gas 4.

4 Brush a little oil over the crêpe or frying pan and preheat it. Pour in enough batter to just cover the base of the pan, tilting to coat evenly.
5 Cook over a high heat till the underside is golden, then turn and cook for a further 1–2 minutes. Tip on to a sheet of greaseproof paper.
6 Repeat till all the batter is used, making 12 crêpes. Divide the filling between them and roll them to enclose the filling. Make Béchamel or tomato sauce.
7 Arrange the crêpes in a greased ovenproof dish and pour sauce over. Bake, uncovered, in the centre of the oven for about 20 minutes. Serve immediately, garnished with extra fluted mushrooms, if liked.

Mash the potato to a fluffy purée, then beat in butter and egg yolks or whole egg

Divide chilled potato into pieces and roll on a floured board into croquette shapes

Below: Croquette potatoes – soft and smooth potato mixture with a crisp golden coating

Croquette potatoes

These are usually very popular with children – it's well worth making up a large quantity and storing some in the freezer. If preferred, fry the croquettes in a large frying pan instead of a deep-fryer, in a mixture of 3 tbsp (3×15ml) oil and 2oz (50g) butter, turning till crisp all over

VEGETABLE Makes 18

Overall timing $1\frac{1}{4}$ hours plus chilling

Equipment Saucepan, 2 plates, deep-fryer

Freezing Prepare to end of Step 4. Place on baking trays and open freeze till firm. Pack in rigid containers, cover, label and freeze. Freezer life: 3 months. To use: shallow fry from frozen

INGREDIENTS

2lb	Floury potatoes	900g
	Salt	
2oz	Butter	50g
3	Egg yolks *or*	3
1	Egg	1
	Freshly-ground black pepper	
	Coating	
2	Egg whites *or*	2
1	Egg	1
8oz	Dried breadcrumbs	225g
	Oil for deep frying	

METHOD
1 Peel and quarter the potatoes. Cover with cold salted water, bring to boil and cook for 20 minutes.
2 Drain thoroughly, return to the pan and mash over a low heat to make a fluffy purée. Remove from the heat and beat in butter and egg yolks (or whole egg). Season to taste. Spread on a plate and leave to cool, then chill for 2–3 hours or till firm.
3 Divide the mixture into 18 even-size pieces and roll each piece on a floured board into a croquette shape.
4 Beat the egg whites (or whole egg) on a plate and roll the croquettes in it till evenly coated. Toss in the breadcrumbs, pressing them on lightly.
5 Heat the oil in the deep-fryer to 360F (180C) and fry the croquettes, a few at a time, for 3–4 minutes till crisp and golden. Drain on kitchen paper and keep hot while you cook the rest. Place in a serving dish and serve immediately, garnished with sprigs of parsley or watercress and lemon wedges if liked.

Potato chips

To preserve as much goodness as possible, use a potato peeler to remove skin with very little flesh attached. Wash well

The size and shape of chips can be what you like – either thick chunky fingers, or very finely cut matchstick lengths

Deep-fryer should only be one-third full of oil and basket a quarter full, or oil will lose heat and chips will be soggy

The first frying blanches the chips, the second one crisps and colours them. Tip on to kitchen paper to drain, then serve

Whether cut finely (*alumettes*), slightly thicker (*mignonettes*) or in thick fingers (*pont-neuf*), potato chips (*pommes frites*) are delicious

VEGETABLE Serves 4

Overall timing 1 hour

Equipment Bowl, deep-fryer

Freezing Prepare to end of Step 2 and cool. Open freeze, pack in polythene, seal and label. Freezer life: 6 months. To use: deep fry from frozen at 360F (180C)

Above: Potato chips – make them thick and succulent, or thin and very crispy

INGREDIENTS

$1\frac{1}{2}$lb	Waxy potatoes	700g
	Oil for deep frying	
	Salt	

METHOD

1 Peel the potatoes and cut into slices $\frac{1}{2}$ inch (12.5mm) thick, then into sticks $\frac{1}{2}$ inch (12.5mm) wide. Alternatively, cut slices $\frac{1}{8}$ inch (3mm) thick, then cut into thin matchsticks. Put into a bowl of cold water and leave to soak for 30 minutes.

2 Heat the oil in a deep-fryer to 360F (180C). Drain the chips and dry thoroughly. Quarter-fill the fryer basket with chips and fry for 4–5 minutes till tender but not brown. Remove and drain on kitchen paper. Repeat till all the chips are blanched.

3 Make sure oil is at right temperature. Quarter-fill the fryer basket with blanched chips and fry till crisp and golden. Drain on kitchen paper and keep hot, uncovered, while the rest are cooked.

4 Arrange on a warmed serving dish and sprinkle with salt. Serve immediately.

OVEN CHIPS

These are a good idea for those who don't like deep frying, but are economical on fuel only if you're using the oven to cook something else. Peel and wash 4 medium-size waxy potatoes, then cut into chips $\frac{1}{2}$ inch (12.5mm) thick. Place in pan, cover with cold salted water and bring to boil. Boil for 2 minutes, then drain, rinse, dry on kitchen paper. Preheat oven to 450F (230C) Gas 8. Spread cold chips in single layer in shallow ovenproof dish. Pour over 1oz (25g) butter melted with 1 tbsp (15ml) oil, turn chips till coated.* Bake above centre of oven for 25–30 minutes, turning chips several times, till golden and tender. Drain on kitchen paper.

*Open freeze at this stage if liked. Pack in shallow foil containers which can go straight in the oven for cooking.

potato nests

Scrape $1\frac{1}{2}$lb (700g) waxy potatoes, wash and dry. Shred coarsely using fluted blade of mandolin. Dry, divide into 4. Use one lot to line bottom part of a nid (potato nest) mould. Secure top part in place. Lower into oil heated to 360F (180C). Fry for 4–5 minutes till crisp, then turn out. Repeat with rest

Courgettes niçoise

This way of cooking courgettes mellows their flavour. For a light lunch or supper dish, stir in 2–3 lightly beaten eggs at the last minute and cook gently till they start to set. Serve with toast

STARTER OR VEGETABLE Serves 6

Overall timing 1 hour

Equipment Large frying pan with lid

Freezing Put in rigid container, cool, cover, label and freeze. Freezer life: 6 months. To use: reheat gently from frozen, stirring from time to time

INGREDIENTS

$1\frac{3}{4}$lb	Tomatoes	750g
2	Large onions	2
3 tbsp	Olive oil	3×15ml
	Salt and pepper	
$1\frac{1}{2}$lb	Small courgettes	700g
1 tbsp	Chopped fresh basil	15ml

METHOD

1 Blanch, peel and chop tomatoes. Peel and thinly slice onions.

2 Heat oil in a large frying pan. Add tomatoes and onions. Season with salt and pepper and cook over a moderate heat for 10–15 minutes, stirring from time to time.

3 Wash courgettes, trim ends and add to pan. Cover and cook for about 30 minutes over a low heat. Sprinkle with chopped basil just before serving. Serve very hot or chilled.

freezing know-how

Leftover plain jacket-baked potatoes can be frozen, although with the reheating time it is not worth baking them specially for freezing. Cut the potatoes in half lengthways and scoop out the flesh. Mash it with a little butter and seasoning (finely-grated cheese can be added if liked) and pile it back into the shells, packing it in firmly. Wrap closely in foil, seal, label and freeze for up to 3 months. Place the foil-wrapped potatoes on a baking tray and reheat at 400F (200C) Gas 6 for about 30 minutes (or while another dish is cooking). Unwrap the potatoes, place on the tray and cook for a further 10–15 minutes till browned.

Sweet-sour red cabbage

This dish complements game or adds extra taste to bland meat. An exciting, spicy way to use red cabbage, it is also a good supper dish, served with frankfurters or gammon

VEGETABLE Serves 4

Overall timing 1 hour 20 minutes

Equipment Large heavy-based casserole with tight-fitting lid

Freezing Pack into containers. Seal, label and freeze. Freezer life: 3 months. To use: reheat slowly from frozen

INGREDIENTS

2lb	Red cabbage	about 1kg
2oz	Streaky bacon	50g
1	Onion	1
1	Cooking apple	1
6	Whole allspice	6
$\frac{1}{2}$ teasp	Salt	2.5ml
2 teasp	Honey	2×5ml
3fl oz	Red wine or wine vinegar	90ml

METHOD

1 Discard any damaged outer leaves of cabbage. Quarter and cut away core and thick ribs then shred leaves.

2 Chop bacon. Peel and chop onion. Cook bacon in casserole over a low heat until fat starts to run. Add onion and cook for 5 minutes, stirring.

3 Core and chop apple and add to casserole with cabbage. Crush allspice and add to casserole with salt, honey and wine or vinegar. Turn mixture over with a wooden spoon. Cover and simmer for 1 hour. If there's too much liquid at the end of cooking time, leave lid off, increase heat and reduce liquid by half. Serve hot.

Below: Sweet-sour red cabbage combines the piquancy of allspice and wine vinegar with the smooth sweetness of honey

DESSERTS

Desserts that can be frozen are a great help when entertaining; make them a week or so ahead as part of a planned menu. Family puddings from the freezer will save you on days when imagination runs out!

Apple and mincemeat tart

The filling is juicy when served hot but is firmer when cold. As the tart freezes well, you can make it in advance, for Christmas, or to serve at any time

HOT OR COLD DESSERT Serves 6

Overall timing 1 hour

Equipment 9½ inch (24cm) loose-bottomed fluted flan tin, bowl, baking tray

Freezing Cook and allow to go cold. Remove from tin, place on thick card and wrap in heavy foil. Label, seal and freeze. Freezer life: 3 months. To use: remove foil, replace tart in flan tin, cover over with foil and reheat at 350F (180C) Gas 4 for about 40 minutes until heated through

INGREDIENTS

7½oz	Frozen pastry	212g
14½oz	Jar of mincemeat	411g
1lb	Bramley apples	450g
3oz	Caster sugar	75g
½ teasp	Ground allspice	2.5ml
1oz	Butter	25g
2 tbsp	Plain flour	2×15ml

METHOD

1 Preheat the oven to 425F (220C) Gas 7.
2 Roll out the pastry and line flan tin.
3 Spread mincemeat evenly over pastry.
4 Peel and finely slice the apples. Mix with 2oz (50g) of sugar and allspice. Arrange in circles on mincemeat.
5 In a bowl, rub the butter into remaining 1oz (25g) sugar and flour until the mixture resembles fine breadcrumbs. Scatter evenly over the apples. Place flan on baking tray.
6 Bake in preheated oven for 15 minutes, then reduce to 375F (190C) Gas 5 for a further 30 minutes. Remove from oven, spoon any topping from baking tray on to tart. Allow to cool. Lift tart from flan tin and place carefully on serving plate.

TO SERVE
Serve warm or cold, with whipped cream or vanilla ice cream.

Above: Apple and mincemeat tart – delicious served warm with a helping of ice cream

pastry know-how

If pastry is hard or tough too much water or not enough fat was used; the mixture was overhandled.
If pastry shrank during cooking it was probably unevenly stretched during rolling and shaping; or was insufficiently rested.

Cranberry tart

An unusually flavoured pastry is used to complement fresh cranberries in this delicious tart. The fruit, which is picked over and washed, is not cooked first but mixed with sugar which draws the juices out

COLD DESSERT Cuts into 12

Overall timing 1 hour 50 minutes plus cooling

Equipment 2 bowls, $10\frac{1}{2}$ inch (26cm) loose-bottom flan tin, piping bag with star nozzle

Freezing When cold, open freeze undecorated tart till firm, then wrap and label. Freezer life: 3 months. To use: thaw at room temperature for 2–3 hours, then decorate with whipped cream

INGREDIENTS

	Pastry	
8oz	Plain flour	225g
	Pinch of salt	
2oz	Icing or caster sugar	50g
4oz	Margarine	125g
2 tbsp	Soured cream	2×15ml
1 tbsp	Rum or water	15ml
	Other ingredients	
1lb	Fresh cranberries	450g
8oz	Caster sugar	225g
1	Egg white	1
4fl oz	Carton of double cream	113ml

METHOD

1 Sift flour, salt and sugar of choice into bowl. Add the margarine, cut into small pieces, and rub in till mixture resembles fine breadcrumbs. Add soured cream, rum or water and mix to a smooth dough. Cover and chill in fridge for 30 minutes.

2 Meanwhile, remove stalks from cranberries, wash and drain. Put them into a bowl and mix in the caster sugar.

3 Preheat the oven to 400F (200C) Gas 6. Grease flan tin.

4 Remove dough from fridge. Set aside a quarter of the dough for decoration. Roll out the rest on a lightly floured board, then line the flan tin.

5 Spread the cranberry and sugar mixture evenly over the dough. Roll out reserved dough, cut into thin strips and make a lattice pattern over the cranberries (see picture).

6 Lightly whisk the egg white in a cup and brush over the top of the tart. Bake in the centre of the oven for 45 minutes. Remove tart from tin and leave to cool.

7 In a bowl, whip cream till stiff peaks form. Spoon into a piping bag fitted with a star nozzle and pipe small rosettes around the edge of the cooled tart.

Below: Cranberry tart – crisp, sweet pastry with a fresh fruit and sugar filling

Apricot tart

A tart that makes the most of fresh apricots. If you're pushed for time, you can use bought shortcrust pastry instead of the sweet flan pastry

HOT DESSERT Serves 4

Overall timing $1\frac{1}{2}$ hours

Equipment Mixing bowl, 9 inch (23cm) flan tin or ring, baking tray, saucepan

Freezing Cool quickly then open freeze. When firm, wrap, label and freeze. Freezer life: 1 month. To use: thaw at room temperature for 2–3 hours. Refresh in oven at 400F (200C) Gas 6 for about 10 minutes

INGREDIENTS

7oz	Plain flour	200g
	Pinch of salt	
1 tbsp	Caster sugar	15ml
4oz	Butter	125g
	Water to mix	
1lb	Fresh apricots	450g
4oz	Granulated sugar	125g
2 tbsp	Apricot jam	2×15ml
2 tbsp	Kirsch	2×15ml
1 tbsp	Split almonds	15ml

METHOD

1 Put flour, salt and caster sugar into bowl, making a well in the centre. Cut the softened butter into small pieces and put into the well. Rub in with fingertips till mixture resembles fine breadcrumbs. Add cold water a little at a time. Gather mixture together and knead lightly. Wrap dough in foil and put in fridge for at least half an hour.

2 Wash, dry and halve apricots. Remove stones. Preheat oven to 425F (220C) Gas 7.

3 Roll dough out fairly thickly on a floured board. Line flan tin or ring first placing it on a baking tray.

4 Sprinkle 1oz (25g) of the sugar over the pastry. Arrange apricots on top, hollow side up, so that the juice doesn't run out during cooking. Sprinkle on the rest of the sugar.

5 Cook for about 45 minutes in the oven until apricots begin to caramelize.

6 Prepare syrup by putting apricot jam and Kirsch into a saucepan. Stir together over a low heat.

7 Remove tart from tin or ring and immediately pour on the syrup. Sprinkle on the almonds and serve hot with vanilla ice cream or whipped cream.

Below: Apricot tart – French speciality with syrup and almond topping

Apple charlotte

The chef who created this dish has long been forgotten, but Charlotte, wife of George III for whom he created it, has not. The dessert with its topping and surround of bread has become a world favourite. It is most important that the apple filling be thick or the charlotte will collapse when it is removed from the dish

COLD DESSERT Serves 4

Overall timing 45 minutes plus cooling time

Equipment Saucepan, 6in (15cm) soufflé dish or charlotte tin

Freezing Freeze in the dish. Pack in polythene bag, seal, label and freeze. Freezer life: 3 months. To use: thaw in dish for about 2 hours at room temperature

INGREDIENTS

2lb	Cooking apples	900g
	Grated rind of ½ a lemon	
2 tbsp	Caster sugar	2×15ml
5 tbsp	Icing sugar	5×15ml
4oz	Butter	125g
9oz	Bread	250g

METHOD

1 Peel, core and slice the apples. Place in saucepan with lemon rind and caster sugar. Cover and cook over a low heat for 15 minutes.

2 Remove pan from heat. Sieve the icing sugar into the apples and beat well with a wooden spoon to make a purée.

3 Preheat the oven to 450F (230C) Gas 8. Grease soufflé dish with some butter.

4 Thinly slice the bread and butter it. Toast till golden on both sides. Cut off crusts, then cut 1 or 2 slices into triangles to line base, and the rest into fingers to line sides of the soufflé dish, overlapping the fingers.

5 Place the apples in the middle of the dish, making sure the toast stays in place. Cook in the oven for 10 minutes, then lower the heat to 425F (220C) Gas 7 and cook for a further 15 minutes. Allow to cool completely before trimming toast, then turn out (run knife carefully round edge of dish first) on to a flat plate.

Above: New England apple pie – with an unusual mix of spices including aniseed

New England apple pie

The unusual thing about this pie – and what makes it so American – is that the fruit is placed between two crusts of unsweetened pastry. The apples, dark brown sugar and spices which make up the filling are reckoned to give sufficient sweetness, while the sugar crystals on top provide crunch as well as a decorative look. A pie that repays mass-production as it freezes well

DESSERT Serves 8

Overall timing $1\frac{3}{4}$ hours

Equipment 2 bowls, 8 inch (20cm) springform tin

Freezing Foil-wrap, seal, label and freeze. Freezer life: 6 months. To use: thaw in wrappings for 4–6 hours at room temperature. Refresh at 400F (200C) Gas 6 for 20 minutes and serve hot or cold

INGREDIENTS

	Pastry	
8oz	Plain flour	225g
	Salt	
4oz	Butter or margarine	125g
1 tbsp	Lemon juice	15ml
1 tbsp	Cold water	15ml
	Filling	
2lb	Dessert apples	900g
3oz	Dark soft brown sugar	75g
3oz	Fresh brown breadcrumbs	75g
½ teasp	Grated nutmeg	2.5ml
1 teasp	Ground cinnamon	5ml
¼ teasp	Ground aniseed	1.25ml
¼ teasp	Vanilla essence	1.25ml
	Grated rind of 1 lemon	
2oz	Melted butter	50g
1	Egg yolk	1
2 tbsp	Coarse sugar crystals	2×15ml

METHOD

1 Sift flour into a bowl with a pinch of salt. Rub fat into the flour till the mixture resembles fine breadcrumbs. Add the lemon juice and water and mix to a soft dough. Knead lightly till smooth, wrap and chill for 30 minutes.

2 Meanwhile, peel and core the apples and dice finely. Put into a bowl with the brown sugar, breadcrumbs, spices, vanilla and lemon rind and toss lightly. Pour melted butter over and mix well. Preheat the oven to 400F (200C) Gas 6.

3 Reserve one-third of the pastry. Roll out rest and use to line the tin.

4 Pile the apple mixture into the case and smooth the top. Roll out remaining pastry and use to cover. Crimp edges.

5 Brush egg yolk over the pastry lid and sprinkle the sugar over the top.

6 Bake just above the centre of the oven for 30 minutes. Reduce temperature to 350F (180C) Gas 4 and cook for a further 20 minutes.

7 Carefully run knife round edge, then remove from the mould. Serve hot or cold with pouring cream or ice cream.

Le poirat

Normandy, land of orchards and dairy cattle, is the natural home of this rich pear pie. Cinnamon and walnuts are mixed into the pastry to make a spicy case for the fruit – use large, round pears for this dish, not the long, Conference-type pear

COLD DESSERT Serves 6–8

Overall timing 1 hour plus chilling time

Equipment 3 bowls, rolling-pin, 8 inch (20cm) diameter fluted flan ring or dish, 3 inch (7.5cm) diameter plain pastry cutter, pastry brush, piping bag and small star nozzle

Freezing Omit cream decoration. Open freeze pie till firm, then overwrap with foil, label and return to freezer. Freezer life: 3 months. To use: remove wrappings and thaw at room temperature for about 6 hours. Decorate with cream as Step 9

INGREDIENTS

	Pastry	
6oz	Plain flour	175g
4oz	Butter	125g
2oz	Caster sugar	50g
2oz	Finely-chopped walnuts	50g
2 teasp	Ground cinnamon	2×5ml
1	Egg	1
3 tbsp	Water	3×15ml
	Filling	
4	Ripe dessert pears	4
1½oz	Caster sugar	40g
¼ pint	Whipping cream	150ml

METHOD

1 First make the pastry. Sift the flour into a large bowl. Add the butter, cut up in small pieces, and rub it in with the fingertips until the mixture resembles fine breadcrumbs.
2 Stir in the caster sugar, walnuts and cinnamon. Make a well in the centre and add the egg. Stir it into the flour mixture, adding the water a little at a time and gradually binding the mixture to a firm dough.
3 Knead dough lightly on a floured surface until smooth. Wrap in polythene and chill for 1 hour.
4 To make the filling: peel and quarter the pears and remove the cores. Keep pears under water in a bowl to prevent them from browning.
5 Preheat the oven to 375F (190C) Gas 5. Remove pastry from fridge and unwrap.
6 Roll out two-thirds of the pastry to a 9 inch (23cm) round and line the base and sides of the flan ring or dish. Drain pears thoroughly on kitchen paper and arrange over pastry in a circle, core-side downwards and with the stem ends pointing towards the centre but not joining up. Sprinkle with 1oz (25g) caster sugar.
7 Roll out remaining pastry to an 8 inch (20cm) round and place over pears. Trim edges and pinch together to seal. Using the pastry cutter, cut a circle out of the centre of the pastry lid.
8 Brush pastry with lightly beaten egg white and dredge with remaining caster sugar. Bake towards the top of the oven for 15 minutes, then reduce oven temperature to 350F (180C) Gas 4 and bake for a further 25 minutes.
9 Remove pie from oven and cool. Just before serving whip the cream in a bowl until it holds soft peaks. Spoon into the piping bag fitted with the star nozzle, and pipe rosettes into the centre of the flan.

Fruit crumble

Use any stewed fruit or mixture of fruit for the filling. Try rhubarb, gooseberries, blackberry and apple. Or use uncooked fruit and add 5 minutes to the baking time

DESSERT Serves 4

Overall timing 50 minutes

Equipment Shallow ovenproof dish, bowl

Freezing Make crumble in foil container then wrap, label and freeze, baked or unbaked. Freezer life: 2 months. To use: bake from frozen at 350F (180C) Gas 4 for 30 minutes, 45 minutes if previously unbaked

INGREDIENTS

2lb	Stewed fruit	900g
3oz	Butter	75g
5oz	Plain flour	150g
3oz	Demerara sugar	75g

METHOD

1 Preheat the oven to 400F (200C) Gas 6. Place stewed fruit in ovenproof dish.
2 Rub fat into flour in a bowl until the mixture resembles fine breadcrumbs. Stir in the sugar, then sprinkle over fruit.
3 Cook in the oven for 20–30 minutes or until crisp and golden. Serve with custard or pouring cream.

VARIATIONS

Add 2 teasp (2×5ml) grated lemon, orange or lime rind; 1oz (25g) candied fruit; 1oz (25g) chopped nuts; 1 teasp (5ml) ground cinnamon, cloves, mixed spice or ginger. Or, replace 2oz (50g) of the flour with the same weight of rolled oats.

Below: Le poirat – Normandy pear pie flavoured with cinnamon

Above: *Banana pudding with rum sauce — a delicious dessert with an exotic finish*

Peel and roughly cut the bananas into slices. Put through a food mill, or mash, until the mixture is really smooth and creamy

Separate the eggs and add the yolks, one by one, to the banana mixture. Beat well until absorbed into the mixture

Place the egg whites in a bowl and beat or whisk until really stiff — the mixture should stand in peaks

When the egg whites are very stiff, fold dollops gently into the banana mixture — there should be no pockets of white

Banana pudding with rum sauce

The combination of rum and bananas will bring a taste of the Caribbean to your table whether the sun is out or not

DESSERT Serves 6

Overall timing $1\frac{1}{4}$ hours

Equipment Food mill, 2 mixing bowls, large pudding basin and ovenproof bowl

Freezing Cool, wrap, label and freeze. Freezer life: 3 months. To use: thaw for 4—5 hours, then heat in moderate oven

INGREDIENTS

2lb	Bananas	900g
$3\frac{1}{2}$oz	Caster sugar	100g
2oz	Softened butter	50g
2oz	Plain flour	50g
	Grated nutmeg	
2	Eggs	2
2 tbsp	Icing sugar	2×15ml
1 tbsp	Rum	15ml
$\frac{1}{4}$ pint	Carton of single cream	150ml

METHOD

1 Preheat the oven to 350F (180C) Gas 4.

2 Reserve half a large or 1 medium-sized banana for decoration. Peel the rest. Mash them with a fork or put them through a Moulinette (see step by step picture, right). Put into a bowl with sugar, butter, flour and a pinch of nutmeg.

3 Separate the eggs. Add yolks to banana mixture and beat well with a wooden spoon until smooth and creamy. Beat the egg whites till very stiff then gently fold into the banana mixture.

4 Lightly grease and flour a pudding basin. Fill with the banana mixture and cook in the oven for 1 hour.

5 Remove from oven. Leave to cool slightly then turn out on to serving plate. Sprinkle with icing sugar and decorate. Mix rum into single cream and serve separately.

Basic sponge pudding

This recipe can be adapted to make almost any steamed sponge pudding

DESSERT Serves 4–6

Overall timing $1\frac{3}{4}$ hours

Equipment Bowl, 2 pint (1.1 litre) pudding basin, foil and saucepan or 8 inch (20cm) square cake tin

Freezing Make pudding in foil container, cover, label and freeze. Freezer life: 3 months. To use: thaw at room temperature for 2 hours, then heat in oven at 375F (190C) Gas 5 for 30 minutes

INGREDIENTS

4oz	Butter or margarine	125g
4oz	Caster sugar	125g
2	Eggs	2
6oz	Self-raising flour	175g
3 tbsp	Milk	3×15ml

METHOD

1 Cream the fat and sugar in a bowl till pale and fluffy. Gradually beat in the eggs one at a time.
2 Fold in the sifted flour with a metal spoon, adding milk to give a soft dropping consistency.
3 Place in greased basin and cover with greased foil. Put basin into a pan and fill up to rim of basin with boiling water. Cover and steam for $1\frac{1}{2}$ hours. Turn out of mould and serve immediately with custard or pouring cream.

Orange upside down pudding

A warming oven-baked sponge dessert that's perfect for a wintry day

DESSERT Serves 4–6

Overall timing 1 hour 10 minutes

Equipment 8 inch (20cm) square cake tin, bowl

Freezing As for basic sponge pudding (see above)

Left: a selection of puddings all made from one basic sponge mix. Top, Orange upside down pudding; bottom left, Cherry pudding with jam sauce and left, Chocolate castles

INGREDIENTS

	Basic sponge pudding mix	
3	Large thin-skinned oranges	3
4 tbsp	Finely shredded marmalade	4×15ml

METHOD

1 Preheat the oven to 375F (190C) Gas 5. Generously grease cake tin and base-line.
2 Make up basic sponge pudding according to instructions on this page, adding the finely grated rind of one of the oranges to the mixture.
3 Spread marmalade over base of prepared tin. Cut the peel and pith away from the oranges with a serrated-edge knife, then thinly slice flesh across the segments. Arrange slices, overlapping, over base of tin. Spread sponge mixture over oranges with a spoon and smooth down the surface with a wetted palette knife.
4 Bake in the centre of the oven for about 45 minutes or until firm to the touch. Turn out on to serving dish and serve with custard or pouring cream.

Chocolate castles

Individual chocolate sponge puddings that taste as good as they look

DESSERT Serves 4

Overall timing 45 minutes

Equipment 8 dariole moulds or 8 inch (20cm) square cake tin, bowl, saucepan

Freezing As for basic sponge pudding. Do not freeze sauce

INGREDIENTS

	Basic sponge pudding mix	
1oz	Cocoa	25g
4oz	Chocolate dots	125g
	Sauce	
1 tbsp	Cornflour	15ml
$\frac{1}{2}$ pint	Milk	300ml
$\frac{1}{2}$oz	Butter	15g
1oz	Sugar	25g

METHOD

1 Preheat the oven to 375F (190C) Gas 5. Grease the individual dariole moulds or square cake tin.
2 Make the basic sponge pudding, substituting the cocoa for 1oz (25g) of the flour. Fold in half the chocolate dots.
3 Divide mixture between dariole moulds or cake tin. Bake in the centre of the oven for 20–25 minutes (35 minutes if using cake tin).
4 To make the sauce, blend the cornflour with 2 tbsp (2×15ml) of the milk. Melt the remaining chocolate dots with the butter and sugar in the rest of the milk. Add cornflour mixture and bring to the boil, stirring, Cook, stirring, until thick and smooth.

TO SERVE

Turn puddings out of moulds and serve with a little of the sauce poured over, or cut into squares and serve cold with ice cream and the hot sauce.

Cherry pudding with jam sauce

A variation on the basic steamed pudding with a red jam sauce

DESSERT Serves 4–6

Overall timing $1\frac{3}{4}$ hours

Equipment 2 pint (1.1 litre) pudding basin, bowl, foil, 2 saucepans

Freezing As for basic sponge pudding. Not recommended for sauce

INGREDIENTS

	Basic sponge pudding mix	
4oz	Glacé cherries	125g
$\frac{1}{2}$ teasp	Almond essence	2.5ml
	Sauce	
4 tbsp	Red jam	4×15ml
$\frac{1}{4}$ pint	Water	150ml
1 teasp	Arrowroot	5ml
1 tbsp	Lemon juice	15ml

METHOD

1 Grease pudding basin. Follow Step 1 of basic sponge pudding method. Wash and dry cherries and toss in the flour. Complete Step 2 of the pudding method, adding the almond essence.
2 Turn mixture into prepared basin and cover with greased foil. Place basin in large saucepan and fill with boiling water up to basin rim. Cover and boil for $1\frac{1}{2}$ hours.
3 To make the sauce, melt the jam with the water in a small pan, then sieve. Blend arrowroot with lemon juice and stir into sauce. Bring to the boil stirring.

TO SERVE

Turn pudding out of mould and serve immediately with the hot jam sauce.

Left: Chocolate layer dessert, party-size. Just double the quantities given and make thick rather than thin layers of the biscuits and chocolate cream

Chocolate layer dessert

Adult-style treat – a rich combination of sherry-flavoured biscuits and chocolate cream

COLD DESSERT OR CAKE 8 servings

Overall timing 15 minutes plus 1–3 hours refrigeration

Equipment Dessert: shallow dish, heatproof bowl and saucepan (or double saucepan), mixing bowl, glass serving dish. Cake: as dessert but see Step 7

Freezing Dessert: make up recipe and arrange in a foil container. Cover, label and freeze. Cake: when chilled remove from tin. Open freeze until fim. Wrap, label and return to freezer. Freezer life (for both): 3 months. To use: thaw at room temperature for about 3 hours

INGREDIENTS

7oz	Packet of rich tea finger biscuits	200g
$\frac{1}{4}$ pint	Sweet or Amontillado sherry	150ml
8oz	Plain chocolate	225g
4 tbsp	Water	4×15ml
4oz	Butter	125g
$\frac{1}{4}$ pint	Cartons of single cream *and* double cream	150ml
	Chocolate curls	

METHOD

1 To make dessert: put biscuits into a shallow dish and sprinkle with sherry. The biscuits should absorb the sherry but not disintegrate.

2 Meanwhile, break chocolate into pieces and put them with the water into a heatproof bowl over a saucepan of hot water (or use a double saucepan). When chocolate has melted, chop butter into small pieces and add to bowl. Stir gently until smooth and well combined. Remove from heat and cool.

3 Whip single and double creams together until thick. Put $\frac{1}{4}$ of the cream to one side for topping.

4 Stir cool chocolate mixture gradually into the remaining whipped cream.

5 Cover base of glass serving dish with a single layer of biscuits and spoon over some of the chocolate mixture. Continue with alternate layers, in this way, ending with biscuits.

6 Spread reserved cream over the top and decorate with chocolate curls. Put in fridge for 1 hour.

7 To make cake: follow steps 1 to 5 of dessert, but arrange layers in a lightly-oiled, loose-bottomed cake tin. After last layer of biscuits, cover with foil and a weight and leave for at least an hour to settle layers. Remove cake from tin, cover with cream and chocolate curls and chill for 3 hours or overnight. During this time the mixture will become firmer and so will slice easily.

No-cook sherry dessert

A simple and deliciously rich dessert that is really improved by being made well ahead of the time that it's wanted

COLD DESSERT 4–6 servings

Overall timing 5–10 minutes plus 3 hours refrigeration

Equipment Shallow dish, glass serving dish or soufflé dish

Freezing Make up recipe using a foil container. Cover, label and freeze. Freezer life: 3 months. To use: thaw overnight in fridge

INGREDIENTS

$\frac{1}{4}$ pint	Sweet sherry	150ml
7oz	Packet of chocolate chip biscuits	200g
$\frac{1}{2}$ pint	Carton of whipping cream	284ml
	Chocolate curls or flake	

METHOD

1 Put sherry into a shallow dish and soak biscuits a few at a time. They should absorb the sherry but not disintegrate.

2 Lift them out carefully with an egg slice and arrange a single layer on the base of a glass or soufflé dish.

3 Lightly whip the cream.

4 Cover biscuits with a layer of whipped cream and continue with alternate layers of biscuits and cream, ending with a layer of cream.

5 Chill dessert for at least 3 hours. Decorate dessert before serving with chocolate curls or crumbled flake.

Rum babas

Scrumptious honey and rum soaked yeast cakes named after Ali Baba

DESSERT OR TEA-TIME Makes 8

Overall timing 1¼ hours plus proving and chilling

Equipment 8 small ring moulds, baking tray, 2 saucepans, 2 bowls, piping bag

Freezing Complete Step 6, remove from moulds and cool completely. Foil-wrap, place in a rigid container, cover, label and freeze. Freezer life: 3 months. To use: unwrap and thaw for 1 hour at room temperature. Complete Steps 7–9

INGREDIENTS

3oz	Seeded raisins	75g
3 tbsp	Milk	3×15ml
½oz	Fresh yeast	15g
1 tbsp	Caster sugar	15ml
4oz	Strong flour	125g
¼ teasp	Salt	1.25ml
2oz	Softened butter	50g
2	Eggs	2
4 tbsp	Runny honey	4×15ml
2 tbsp	Water	2×15ml
5 tbsp	Rum	5×15ml
½ pint	Carton of whipping cream	284ml

METHOD

1 Grease the ring moulds and arrange on a baking tray. Divide the raisins between the moulds.

2 Warm the milk and pour into a bowl. Add the yeast and a pinch of the sugar, and cream till smooth. Stir in 3 tbsp (3×15ml) of the flour, mix well and leave in a warm place for about 15 minutes till frothy.

3 Sift the remaining flour and salt into a bowl and make a well in the centre. Add the yeast mixture, remaining sugar, butter and eggs and beat for 2–3 minutes with a wooden spoon.

4 Divide the mixture between the moulds. Cover lightly with oiled polythene and leave to prove in a warm place till the mixture has almost filled the moulds.

5 Preheat the oven to 400F (200C) Gas 6.

6 Bake the babas just above the centre of the oven for 15–20 minutes till springy.

7 Meanwhile, put the honey and water in a saucepan and heat gently till dissolved. Remove from the heat and add 4 tbsp (4×15ml) of the rum.

8 Turn the babas out on to a large dish and spoon the syrup over while still hot. Leave to cool, then chill for 1 hour.

9 Whip the cream till stiff peaks form. Fold in the remaining rum. Put into a piping bag fitted with a star nozzle. Arrange the babas on individual plates and pipe the cream into the centres.

Tipsy cake

Brandy-laced cake filled with jam and apricots, covered with cream

DESSERT Serves 8

Overall timing 2 hours plus chilling

Equipment Deep 8 inch (20cm) cake tin, 2 bowls, skewer, saucepan, piping bag

Freezing Complete to end of Step 3 and cool. Remove from tin, foil-wrap, seal, label and freeze. Freezer life: 3 months. To use: unwrap, thaw at room temperature for 4 hours, then complete

INGREDIENTS

	Cake	
6oz	Butter or margarine	175g
6oz	Caster sugar	175g
3	Eggs	3
2oz	Ground almonds	50g
½ teasp	Almond essence	2.5ml
6oz	Self-raising flour	175g
2 tbsp	Milk	2×15ml
	Filling and topping	
14oz	Can of apricot halves	397g
5 tbsp	Brandy	5×15ml
2 tbsp	Apricot jam	2×15ml
½ pint	Carton of whipping cream	284ml
2oz	Toasted flaked almonds	50g

METHOD

1 Preheat the oven to 325F (170C) Gas 3. Grease and base-line the tin.

2 Cream the fat and sugar together till pale and fluffy. Add the eggs one at a time, beating well between each addition. Add the almonds and essence. Sift the flour over, add the milk and fold into the mixture with a metal spoon.

3 Spread the mixture into the tin, smooth the surface and bake in the centre of the oven for about 1¼ hours till a skewer inserted in the centre of the cake comes out clean.

4 To make filling, drain the apricots and put the syrup into a small saucepan. Bring to the boil and boil till reduced to ¼ pint (150ml). Remove from the heat and allow to cool. Add the brandy. Reserve 8 of the apricot halves for decoration and chop the rest.

5 Remove the warm cake from the tin and cut it in half through the centre. Return the bottom half to the tin and spoon half the brandy syrup over it. Spread the jam on top and cover with the chopped apricots. Replace second half of cake. Pierce in several places with a skewer and spoon the remaining syrup over. Press a plate on top and chill for 2 hours.

6 Turn the cake carefully out of the tin on to a flat serving dish or board. Whip the cream till it forms stiff peaks. Spread two-thirds over the sides and top of the cake and smooth the surface. Mark the top into 8 wedges.

7 Press the toasted almonds against the sides of the cake, reserving a few for the top. Put the remaining cream into a piping bag fitted with a star nozzle and pipe a large swirl on each wedge. Top each with an apricot half, scatter reserved almonds in the centre of the cake. Chill for 1 hour before serving.

Swedish cherry pudding

An easy-to-make layered pudding

DESSERT Serves 6

Overall timing 50 minutes

Equipment Saucepan, ovenproof dish

Freezing Cook in foil container, cool, seal and label. Freezer life: 3 months. To use: thaw for 2 hours at room temperature

INGREDIENTS

6oz	Butter	175g
8oz	Breadcrumbs	225g
3 tbsp	Caster sugar	3×15ml
2 teasp	Cinnamon	2×5ml
2×14oz	Cans of cherry pie filling	2×397g

METHOD

1 Preheat the oven to 375F (190C) Gas 5.

2 Melt 4oz (125g) of the butter in a saucepan. Add breadcrumbs, sugar and cinnamon and cook, stirring, till golden brown.

3 Grease an ovenproof dish with a little of remaining butter, line base with a ½ inch (12.5mm) layer of the bread mixture. Cover with layer of pie filling. Continue building layers till all the ingredients are used, then dot the surface with rest of butter.

4 Bake for 25 minutes. Remove from oven and leave to cool. Serve with custard or whipped cream.

Chocolate rum flan

The mousse filling for this flan could also be made and served separately

DESSERT Serves 6

Overall timing 1 hour plus chilling time

Equipment 3 bowls, 9½ inch (24cm) loose-bottomed deep flan tin, saucepan

Freezing Open freeze until hard, then wrap in foil, label and refreeze. Freezer life: 1 month. To use: remove wrappings and thaw in fridge for 3 hours

INGREDIENTS

4oz	Plain flour	125g
1oz	Ground almonds	25g
1oz	Butter	25g
1 tbsp	Soft brown sugar	15ml
1	Egg	1
	Filling	
5oz	Plain chocolate	150g
3oz	Butter	75g
3	Eggs	3
3 tbsp	Caster sugar	3×15ml
	Salt	
1 tbsp	Rum	15ml
¼ pint	Carton of double or whipping cream	150ml

Melt chocolate with butter, then add egg yolks and sugar and beat well

Fold beaten egg whites into chocolate, add rum, then pour into flan case

Above: Chocolate rum flan – almond pastry

METHOD

1 Put flour and ground almonds in a bowl, rub in the butter until it resembles breadcrumbs, stir in sugar, then mix in egg to form a firm dough. Chill for 30 minutes. Preheat the oven to 400F (200C) Gas 6.

2 On a floured board, roll out dough to fit greased tin. Press into base and sides of tin with your fingers. Line with foil and baking beans or crusts and bake blind for 15 minutes. Then remove foil, reduce oven to 350F (180C) Gas 4, return flan to oven and continue baking for about 10 minutes until pastry is set and golden brown. Cool a little, then carefully remove from tin and place on flat serving dish to cool completely.

3 To make the filling, break chocolate into small pieces and melt in a bowl over a pan of hot water, together with half the butter, stirring often.

4 When melted, remove pan from heat. Separate the eggs. Add egg yolks, the remaining butter in pieces and 2 tbsp (2×15ml) of the sugar to the chocolate mixture. Beat well, then allow to cool.

5 In another bowl beat the egg whites with a pinch of salt until stiff. Stir 1 tbsp (15ml) of the caster sugar into the egg whites, then fold them into the chocolate until no white specks show.

6 Stir in the rum, then pour the filling into the flan case. Chill for 1–2 hours till firm, then pipe whipped cream on top to decorate just before serving.

Chocolate sauce

A sauce to be eaten hot rather than cold. It is especially good over ice cream with a sprinkling of nuts, or fresh or grilled bananas

HOT DESSERT SAUCE Makes ½ pint (300ml)

Overall timing 15 minutes

Equipment Bowl, saucepan

Freezing Cool, then pour into rigid container. Cover, label and freeze. Freezer life: 1 month. To use: thaw for 1 hour, then heat gently

INGREDIENTS

2 teasp	Cornflour	2×5ml
½ pint	Cold milk	300ml
2oz	Plain dessert chocolate or chocolate dots	50g
2 tbsp	Granulated sugar	2×15ml
½ teasp	Vanilla essence	2.5ml

METHOD

1 Blend the cornflour in a bowl with a little milk. Put rest of milk in saucepan with the broken up chocolate or chocolate dots. Heat slowly until the chocolate melts, then stir in cornflour.

2 Cook, stirring constantly, until the sauce comes to the boil and thickens. Stir in sugar and essence and cook, stirring, for 3 minutes more. Serve.

Chocolate profiteroles

A classic recipe – choux balls, cream-filled and coated with chocolate sauce. Don't open oven till choux have baked for 20 minutes

DESSERT Serves 4–6

Overall timing 1½ hours

Equipment 2 saucepans, 2 baking trays, piping bag with small plain nozzle, 2 bowls

Freezing Unbaked: pipe shapes on to baking trays lined with greased foil or non-stick cooking paper. Unbaked or baked: open freeze till firm, then pack in polythene bags or rigid container, cover, label and freeze. Freezer life: unbaked – 3 months, baked – 6 months. To use: unbaked – bake from frozen on greased baking tray in hot oven 425F (220C) Gas 7, allowing extra 5 minutes baking time. Baked – place frozen shapes on greased baking tray and refresh for 10 minutes in oven at 325F (170C) Gas 3. Then complete from Step 6

INGREDIENTS

4oz	Plain flour	125g
8fl oz	Water	220ml
3oz	Unsalted butter	75g
¼ teasp	Salt	1.25ml
3	Eggs	3
	Filling	
1 pint	Whipping cream	560ml
1 tbsp	Caster sugar	15ml
¼ teasp	Vanilla essence	1.25ml
	Chocolate sauce	
6oz	Plain chocolate cake covering	175g
1oz	Butter	25g
2 tbsp	Water	2×15ml

METHOD

1 Preheat the oven to 425F (220C) Gas 7. Sift flour on to sheet of greaseproof paper. Put water, butter, cut into small pieces, in a saucepan and heat gently till the butter has melted. Bring rapidly to the boil, remove pan from heat and add the flour all at once.

2 Beat vigorously with a wooden spoon, then return pan to heat.

3 Continue beating until the paste is a single smooth mass, leaving the sides of the pan cleanly (about 45 seconds). Remove pan from heat immediately, cool paste slightly, then add the eggs, one at a time, beating till each egg is mixed in and forms a soft, glossy mass, before adding the next.

4 Using a teaspoon, drop spoonfuls of paste in balls on to the greased baking trays, easing them off with a second teaspoon. Leave plenty of space between them for expansion during baking. Bake for 20–25 minutes till they are golden and crisp.

5 Remove buns from oven and transfer to a wire rack. Make a slit in the side of each one with a knife point to release steam. Leave them to cool.

6 In a bowl beat till thick the whipping cream, sugar and vanilla essence. Spoon the mixture into the piping bag. Place nozzle in slits already made in buns and pipe flavoured cream into the centre of each.

7 To make chocolate sauce: break chocolate into pieces. Place in bowl over saucepan of hot water and melt with the butter and water. Whisk till smooth.

TO SERVE

Pile up profiteroles on a serving plate. Allow the sauce to cool a little, then pour over buns. Serve immediately.

Return pan to heat, beating constantly. (Some cooks prefer not to return the paste to the heat, others feel that the flour doesn't cook through otherwise – experience is the best guide)

The paste suddenly changes from being a loose mix, to a unified whole. When this happens, remove at once from heat and add the eggs – whole or beaten, one at a time, till glossy

Left: Chocolate profiteroles – melting sauce, tender pastry and creamy centres

Black Forest gâteau

The lusciously indulgent *Schwarzwalder kirschtorte* – the most famous of the specialities of Germany's Black Forest. Layers of crisp biscuit, chocolate sponge and cherry sauce are coated with whipped cream sweetened with Kirsch and sugar. It takes time to make, but well worth it for a really special occasion

DESSERT OR TEA-TIME Cuts into 12

Overall timing $1\frac{3}{4}$ hours plus cooling time

Equipment 9 inch (23cm) loose-bottom round cake tin, 3 large bowls, electric or rotary whisk, 2 saucepans, pastry brush, palette knife, piping bag with star nozzle

Freezing Open freeze until firm. Wrap carefully, seal and label. Freezer life: 4 months. To use: unwrap, place on serving plate, thaw overnight in fridge

Above: Black Forest gâteau – layers of sponge and cream, black cherries, liqueur and chocolate

INGREDIENTS

	Sponge	
6	Eggs	6
6 tbsp	Hand-hot water	6×15ml
5oz	Caster sugar	150g
	Pinch of salt	
2oz	Plain flour	50g
3oz	Cornflour	75g
2oz	Cocoa	50g
	Biscuit base	
5oz	Plain flour	150g
1	Egg yolk	1
3oz	Caster sugar	75g
	Pinch of salt	
	Grated rind of $\frac{1}{2}$ a lemon	
5oz	Butter	150g
	Filling and topping	
2×15oz	Cans of pitted black cherries*	2×425g
2 teasp	Arrowroot	2×5ml
8 tbsp	Kirsch or Cognac	8×15ml
3 tbsp	Redcurrant jelly	3×15ml
1 tbsp	Caster sugar	15ml
1 pint	Double cream	560ml
$\frac{1}{2}$ pint	Single cream	284ml
2 tbsp	Icing sugar	2×15ml
2oz	Plain dessert chocolate	50g

*Use $1\frac{1}{2}$lb (700g) fresh morellos if available. Remove stones, keep 12 whole but quarter rest. Cook all in sugar syrup till just tender.

METHOD

1 To make the sponge, grease and base-line the tin. Preheat the oven to 350F (180C) Gas 4. Separate eggs. Put yolks in large bowl with water and caster sugar. Whisk at high speed for about 3 minutes till blades leave a trail when lifted which "holds" for 15 seconds. Wash whisk. In another bowl, whisk whites with salt till mixture forms soft peaks. Fold whites into yolks with metal spoon and gentle figure of eight action.

2 Sift flour, cornflour and cocoa into a bowl and resift half at a time into egg mixture. Fold in, then pour mixture into tin. Bake in centre of oven for 1 hour.

3 To make the biscuit base, sift flour into bowl and make a well in the centre. Add egg yolk, sugar, salt and lemon rind. Cut butter into small pieces and rub in to a smooth dough. Chill until cake is cooked. Remove cake from oven and turn out of tin. Wash and dry the tin. Place biscuit dough in centre of the tin base and roll out to fit. Replace base in tin and bake for 30 minutes.

4 Drain cherries, saving juice and set aside 12 cherries for decoration. Roughly chop remaining cherries and put in saucepan with 8 tbsp (8×15ml) of the juice. Blend arrowroot with 2 tbsp (2×15ml) of juice and stir into cherries. Bring to the boil, stirring. Remove from heat and stir in 4 tbsp (4×15ml) Kirsch or Cognac. Cool.

5 Remove biscuit base from oven and place on flat serving plate. Cool. Meanwhile, place redcurrant jelly and caster sugar in a small pan and bring to the boil, stirring till smooth. Remove from heat and add 1 tbsp (15ml) Kirsch or Cognac. Brush biscuit base with glaze, reserving 1 tbsp (15ml).

6 Cut cooled sponge into 3 layers and place top layer, cut side up, on glazed biscuit base. Spread with half the cold cherry sauce.

7 Place double and single creams in a large bowl and whisk until stiff. Whisk in icing sugar and remaining Kirsch or Cognac. Divide cream into five. Spread a fifth of cream over the cherries with a palette knife, and cover with second sponge layer. Spread over rest of cherry sauce and one more fifth of cream. Top with final sponge layer. Smooth two-fifths of cream over top and sides of gâteau.

8 Grate chocolate coarsely. Save some for the top of the gâteau and flick rest on to sides with a palette knife. Mark top of gâteau into 12 slices. Put remaining fifth of cream in piping bag fitted with star nozzle and pipe a whirl on each slice.

9 Top each whirl of cream with a whole black cherry and brush carefully with the 1 tbsp (15ml) reserved redcurrant glaze. Sprinkle the remaining chocolate over centre of gâteau. Chill well.

1 To make sponge, beat yolks, water and sugar till thick enough for blades when lifted to leave a trail for 15 seconds

2 Sift dry ingredients into bowl and resift half at a time into yolk/white mix. Fold in carefully with a metal spoon

3 To make biscuit base, add yolk and butter to dry ingredients, and mix with fingertips to give a smooth dough

4 Place chilled biscuit dough in centre of tin base and roll out to fit. Replace base in tin and bake for 30 minutes

5 To make cherry sauce, combine cherries, arrowroot and juice. Remove from heat and stir in Kirsch. Leave to cool

6 To assemble gâteau, place cooked and cooled biscuit base on serving dish. Brush with prepared redcurrant glaze

7 Cut cooled sponge into 3 layers. Place top layer on glazed biscuit base. Spread with half cold cherry sauce

8 Smooth whipped cream over cherry layer, cover with second sponge, repeat layering. Smoothly coat top and sides

9 Flick coarsely grated chocolate on to sides of gâteau with knife. Pipe on cream whirls, add cherries, rest of chocolate

Almond and coffee meringue gâteau

An eye-catching meringue dessert that doubles up as a special tea-time cake. If you have no flan rings, instead mark out circles on non-stick cooking paper on baking trays and spread meringue evenly within circles

DESSERT OR TEA-TIME Serves 6–8

Overall timing $1\frac{1}{2}$ hours plus cooling

Equipment 2 bowls, three 10 inch (25cm) flan rings, 3 baking trays, non-stick cooking paper, spatula or flat-bladed knife

Freezing Pack cooled meringues in rigid container, with sheet of greaseproof paper between each one. Cover, label and freeze. Freezer life: 3 months. To use: remove from container and thaw at room temperature for 1 hour. Complete as recipe

INGREDIENTS

2oz	Chopped almonds	50g
4	Egg whites	4
3oz	Ground almonds	75g
5oz	Icing sugar	150g
	Butter cream	
4	Egg yolks	4
4oz	Icing sugar	125g
2 tbsp	Coffee essence	2×15ml
4oz	Softened butter	125g

To make butter cream, whisk the eggs, icing sugar and coffee essence over hot water

When thickened, leave to cool, then beat in butter. Sandwich meringues with cream

METHOD

1 Preheat the oven to 250F (130C) Gas $\frac{1}{2}$. Place chopped almonds under the grill and toast for 7–10 minutes. Set aside.

2 In a bowl, whisk egg whites till they hold stiff peaks. Using a metal spoon, lightly fold in the ground almonds and icing sugar, sifted.

3 Well grease and flour flan rings and place each on a baking tray, covered with non-stick cooking paper. Using a spatula or flat-bladed knife, spread one third of meringue mixture into each ring. Place baking trays in oven and cook for about 1 hour until meringues are crisp and dry. Change round baking positions twice so all meringues cook at same temperature. Cool before lifting off flan rings.

4 To make butter cream: put yolks and icing sugar in a bowl, place over a pan of hot water and whisk until light and fluffy.

5 Stir in coffee essence and continue whisking until the mixture is thick and foamy, then remove from heat. Leave to cool completely, then beat in softened butter a little at a time.

6 Place 1 meringue round on serving plate, then sandwich all 3 meringues together with two-thirds of the butter cream. Spread remaining cream on top and sprinkle with reserved almonds.

Above: Almond and coffee meringue gâteau – topped with butter cream and chopped almonds

Coffee charlotte

Traditionally, this type of dessert was made in a special charlotte tin. But for easier removal, a springform cake tin that unclips is better

COLD DESSERT Serves 8

Overall timing 50 minutes plus chilling

Equipment 10 inch (25cm) springform tin, 2 saucepans (1 heavy-based), dish, piping bag and star nozzle

Freezing Leave charlotte in tin. Cover with cling film or foil, then place in polythene bag, seal, label and freeze. Freezer life: 2 months. To use: remove wrappings and thaw at room temperature for about 5 hours. Serve chilled

INGREDIENTS

30	Sponge fingers	30
2 tbsp	Brandy	2×15ml
$\frac{1}{4}$ pint	Water	150ml
5oz	Caster sugar	150g
3 tbsp	Water	3×15ml
$\frac{1}{4}$ pint	Freshly-made strong black coffee	150ml
1 tbsp	Powdered gelatine	15ml
4	Egg yolks	4
2 tbsp	Vanilla sugar	2×15ml
$\frac{1}{2}$ pint	Carton of double cream	284ml
15	Sugar coffee beans	15

METHOD

1 Lightly grease cake tin. Trim sponge fingers so the tops are level with the edge of the tin. Mix the brandy and $\frac{1}{4}$ pint (150ml) water in a shallow dish. Dip sponge fingers quickly in and out of brandy mixture to moisten them but not so they collapse.

2 Line inside of mould with the sponge fingers in upright position, placing cut ends on base and sugared sides against side of tin. Press lightly into place.

3 Put caster sugar and 3 tbsp (3×15ml) water in heavy-based saucepan. Heat gently, stirring all the time, until sugar is dissolved, then heat until it becomes golden brown. Remove pan from heat and leave for 45 seconds, then add the hot coffee slowly and very carefully as caramel mixture can splatter. Simmer for 2 minutes till dissolved. Cool.

4 Put gelatine in a bowl with 2 tbsp (2×15ml) cold water and leave for at least 5 minutes to soften, then place bowl in a pan of hot water and stir until gelatine is dissolved.

Above: Coffee charlotte – sponge fingers surround a thickened, coffee-flavoured cream

5 Put egg yolks and vanilla sugar in a bowl and whisk together till light and foamy. Place over a pan of hot water. Stir coffee caramel into egg mixture and whisk continuously until it starts to thicken.

6 Stir gelatine liquid into coffee mixture, then leave to cool until just on the point of setting and forming small lumps but still liquid enough to pour.

7 In a bowl, whisk two-thirds of the cream until it holds soft peaks. Using a metal spoon, fold lightly into coffee mixture until well blended. Pour into centre of sponge finger-lined tin and place in fridge to set.

TO SERVE

When set, unclip tin and carefully transfer charlotte to a serving plate. In a bowl, whip remaining cream until it holds stiff peaks. Spoon into a piping bag, fitted with a star nozzle, and pipe 15 rosettes of cream round edge of charlotte. Place a coffee bean on top of each one. Pipe smaller rosettes of cream all the way round the base of the charlotte.

Blackcurrant charlotte

There's no cooking involved in making this dessert, which is a combination of fresh fruit and jam, and sponge fingers which are moistened with liqueur. It's a dish to serve on a special occasion because it can be made well in advance

DESSERT Serves 8

Overall timing 30 minutes plus overnight chilling

Equipment 2 bowls, 6 inch (15cm) loose-bottom cake tin or charlotte mould

Freezing Freeze charlotte while still in mould. Turn out when frozen and store, wrapped in foil. Freezer life: 2 months. To use: leave overnight in fridge. Decorate before serving

INGREDIENTS

4oz	Blackcurrants	125g
2oz	Caster sugar	50g
3 tbsp	Kirsch or Cointreau	3×15ml
$\frac{1}{4}$ pint	Water	150ml
40	Sponge fingers	40
$\frac{1}{2}$ pint	Carton of double cream	284ml
2oz	Icing sugar	50g
8oz	Jar of blackcurrant jam	227g

METHOD

1 Top and tail blackcurrants, then wash under running water in a sieve. Place in a bowl and sprinkle over caster sugar.

2 Mix Kirsch or Cointreau and water in a bowl. Quickly dip the sponge fingers one at a time into the liquid without soaking them. Use about 8 fingers to line the base of the cake tin or charlotte mould, and about 20 round the sides. Trim if sponges come above the top edge of the tin.

3 Whip the cream with the icing sugar until stiff, then fill the mould with alternate layers of blackcurrant jam, sponge fingers, sugared blackcurrants and whipped cream. Reserve some of the whipped cream and blackcurrants for decoration.

4 Cover the charlotte with a plate, place a weight on top and chill for 12 hours or overnight.

5 When ready to serve, turn the charlotte out on to a serving plate and decorate with remaining whipped cream and blackcurrants.

Raspberry cream mould

Roughly crushed meringue shells give this rich ice cream its unusually crunchy texture. The mould is generously decorated with fresh fruit and accompanied by a thick sauce made from raspberries, Cointreau and sugar

DESSERT Serves 6

Overall timing 45 minutes plus freezing and chilling

Equipment 2 bowls, 6 inch (15cm) charlotte mould or loose-bottom cake tin, saucepan

Freezing Freeze in mould or tin, cover and label. To freeze sauce, cool, pour into a rigid container, leaving $\frac{1}{2}$ inch (12.5mm) headspace, cover, label and freeze. Freezer life: 2 months. To use: turn out on to serving dish and leave in fridge for 30 minutes to soften. Thaw sauce at room temperature for 2–3 hours

Below: Raspberry cream mould – exciting ice cream dish with a liqueur-laced sauce

INGREDIENTS

$\frac{3}{4}$ pint	Double cream	400ml
4oz	Icing sugar	125g
1 teasp	Vanilla essence	5ml
	Red food colouring	
4oz	Meringue shells	125g
1lb	Raspberries	450g
2 tbsp	Caster sugar	2×15ml
3 tbsp	Cointreau	3×15ml

METHOD

1 Put the cream, sifted icing sugar and vanilla essence in a bowl with a few drops of red food colouring and whisk till soft peaks form. Roughly crush the meringue shells and fold into the cream mixture.

2 Pour into the mould or tin, cover with a plate and put a weight on top. Freeze for about 4 hours till firmly set.

3 Meanwhile, hull and pick over the raspberries. Reserve half the fruit and put the rest into a bowl with the caster sugar and liqueur and leave to macerate for 15 minutes.

4 Put into a saucepan and stir over a low heat till the sugar dissolves. Pour into a bowl, allow to cool, then chill for 2 hours.

5 Dip the mould or tin into hot water for 10 seconds and turn out on to a serving dish. Score the sides with a fork and decorate with the reserved raspberries. Serve the raspberry and liqueur sauce separately.

Above: Bavarois à la vanille – one of the most popular European desserts

Bavarois à la vanille

A lightly textured moulded cream dessert popular in many parts of Europe. It's not known whether it originated in Bavaria or was in fact created by a chef in that country's honour

COLD DESSERT Serves 4–6

Overall timing 40 minutes plus cooling and setting

Equipment 3 bowls, 2 saucepans, cup, ring mould

Freezing Open freeze in mould till firm. Remove from mould, wrap well, seal and label. Freezer life: 2 months. To use: remove wrappings, place on serving plate and thaw in fridge. Decorate

INGREDIENTS

4	Eggs	4
3oz	Caster sugar	75g
½ pint	Milk	300ml
1 teasp	Vanilla essence	5ml
1 teasp	Powdered gelatine	5ml
3 tbsp	Water	3×15ml
½ pint	Carton of double cream	284ml
2oz	Glacé cherries	50g

METHOD

1 Separate the eggs. Put the yolks and 2oz (50g) of the caster sugar in a bowl placed over a pan of hot water. Whisk till pale and frothy.

2 Warm the milk and vanilla essence in a pan, then gradually stir into yolk mixture. Strain back into pan and cook very gently, stirring frequently, for 15–20 minutes or until mixture thickens. Do not boil or the mixture will curdle. Remove from heat and allow to cool. Stir from time to time to prevent a skin forming.

3 In a cup, soak the gelatine in the water for about 5 minutes till spongy, then put cup in a pan of boiling water to dissolve gelatine. Cool slightly, then trickle into cooled custard, stirring. Chill bowl of iced water to which ice cubes have been added, stirring mixture from time to time, until thick but not set.

4 In a bowl, beat the cream till soft peaks form. Stir in remaining 1oz (25g) sugar, then fold into chilled custard mixture.

5 Whisk egg whites till stiff, then carefully fold into cream and custard mixture. Turn into wetted mould and put in fridge to set.

TO SERVE

Immerse mould up to the rim in hot water, then invert on to serving plate. Decorate around the base with glacé cherries and serve at once. Eat the same day.

Strawberry flummery

This is like a *bavarois*, but of British or Irish origin. It has a fresh summery taste because of the strawberries, though you could achieve the same thing in the depths of winter with frozen fruit

COLD DESSERT Serves 6

Overall timing 35 minutes plus chilling

Equipment 3 bowls, saucepan, 1½ pint (850ml) mould or individual dishes

Freezing Put into rigid container, seal, label and freeze. Freezer life: 2 months. To use: thaw in fridge for 3 hours, then decorate with fresh strawberries and serve

INGREDIENTS

2 teasp	Powdered gelatine	2×5ml
½ pint	Milk	300ml
4oz	Caster sugar	125g
1lb	Fresh or frozen strawberries	450g
½ pint	Carton of double or whipping cream	284ml
2 tbsp	Sherry *or*	2×15ml
1 tbsp	Brandy	15ml

METHOD

1 Put the gelatine in a bowl with ¼ pint (150ml) of the milk and leave till spongy.

2 Bring remaining milk to the boil in a pan. Remove from heat and stir in sugar. Stir milk gradually into gelatine mixture and leave to cool.

3 Hull the strawberries and wipe over if using fresh. Make sure frozen ones are thawed. Reserve a few whole strawberries for the decoration. Purée the rest in a blender or press through a sieve into a bowl.

4 Beat cream in a bowl till it holds stiff peaks, then lightly stir in sherry or brandy. Lightly fold cream mixture into strawberry purée.

5 As soon as the gelatine mixture starts to set, lightly whisk it into the strawberry and cream mixture. Pour into a wetted mould or individual dishes if preferred and place in fridge.

6 When firm, turn out, decorate with reserved strawberries and serve with langue de chat biscuits.

Strawberry syllabub

A very quick, easy-to-make sherry or Cointreau flavoured strawberry cream. If you like, roughly crush macaroons or ratafia biscuits, place in the bottom of each glass and pour syllabub over, or fold straight into syllabub

DESSERT Serves 6

Overall timing 20 minutes plus maceration and chilling

Equipment Sieve, 2 bowls, 6 individual serving glasses

Freezing Turn into rigid container, cover, label and freeze. Freezer life: 1 month. To use: thaw overnight in fridge, or for 4 hours at room temperature, then spoon into individual glasses and chill for 30 minutes in fridge before serving

INGREDIENTS

12oz	Strawberries	350g
1	Lemon	1
4 tbsp	Sherry or Cointreau	4×15ml
¾ pint	Double cream	400ml
4oz	Caster sugar	125g

METHOD

1 Wipe and hull strawberries and rub through a sieve into a bowl. Finely grate the rind of the lemon then squeeze out the juice. Add to strawberries with the sherry or Cointreau and leave to macerate for 15 minutes.

2 Put the cream into a bowl with half the fruit mixture and whisk till soft peaks form. Add the sugar and remaining fruit mixture and whisk till thick.

3 Spoon into glasses and chill for 1 hour before serving with sponge fingers.

American shortcakes

One of the American classics, this dessert is popular in every State and was traditionally made with the first strawberries of the season. The rich and buttery shortcake is made with double cream and more cream is used as a topping. Reserve the best looking strawberries for decoration and try to match them for size. Serve for dessert or at tea-time – one per person is plenty!

DESSERT OR TEA-TIME Serves 6

Overall timing 1¼ hours

Equipment 2 bowls, saucepan, pastry cutters, baking tray, piping bag with star nozzle

Freezing Wrap cooled and separated cakes in foil. Seal, label and freeze. Freezer life: 2 months. To use: remove wrappings and thaw for 2 hours, then complete Steps 6 and 7

INGREDIENTS

1lb	Plain flour	450g
2 teasp	Baking powder	2×5ml
½ teasp	Salt	2.5ml
3 tbsp	Caster sugar	3×15ml
5oz	Butter	150g
½ pint	Carton of double cream	284ml
	Topping	
1½lb	Strawberries	700g
2 tbsp	Caster sugar	2×15ml
½ pint	Carton of double cream	284ml

METHOD

1 Preheat the oven to 400F (200C) Gas 6.

2 Sift the flour and baking powder into a bowl and add the salt and sugar. Rub in 3oz (75g) of the butter till the mixture resembles fine breadcrumbs.

3 Mix in the cream with a spoon to make a firm dough. Knead lightly till smooth, then chill for 15 minutes. Meanwhile, melt the remaining butter in a pan.

4 Roll the dough out on a lightly floured surface to ½ inch (12.5mm) thickness, then cut out six 4 inch (10cm) rounds. Gather up the trimmings, roll out lightly to same thickness and cut six 3 inch (7.5cm) rounds.

5 Arrange the large rounds on a lightly floured baking tray. Brush with melted butter and top with the smaller rounds. Bake for 15–20 minutes till firm and golden. Remove from oven and cool.

6 Meanwhile, wipe and hull strawberries. Reserve best for decoration and cut the rest in half.

7 Separate the small cakes from the large and arrange halved strawberries on the large ones. Sprinkle with caster sugar, top with small cakes and decorate with whole strawberries. Just before serving, whip the cream and pipe on top.

Below: American shortcakes – make in advance and top with the cream just before serving

Saint-Emilion au chocolat

A splendid gâteau – named after a town in France famous for macaroons

DESSERT Serves 8

Overall timing 1 hour plus chilling

Equipment 4 bowls, saucepan, 6 inch (15cm) charlotte mould, plate, weight

Freezing Remove from mould, open freeze, pack in rigid container, cover and label. Freezer life: 2 months. To use: thaw in fridge overnight, then cover with topping

INGREDIENTS

3½oz	Plain dessert chocolate	100g
1	Egg yolk	1
¼ pint	Warm milk	150ml
4oz	Unsalted butter	125g
4oz	Caster sugar	125g
5 tbsp	Cognac	5×15ml
1lb	Macaroons	450g
	Topping	
2oz	Plain dessert chocolate	50g
½oz	Butter	15g

METHOD

1. Break the chocolate into small pieces and put into a bowl with 1 tbsp (15ml) of cold water. Place over a pan of simmering water to melt.
2. Mix egg yolk and milk in a bowl and stir in the melted chocolate. Cool.
3. Meanwhile, put butter and sugar in a bowl and cream till light and fluffy.
4. Add the chocolate mixture to the creamed mixture a little at a time and beat till smooth. Grease mould.
5. Place Cognac and 5 tbsp (5×15ml) of water in a bowl. Quickly dip macaroons in, a few at a time, and use to line the base and sides of the mould with the flat sides facing out. Pour in a thick layer of the chocolate cream, cover with macaroons, and continue till all ingredients have been used, ending with a layer of macaroons.
6. Cover with a plate, add a weight and chill for 12 hours. Immerse mould up to rim in hot water then turn out on to serving plate.
7. To make topping, break up the chocolate and put into a small saucepan with 1 tbsp (15ml) of cold water. Melt over a very low heat, then beat in the butter and pour over the top of the cake so that it flows down the sides. Serve.

Above: Avocado and banana fool – two fruits blended to make a delicious, colourful treat

Avocado and banana fool

A perfect dessert for a summer day – sweet and smooth with an intriguing flavour that's lifted with a touch of white rum. Serve really well chilled

DESSERT Serves 6

Overall timing 20 minutes plus chilling

Equipment Blender, 2 bowls

Freezing Prepare to end of Step 2. Put into a rigid container, cover, label and freeze. Freezer life: 3 months. To use: thaw in fridge for 2–3 hours, then divide between individual dishes

INGREDIENTS

2	Ripe avocados	2
3	Large bananas	3
3 tbsp	Lemon juice	3×15ml
2 tbsp	White rum	2×15ml
6 tbsp	Light soft brown sugar	6×15ml
¼ pint	Carton of double cream	150ml
	Green food colouring (optional)	

METHOD

1. Cut the avocados in half and discard the stones. Scoop out the flesh and put into a blender. Peel the bananas, add to the blender with the lemon juice, rum and sugar and blend till smooth. Transfer to a large bowl.
2. Whip the cream till soft peaks form, then fold into the purée with a metal spoon, adding a few drops of green colouring if liked.
3. Divide between individual dishes and chill for at least 2 hours before serving.

VARIATIONS

For a tropical dessert, replace the avocados with the pulp of 1 large mango and blend with the bananas as above. Or, use 13oz (375g) canned crushed pineapple, draining the juice well before blending. For a lighter dessert, whisk 2 egg whites till soft peaks form and fold into the blended fruit purée with a metal spoon after the whipped cream has been added.

Liqueur fruit salad

The addition of liqueur makes this a special dish for a dinner party

DESSERT Serves 4

Overall timing 15 minutes plus chilling

Equipment Bowl

Freezing Cover fruit with syrup in a rigid container. Cover, label and freeze. Freezer life: 3 months. To use: thaw overnight in fridge

INGREDIENTS

2lb	Mixed fresh fruit	900g
1	Lemon	1
1	Orange	1
4 tbsp	Caster sugar	4×15ml
3 tbsp	Curaçao or Grand Marnier	3×15ml

METHOD

1 Wash and prepare fruit, cutting into small chunks as necessary, and put into a bowl.

2 Pare away a small strip of lemon rind and add to bowl. Squeeze juice from lemon and orange and add to fruit with the sugar and liqueur. Mix carefully without damaging the fruit.

3 Cover and chill for 2–3 hours. Remove lemon rind and serve with whipped cream and crisp biscuits.

Rødgrød med fløde

Delicious berry fruits of summer are combined in this delectable dessert from Denmark. As the fruits are gently cooked before being thickened, the dish could be made in winter with frozen fruit

DESSERT Serves 6

Overall timing 20 minutes plus cooling and chilling

Equipment Saucepan, measuring jug, serving dish

Freezing Do not decorate. Cool, pour into rigid container, cover, label and freeze. Freezer life: 3 months. To use: thaw overnight in fridge, then decorate and serve

Below: Rødgrød med fløde – a red fruit jelly popular in Denmark. The fruits are cooked till soft but still whole, then the juice is strained off and thickened. The dessert should be served chilled

INGREDIENTS

1½lb	Mixed soft fruit (raspberries, strawberries, blackcurrants, redcurrants, blackberries, loganberries)	700g
4oz	Caster sugar	125g
	Arrowroot	
1oz	Toasted flaked almonds (optional)	25g

METHOD

1 Wash and prepare fruit. Put into a saucepan and add enough water to just cover. Bring gently to the boil and simmer for about 5 minutes or until soft. Strain fruit and measure amount of juice. Place fruit in serving dish.

2 Return juice to pan, add sugar and heat gently till sugar dissolves.

3 Allowing 2 teasp (2×5ml) per pint (560ml) of fruit juice, measure out arrowroot and mix with a little cold water. Stir into pan and heat gently for 2 minutes, stirring constantly until slightly thickened and glossy. Do not boil.

4 Pour over fruit in serving dish, and leave to cool. Chill for 1 hour, then decorate with flaked almonds and serve with unsweetened whipped cream.

Choose 12 large apricots, wash and dry them and carefully remove the stones

Chop almonds, macaroons and candied peel, mix in with custard and add cinnamon

Baked apricots

Above: Baked apricots – a creamy, nutty filling and a redcurrant and Kirsch sauce

A simple but delicious way of serving apricots when they are in season. As they freeze well, you can store them away for a mid-winter treat. You'll get an equally appetizing result if you use peaches, pears or nectarines instead of the apricots

DESSERT Serves 6–8

Overall timing 1 hour

Equipment 2 small saucepans, baking tray or shallow ovenproof dish

Freezing Prepare to end of Method, Step 5. Cool, open freeze, then pack in a rigid container, seal and label. Freezer life: 3 months. To use: remove from container and place on baking tray. Heat in oven at 400F (200C) Gas 6 for 15 minutes, then carry out Step 6

INGREDIENTS

12	Large apricots	12
½ pint	Milk	300ml
2 tbsp	Custard powder	2×15ml
1 tbsp	Caster sugar	15ml
4oz	Blanched almonds	125g
5oz	Macaroons	150g
1½oz	Candied orange peel	40g
	Pinch of cinnamon	
6 tbsp	Redcurrant jelly	6×15ml
4 tbsp	Kirsch (optional)	4×15ml
4 tbsp	Water	4×15ml

METHOD

1 Preheat oven to 400F (200C) Gas 6. Wash, dry and halve apricots. Remove stones. (See step-by-step pictures.)

2 Prepare the custard according to packet instructions, using the milk, custard powder and sugar. Cool quickly by standing the pan in cold water. Stir the custard frequently to prevent a skin forming.

3 Chop almonds, macaroons and candied peel finely, mix in with the custard and add cinnamon.

4 Grease a baking tray or shallow oven-proof dish. Arrange the prepared apricot halves on it.

After apricots have cooked for 30 minutes, spoon redcurrant syrup over them

5 Fill apricot halves with custard mixture. Bake in oven for 30 minutes.

6 Meanwhile, mix together the red-currant jelly, Kirsch, if you are using it, and water in a small pan over a low heat. Spoon syrup carefully over the apricots and return tray to oven for a further 10 minutes.

TO SERVE

Serve hot with whipped cream, or leave to cool then chill and serve with ice cream or with a bowl of whipped cream.

Vanilla ice cream

A rich, creamy yellow ice made from a custard base. The added cream increases the fat content and gives the mixture a wonderfully smooth texture. It is beaten twice at the half-frozen stage so that the ice crystals are broken down

DESSERT Makes 1 pint (560ml)

Overall timing 40 minutes plus freezing

Equipment 3 bowls, 2 saucepans, sieve and muslin, freezer tray or mould

Freezing Freeze in tray or mould, or make scoops and arrange on plastic tray, then cover, label and refreeze. Freezer life: 2 months. To use: soften before serving by placing tray or mould in fridge for 30 minutes, scoops on tray 15 minutes

INGREDIENTS

2	Egg yolks	2
2oz	Caster sugar	50g
½ pint	Milk	300ml
1	Vanilla pod *or*	1
1 teasp	Vanilla essence	5ml
¼ pint	Carton of double cream	150ml

METHOD

1 Put the egg yolks and sugar in a large bowl and beat until creamy.
2 Put milk and vanilla pod or essence into a pan and bring to just under boiling point. Remove from heat and take out vanilla pod if used.
3 Pour milk in a thin stream on to creamed mixture, stirring continuously. Place bowl over a pan of simmering water and cook for about 10 minutes without boiling, stirring continuously until mixture coats the back of the spoon.
4 Remove from heat and strain through a muslin-lined sieve into a bowl. Beat until cool to prevent skin forming.
5 Whisk the cream until it just holds its shape, then fold into cold custard. Pour into freezer tray or mould and freeze for about 1½ hours or until mushy.
6 Turn ice cream into a bowl and beat well. Pour back into container and return to freezer. Freeze till mushy.
7 Repeat beating process, then return to freezer and freeze till firm.

Above: Vanilla ice cream served in scoops

1 *Put the egg yolks and sugar into a bowl and beat with a wooden spoon until creamy*

2 *Put milk and vanilla pod into a saucepan and bring to just under boiling point*

3 *Pour hot milk on to creamed mix in a thin stream, stirring continuously, then cook*

4 *Strain custard, beat until cool, fold in whipped cream. Pour into tray or mould*

To give citrus water ices extra flavour, add finely pared rind (be careful not to include bitter pith) to the sugar syrup

When the fruit juice has been added, strain mixture into freezer tray to make a water ice, or granita

To make a sherbet, *remove mixture from freezer when mushy, turn into bowl and beat well. Whisk 1 egg white till soft peaks form, then fold into beaten mix. Freeze till firm, then serve*

To make a sorbet, *whisk 2 egg whites and proceed as for sherbet. To give a very soft texture, make the sorbet with gelatine which prevents the formation of ice crystals. Sprinkle 2 teasp (2×5ml) of powdered gelatine over 2 tbsp (2×15ml) water, wine or liqueur in a cup and leave to sponge. After syrup has simmered for 10 minutes, add the soaked gelatine and stir till dissolved. Freeze till mushy, then beat. Whisk 2 egg whites till stiff, then whisk into beaten mixture. Cover, freeze till firm*

To freeze sorbets in shells, *make the syrup adding gelatine as above. Fold whisked whites into beaten mixture, then pile into shells, pack into rigid container, cover and freeze*

Basic water ice

The most refreshing of desserts, water ices are simple to make and are useful freezer standbys. Vary the flavour with different types of fruit juice, or use a purée of soft fruit. To make sherbets and sorbets, see the captions, right

DESSERT Serves 6

Overall timing 20 minutes plus freezing

Equipment Saucepan, sieve, 2 pint (1.1 litre) freezer tray, 2 bowls

Freezing Freeze in tray. Freezer life: 6 months. To use: serve from frozen

INGREDIENTS

8oz	Caster sugar	225g
1 pint	Water	560ml
¼ pint	Fruit juice	150ml

Above: Lemon sherbet – a basic water ice which has been made fluffy with the addition of a softly whisked egg white. To make lemon granita, leave out the egg white, and to make a sorbet, see right

METHOD

1. Put the sugar and water in a pan and heat slowly, stirring until sugar dissolves. Bring to the boil and simmer for 10 minutes without stirring – do not let it colour. Remove from heat and leave to cool.
2. Add fruit juice to syrup, strain into freezer tray and freeze until mushy.
3. Remove mixture from freezer, turn into a bowl and beat well to break down crystals. Return to freezer tray and freeze till firm.

Above: French parfait – refreshingly cool

French parfait

A simply made ice that doesn't have to be stirred during freezing

DESSERT Makes 1 pint (560ml)

Overall timing 30 minutes plus chilling and freezing

Equipment Saucepan, 2 bowls, electric whisk, freezer tray

Freezing Freeze in tray and cover. Freezer life: 2 months. To use: soften in fridge for 30 minutes before serving

INGREDIENTS

$\frac{1}{4}$ pint	Water	150ml
2oz	Caster sugar	50g
1	Vanilla pod	1
4	Egg yolks	4
$\frac{1}{2}$ pint	Carton of double cream	284ml

METHOD

1 Put the water and sugar into a pan and stir over a low heat until sugar dissolves. Add the vanilla pod and boil gently for 5 minutes. Remove from heat, take out vanilla pod and cool slightly.

2 Place egg yolks in a bowl and beat with an electric whisk until pale and thick. While still beating, trickle in the syrup in a thin stream. Continue whisking until mixture is cool. Chill in fridge for 30 minutes.

3 Whisk cream to soft peaks and fold into the yolk mixture. Pour into freezer tray and freeze till firm. Serve in individual glasses with crisp biscuits.

VARIATION

To make a liqueur-flavoured parfait, omit the vanilla pod and add 4 tbsp (4×15ml) liqueur when you fold the cream into the chilled mixture.

Fruit mousse

Whisked egg whites lighten this rich cream and puréed fruit mixture

DESSERT Makes $1\frac{1}{2}$ pints (850ml)

Overall timing 15 minutes plus chilling and freezing

Equipment Blender, sieve, 3 bowls, freezer tray or rigid container

Freezing Freeze in tray and cover. Freezer life: 2 months. To use: soften in fridge for 30 minutes before serving

INGREDIENTS

12oz	Fresh or stewed fruit (strawberries, raspberries, peaches, plums, blackcurrants)	350g
1–2oz	Caster sugar	25–50g
1–2 tbsp	Lemon juice	1 or 2 ×15ml
$\frac{1}{2}$ pint	Carton of double cream	284ml
3	Egg whites	3

METHOD

1 Purée the fruit in a blender and if necessary press through a sieve to remove seeds. Add sugar and lemon juice and chill for 30 minutes.

2 Whisk cream until soft peaks form. Fold into fruit purée. Whisk egg whites till stiff but not dry and gently fold into the mixture with a metal spoon.

3 Pour mixture into freezer tray or container and freeze till firm.

VARIATION

To make chocolate mousse, melt 4oz (125g) plain dessert chocolate with 2 tbsp (2×15ml) caster sugar and 4 tbsp (4×15 ml) water in a bowl placed over a pan of simmering water. Allow to cool, then fold into mixture before freezing.

Zuccotto

The Italians are not over fond of hot, heavy puddings. Instead, they prefer fruit, ice cream or sponge cakes. In this recipe, all three are combined to make a glorious sponge-lined bombe. There is some dispute over the origin of the term zuccotto – some say it refers to the amount of sugar (zucchero) in the dessert; while others believe that the literal translation of the word – skullcap – refers to the finished shape. Whatever the case, this rich, liqueur-flavoured dessert is well worth trying

Line base and sides of mould with sponge cake pieces, then sprinkle with liqueur

Spoon softened ice creams into the mould and smooth surface. Cover with sponge

Right: Zuccotto – liqueur-flavoured sponge mould filled with ice cream. If you like, use Fruit mousse (recipe left) for the second layer rather than tutti-frutti ice cream

DESSERT Serves 6–8

Overall timing $1\frac{3}{4}$ hours

Equipment 2 pint (1.1 litre) mould or pudding basin

Freezing Freeze in basin and cover. Freezer life: 2 months. To use: soften in fridge for 30 minutes before serving

INGREDIENTS

1 pint	Chocolate and nut ice cream	560ml
1 pint	Tutti-frutti ice cream	560ml
8oz	Sponge cake	225g
2 tbsp	Liqueur	2×15ml

METHOD

1 Remove both ice creams from freezer and leave in fridge to soften for about 20 minutes. The ice cream should be soft enough to work with, but not runny.

2 Cut cake into thin slices. Use three quarters of the cake to line the base and sides of the mould. Sprinkle sponge with liqueur (any kind would do, but Curaçao, Cognac or Kirsch would complement the ice cream flavours).

3 Working quickly, spoon softened chocolate and nut ice cream into sponge-lined mould and smooth surface. Top with tutti-frutti ice cream, smooth surface and cover with remaining sponge pieces. Cover and freeze till firm.

TO SERVE

Transfer mould to fridge 30 minutes before serving. Run a knife around the edge to loosen and turn out on to a chilled serving dish. Decorate with whipped cream and glacé cherries if liked.

Cassata gelata

An Italian speciality, a cassata consists of layers of different flavoured ice creams frozen in a mould. It's important to get the consistency of the ice creams just right so you can spread them against the sides of the mould with a spoon

DESSERT Serves 8

Overall timing $1\frac{3}{4}$ hours

Equipment $2\frac{1}{2}$ pint (1.5 litre) bombe mould or pudding basin

Freezing Freeze in mould or basin. Freezer life: 2 months. To use: soften in fridge for 20 minutes before serving

INGREDIENTS

1 pint	Vanilla ice cream	560ml
1 pint	Chocolate ice cream	560ml
$\frac{1}{2}$ pint	Tutti-frutti ice cream	300ml

Above: Cassata gelata – serve in slices

METHOD

1 Chill mould. Remove vanilla ice cream from freezer and soften in fridge for 15–20 minutes. Spoon two-thirds of the vanilla ice cream into the mould, pressing it firmly to cover shape of mould. Place remaining vanilla ice cream and mould in freezer and leave till firm. Meanwhile, remove chocolate ice cream from freezer and leave to soften in fridge.

2 Take mould out of freezer and press in layer of chocolate ice cream following shape of mould and leaving space in middle. Return mould to freezer for 20 minutes. Meanwhile, remove remaining vanilla ice cream from freezer and leave to soften in fridge.

3 Spread over chocolate layer, leaving space in middle, and return to freezer for 20 minutes. Meanwhile, remove tutti-frutti ice cream from freezer and soften in fridge.

4 Remove mould from freezer and fill centre with tutti-frutti ice cream. Smooth surface. Cover with lid or foil and freeze till firm.

TO SERVE

Place mould in fridge for 30 minutes. Dip mould in hot water for a few seconds to loosen ice cream. Turn out on to plate.

CAKES AND BAKING

Home-made cakes, breads and crisp, buttery pastries are family favourites. Bake on a day when you have time to spare and keep them in readiness in the freezer. Icings can be frozen for a short time but are often better added after thawing

Cream sponge

Whisking the egg whites separately from the yolks makes this sponge extra fluffy. If you prefer to use self-raising flour, omit the baking powder

TEA-TIME Cuts into 10 slices

Overall timing 30 minutes plus cooling

Equipment Two 8 inch (20cm) sandwich tins, 2 mixing bowls, small saucepan, cake wire

Freezing Cook sponges but do not decorate. Wrap, label and freeze. Freezer life: 4 months. To use: thaw for 1 hour before decorating

INGREDIENTS

2oz	Butter	50g
2 tbsp	Milk	2×15ml
4	Large eggs	4
4oz	Caster sugar	125g
2 tbsp	Warm water	2×15ml
4oz	Plain flour	125g
1 teasp	Baking powder	5ml
4 tbsp	Apricot jam	4×15ml
¼ pint	Carton of double cream	150ml
2 tbsp	Strawberry jam	2×15ml
2oz	Split or flaked almonds	50g

METHOD

1 Grease and flour sandwich tins. Preheat oven to 375F (190C) Gas 5.

2 Melt butter in saucepan, add milk. Set aside. Separate eggs. Place yolks in bowl over hot water and whisk till fluffy. Add sugar and warm water and beat well till beaters leave trail for 3 seconds. Wash and dry beaters. Whip whites till stiff peaks form. Fold carefully into yolk mixture.

3 Sift flour and baking powder. Fold in a little at a time, then mix in butter/milk mixture.

4 Divide mixture between sandwich tins and cook on middle shelf of oven for 20 minutes. Turn on to cake wire.

5 When cold, spread top of one sponge with apricot jam. Place second sponge on top. Whip cream and fold in strawberry jam. Spread cream over top of sponge, then sprinkle almonds over.

Below: Cream sponge – a simple whisked sponge to decorate richly with cream and jam as a tea-time treat

Swiss roll

Above: *Swiss roll – a tea-time favourite*

Whisking gives light and airy sponges for swiss rolls or flans. Eat them quickly – they don't keep – or use up in trifles

TEA-TIME Makes 2

Overall timing 30 minutes plus cooling time

Equipment Mixing bowl, 1 large or 2 small swiss roll tins

Freezing Cook but do not fill. Remove from tins, roll up with greaseproof paper, wrap in foil when cold. Overwrap, label and freeze. Freezer life: 6 months. To use: thaw at room temperature for 2–4 hours. Unroll gently, remove greaseproof and fill. Reroll

INGREDIENTS

3	Large eggs	3
3oz	Plain flour	75g
4 tbsp	Jam	4×15ml
3oz	Caster sugar	75g
$\frac{1}{4}$ teasp	Vanilla essence	1.25ml
	Pinch of salt	
1 tbsp	Warm water	15ml

METHOD

1 Preheat the oven to 400F (200C) Gas 6. Grease tin or tins and line with greaseproof. Separate the eggs. Sift flour into bowl, leave in warm place. Place jam in warm place.

2 Whisk yolks, sugar and vanilla till mixture forms trails when beaters are lifted. Wash the beaters.

3 In another bowl, whisk the whites with salt till mixture forms soft peaks that curl downwards.

4 Fold flour into yolk and sugar mixture with a metal spoon, then fold in whites and warm water.

5 Place mixture in tin or tins, spreading to sides with spoon or spatula. Bake in centre of oven till sides of sponge shrink a little, about 12–15 minutes.

6 Remove tins from oven. Sprinkle large sheet of greaseproof paper with caster sugar and invert tin or tins on to it. Remove tin or tins, then carefully peel away paper from sponge. Trim edges of sponge with a sharp knife.

7 Working quickly, spread jam over sponge. With the help of the greaseproof, roll sponge away from you, so that the jam is inside the roll and the outside is covered in caster sugar. Place seam-side down on wire rack to cool.

Greaseproof is cut slightly larger than tin; corners are mitred so paper comes up sides

Yolks and caster sugar are whisked till pale and thick, and whisk leaves trails

Egg whites, whisked only until soft peaks form, are then folded into yolk and sugar mixture

Invert warm sponge on to sugared greaseproof, trim edges with a sharp knife

Spread jam quickly, roll sponge. Or roll warm sponge with paper inside. When cold unroll, fill with cream, reroll

Chocolate torte

The German *torte* was originally a filled tart or flan. But as these became more extravagant, *torte* was then used to describe the filling rather than the base – as in this richly layered cake made with both plain and milk cooking chocolate

TEA-TIME OR DESSERT Cuts into 12 slices

Overall timing 2 hours

Equipment 5 bowls, 2×9 inch (2×23cm) cake tins, saucepan

Freezing Freeze cooled cake only. Open freeze until firm, wrap, label and freeze. Freezer life: 4 months. To use: thaw at room temperature for about 2 hours

INGREDIENTS

	Cake	
8	Eggs	8
8oz	Caster sugar	225g
7oz	Self-raising flour	200g
4oz	Ground almonds	125g
5oz	Plain cooking chocolate	150g
2 tbsp	Cocoa	2×15ml
4oz	Butter	125g
	Chocolate cream	
8oz	Milk cooking chocolate	225g
1 teasp	Instant coffee powder	5ml
2 tbsp	Caster sugar	2×15ml
$1\frac{1}{4}$ pint	Single cream	700ml
4 teasp	Gelatine	4×5ml
2oz	Chocolate chips or crushed flake	50g

METHOD

1 Preheat the oven to 350F (180C) Gas 4. Grease and base-line the 2 tins. Separate the eggs. Whisk the yolks and 6oz (175g) of the sugar in a bowl over hot water till light and fluffy. In another bowl, beat the remaining sugar and egg whites till very stiff. Gently fold the white into the creamed mixture.

2 Mix the flour, almonds, grated chocolate and cocoa in a bowl. Add the egg mixture and mix till smooth.

3 Melt the butter over a low heat, then stir into the cake mixture. Fill greased tins with mixture and cook in centre of oven for 50 minutes.

4 Remove cakes from oven and allow to cool for 20 minutes in the tins, then turn out on to a wire rack.

5 Meanwhile, to make the chocolate cream, break the chocolate into small pieces and place in a bowl over a saucepan of boiling water. Add the coffee, caster sugar and cream and stir the mixture constantly until the chocolate has melted.

6 Remove pan from heat. Mix gelatine and 1 tbsp (15ml) of water in a cup till spongy. Then place cup in pan of hot water and stir till dissolved. Add to cream, mix well, then pour into a large mixing bowl. Leave to cool, then whisk till very stiff.

7 When cakes are cold, cut each into 2 layers. Spread 1 layer with a fifth of the chocolate cream; place another layer on top, then cream, then cake etc. Cover the top and sides of cake with remaining two-fifths of cream. Decorate the sides with crushed chocolate chips or flake, pressed on to chocolate cream with a spatula. Chill in fridge till wanted and serve with single cream, if using as a dessert.

Below: Chocolate torte – splendid mix of chocolate cake, cream and topping

Mocha gâteau

A simple sponge cake made in classic fashion by whisking the eggs and sugar over hot water before folding in the flour. And with so rich a filling and topping, a plain cake such as this sponge is just what's called for

Above: Mocha gâteau – coffee sponge cake with coffee butter cream filling and topping

TEA-TIME Cuts into 12 slices

Overall timing $1\frac{1}{4}$ hours

Equipment 8 inch (20cm) cake tin, bowls, 2 saucepans, piping bag and star nozzle

Freezing Open freeze, then pack carefully in rigid container. Cover, label, refreeze. Freezer life: 3 months. To use: uncover, thaw at room temperature for 4 hours

INGREDIENTS

2 teasp	Instant coffee powder	2×5ml
1 tbsp	Water	15ml
4	Large eggs	4
4oz	Caster sugar	125g
	Pinch of salt	
2oz	Butter	50g
4oz	Plain flour	125g
	Filling and topping	
1 tbsp	Cornflour	15ml
$\frac{1}{4}$ pint	Milk	150ml
3 tbsp	Caster sugar	3×15ml
1 tbsp	Coffee granules	15ml
1	Egg yolk	1
6oz	Softened butter	175g
3oz	Icing sugar	75g
	Decoration	
2oz	Milk chocolate flake	50g
	Sugar coffee beans	

METHOD

1 Preheat the oven to 375F (190C) Gas 5. Grease and base-line cake tin.

2 Mix coffee with water and stir till dissolved. Place in large bowl over saucepan of hot water, add eggs, sugar and salt and whisk until mixture is very thick and the beaters when lifted leave a trail that lasts 20 seconds. Remove bowl from pan. Melt butter in small pan – do not let it brown.

3 Sift half the flour evenly over bowl and fold in gently with a metal spoon. Pour melted butter round edge of bowl, then fold in gently. Gently fold in remaining sifted flour.

4 Gently pour mixture into tin and bake just above centre of oven for about 40 minutes. The cake is cooked when the top springs back when gently pressed. Run knife round side of tin and turn cake on to wire rack to cool.

5 To make the butter cream, place cornflour in small saucepan and blend in the milk. Add the sugar and coffee and bring to the boil, stirring. Reduce heat and cook for 2–3 minutes, stirring constantly. Remove from heat and leave to cool slightly.

6 Add egg yolk and beat well. Cook over gentle heat for 2 minutes, then remove from heat and leave to cool.

7 In a bowl beat butter and sifted icing sugar till well combined, then add the cooled custard and beat to a smooth creamy consistency.

8 Cut sponge into 2 layers and spread one half with a third of the butter cream. Top with second half, then coat top and sides of cake with most of the remaining butter cream, reserving some for piping swirls on top with a star nozzle.

9 Mark top of cake into 12 equal slices. Pipe swirl of cream on each one, then decorate with crumbled flake and sugar coffee beans.

cook's know-how

When you want grated chocolate for decoration, there is a simple way to make it without getting your fingers sticky. Break up 1oz (25g) plain chocolate and melt it in a small bowl over hot water. Pour it on to a baking tray and spread it thinly with a palette knife. When it is just set, with knife at a 45° angle, scrape chocolate towards you to make curls.

Victoria sandwich

The classic jam sponge cake that makes an English tea complete. The mixture can also be used to make small sponge cakes, sponge castles or swiss rolls, all of which use jam in their ingredients, as the two complement each other very well

TEA-TIME Cuts into 8

Overall timing 40 minutes plus cooling

Equipment Two 7 inch (18cm) sandwich tins, bowl

Freezing Cool cakes but do not sandwich together. Place piece of waxed paper or foil between layers. Wrap in foil, seal, label and freeze. Freezer life: 4 months. To use: thaw in wrapping, then complete Step 6

INGREDIENTS

6oz	Butter or block margarine	175g
6oz	Caster sugar	175g
3	Large eggs	3
6oz	Self-raising flour	175g
4 tbsp	Jam	4×15ml
1 tbsp	Caster sugar	15ml

METHOD

1 Preheat oven to 375F (190C) Gas 5. Grease and base-line tins.
2 Beat fat in a bowl until creamy. Gradually add the sugar and continue beating until pale and fluffy.
3 Beat eggs and gradually add to mixture, beating well after each addition.
4 Sift in the flour. Using a metal spoon, lightly cut through the mixture in a figure of eight action, scraping base and sides of bowl and turning mixture until all the flour is incorporated. Divide between tins and smooth tops.
5 Place both tins on the centre shelf of the oven and cook for 20–25 minutes until well risen and golden and springy when lightly pressed.
6 Turn out of tins on to a wire rack and leave to cool. Place one cake, upside down, on a serving plate and spread with the jam. Place the other cake on top and sieve caster sugar over.

VARIATIONS

Whip ¼ pint (150ml) double cream and spread over the jam before topping with the second sponge. Dredge top with icing sugar. For special occasions, fold one chopped fresh peach into the cream and arrange thin peach slices on the top; glaze with jam.

Coffee ring cake

Grated orange rind and juice give added zest to a moist textured cake – perfect for tea-time

TEA-TIME Cuts into 16 slices

Overall timing 1½ hours

Equipment 2 bowls, 8½ inch (22cm) fluted or plain ring tin

Freezing Open freeze cooled cake, wrap well and label. Freezer life: 3 months. To use: thaw at room temperature for 2–3 hours, then ice and leave to thaw completely

INGREDIENTS

	Cake	
5oz	Softened margarine	150g
5oz	Caster sugar	150g
	Salt	
2	Large eggs	2
1	Orange	1
3 teasp	Instant coffee granules	3×5ml
5oz	Self-raising flour	150g
¼ teasp	Ground cinnamon	1.25ml
2oz	Plain or mocha chocolate	50g
	Icing	
6oz	Icing sugar	175g
2 teasp	Instant coffee granules	2×5ml
1 teasp	Cocoa	5ml
2 tbsp	Hot water	2×15ml
	Vanilla essence	

METHOD

1 Preheat oven to 325F (170C) Gas 3. Grease ring tin well.
2 In a mixing bowl, cream margarine, sugar and salt till light and fluffy. Add eggs one at a time and beat well. Grate orange and add peel to bowl. Squeeze orange, put 3 tbsp (3×15ml) juice in a cup with the instant coffee and mix well.
3 Sift flour and cinnamon and mix half at a time into bowl, alternating with orange/coffee mixture. Grate chocolate and fold in.
4 Spoon mixture evenly into tin, then bake towards top of oven for 40–50 minutes. Turn on to wire rack and leave to cool.
5 To make the icing, place icing sugar in bowl. Dissolve coffee and cocoa in hot water, then add to icing sugar with a few drops of vanilla essence and mix well. Pour over cooled cake and smooth surface with a knife.

Below: Coffee ring cake – orange, coffee and chocolate flavours combined in one cake

Battenberg

Plain and coloured sponge is neatly layered to produce a check design

TEA-TIME Cuts into 10

Overall timing 1½ hours plus cooling

Equipment Greaseproof paper, swiss roll tin, large bowl, saucepan

Freezing As for Neapolitan marble cake but complete with almond paste

INGREDIENTS

8oz	Butter or margarine	225g
8oz	Caster sugar	225g
4	Eggs	4
8oz	Self-raising flour	225g
4 tbsp	Milk	4×15ml
	Red food colouring	
3 tbsp	Apricot jam	3×15ml
	Caster sugar	
8oz	Almond paste	225g

METHOD

1 Preheat the oven to 375F (190C) Gas 5. Cut out a piece of greaseproof paper 2 inches (5cm) wider than the swiss roll tin. Make a 1 inch (2.5cm) pleat down the centre of the paper and place in the centre of the tin so that it divides it in half lengthways. Brush greaseproof lightly with oil.

2 In a large bowl, cream the butter or margarine and the sugar until pale and fluffy. Beat in the eggs one at a time. Sift the flour and gradually fold into creamed mixture with a metal spoon. Add milk and mix to soft consistency.

3 Spread half the mixture into one side of the prepared tin. Add a few drops of food colouring to the remaining mixture and beat well so that colouring is evenly distributed. Spread coloured mixture into other half of the tin.

4 Bake on the centre shelf of the oven for about 45 minutes, or until well risen and firm to the touch. Turn out of tin and leave to cool on wire rack.

5 Trim edges and cut each cake in half lengthways. Warm the jam in a small pan. Spread one strip of plain cake with jam and place one pink strip on top; repeat process with pink strip as base. Stick two halves of cake together with jam.

6 Sprinkle caster sugar over working surface and roll out almond paste to a rectangle large enough to cover cake.

7 Spread remaining jam over the outside of the cake, then wrap in the almond paste, sealing join well. Crimp edges and lightly score top with diamond pattern using a sharp knife.

Above: Battenberg – contrasting sponge squares wrapped in delicious almond paste

Neapolitan marble cake

Food colourings give similar swirls of colour in both cake and icing

TEA-TIME Cuts into 10

Overall timing 1¼ hours plus cooling

Equipment 3½ pint (2 litre) ring mould, 4 bowls, greaseproof paper

Freezing Make cake, but do not ice. Wrap well, seal, label and freeze. Freezer life: 4 months. To use: thaw for 2 hours at room temperature, then ice

INGREDIENTS

	Cake	
8oz	Margarine	225g
8oz	Caster sugar	225g
4	Eggs	4
8oz	Self-raising flour	225g
4 tbsp	Milk	4×15ml
1 tbsp	Cocoa	15ml
	Red food colouring	
	Almond essence	
	Green food colouring	
	Peppermint essence	
	Icing	
8oz	Icing sugar	225g
	Water to mix	
1 teasp	Cocoa	5ml
	Red food colouring	
	Green food colouring	

METHOD

1 Preheat the oven to 350F (180C) Gas 4. Oil ring mould.

2 In a bowl, cream the margarine and sugar till pale and fluffy. Beat in the eggs one at a time, then fold in the sifted flour with a metal spoon. Add milk if necessary to give a soft, dropping consistency.

3 Divide the creamed mixture between 3 bowls. To the first, add the sifted cocoa and a little extra milk if necessary; to the second, add a few drops of red food colouring and almond essence and mix in well; to the third, add a few drops of green food colouring and peppermint essence.

4 Place large dollops of the mixtures in turn round the oiled mould. If you like, carefully swirl the mixtures with a skewer. Do not mix too much or the colours will blur.

5 Bake in the centre of the oven for about 45 minutes or until the cake is well risen and firm and spongy to the touch. Turn out of tin and cool on wire rack.

6 To make the icing, sift the icing sugar into a bowl and mix with water to give a smooth, coating consistency. Spoon two-thirds of the icing over the cooled cake.

7 Divide remaining icing between 3 bowls. Mix cocoa into the first, a few drops red food colouring into the second and green food colouring into the third.

8 Make 3 small greaseproof paper piping bags with a fine hole in the end. Place icing in bags and "drizzle" over the cake in very thin lines, allowing each coloured icing to set before adding another. Or, trickle icing from a small spoon held high above the cake.

Lamingtons

An Australian speciality which can be made with leftover cake if you prefer. Make chocolate lamingtons by using cocoa instead of 1oz (25g) flour

TEA-TIME Makes 20

Overall timing 1¼ hours

Equipment 7×12 inch (18×30cm) swiss roll tin, bowl, heatproof bowl, saucepan, tongs

Freezing Open freeze after completing Step 3. Place in freezer bags, seal, label and freeze. Freezer life: 6 months. To use: thaw for 1 hour at room temperature, then coat with icing and coconut. Leave to thaw completely

Storage Airtight container

INGREDIENTS

	Cake	
6oz	Butter	175g
6oz	Caster sugar	175g
1 teasp	Vanilla essence	5ml
3	Eggs	3
8oz	Self-raising flour	225g
	Pinch of salt	
4 tbsp	Milk	4×15ml
8oz	Icing sugar	225g
2 tbsp	Cocoa	2×15ml
½oz	Butter	15g
4–5 tbsp	Milk or water	4–5× 15ml
	Decoration	
6oz	Desiccated coconut	175g

METHOD

1 Preheat the oven to 350F (180C) Gas 4. Grease tin and base-line.

2 To make cake, in a bowl cream butter and sugar till light and fluffy. Beat in vanilla essence, then eggs, one at a time. Sift flour and salt and add to mixture alternately with milk. Mix well.

3 Pour cake mixture into prepared tin. Bake just above centre of oven for 35 minutes. Remove from oven and leave to cool slightly, then turn cake on to wire rack. Cut into 20 oblongs.

4 To make the icing, sift the icing sugar and cocoa into a bowl. Melt the butter, add the milk, then remove from heat. Stir into dry ingredients, a little at a time, till icing is smooth. Place bowl over saucepan of simmering water so the icing remains liquid.

5 Using tongs, dip oblongs into icing and, when coated and drips have stopped, place on plate covered with coconut. Roll to coat, place on wire rack to dry.

Above: Marble ring cake – an attractive cake with two flavours thinly layered

Marble ring cake

Fine layers of cocoa-flavoured and plain mixtures create this unusual marble effect. Work carefully – the layers shouldn't be too thick

TEA-TIME Cuts into 10 slices

Overall timing 1½ hours

Equipment 7½ inch (19cm) ring mould, 2 bowls, sieve, 2 spatulas

Freezing Cool the cake and foil-wrap or place in a rigid container, seal, label and freeze. Freezer life: 6 months. To use: thaw, wrapped, at room temperature for 4–6 hours

INGREDIENTS

4oz	Margarine	125g
5oz	Caster sugar	150g
3	Eggs	3
7oz	Self-raising flour	200g
5 tbsp	Milk	5×15ml
1oz	Cocoa	25g

METHOD

1 Preheat the oven to 350F (180C) Gas 4. Grease and flour the ring mould.

2 Beat the margarine in a bowl until soft, then gradually beat in the sugar until mixture is pale and fluffy. Beat in the eggs, one at a time.

3 Divide the mixture into two, placing half in the second bowl. Sift 4oz (125g) of the flour into half the mixture and fold in, adding 3 tbsp (3×15ml) of the milk.

4 Sift the rest of the flour and cocoa into the other half and fold in, adding the remaining milk.

5 Spread a little of the plain mixture over the base and sides of the prepared mould. With another spatula, carefully spread a thin layer of the chocolate mixture over the first layer.

6 Repeat the careful layering until both mixtures are used up. Smooth the surface with clean spatula.

7 Bake for 1 hour until well risen and firm to the touch. Cool cake slightly in the mould before turning out on to a wire rack to cool completely.

Orange-flavoured simnel cake

A traditional Easter cake that comes complete with 12 "apostles" on top

TEA-TIME/SPECIAL OCCASION Cuts into 16

Overall timing 3¼ hours

Equipment 8 inch (20cm) round cake tin, 3 bowls, saucepan

Freezing Complete Step 6, foil-wrap, seal, label and freeze. Freezer life: 6 months. To use: thaw in wrappings at room temperature for 6–8 hours. Complete Steps 7–9

INGREDIENTS

6oz	Butter or margarine	175g
6oz	Light soft brown sugar	175g
1	Large orange	1
3	Eggs	3
8oz	Plain flour	225g
	Salt	
½ teasp	Freshly-grated nutmeg	2.5ml
½ teasp	Ground cinnamon	2.5ml
12oz	Sultanas	350g
4oz	Currants	125g
2oz	Chopped mixed peel	50g
	Almond paste	
6oz	Icing sugar	175g
6oz	Caster sugar	175g
12oz	Ground almonds	350g
3	Eggs	3
2 teasp	Lemon juice	2×5ml
	Glaze	
1 tbsp	Apricot jam	15ml
1	Egg white	1

METHOD

1 Preheat the oven to 325F (170C) Gas 3. Grease and base-line the cake tin.

2 Cream the fat and sugar together till pale and fluffy. Wash and dry the orange and grate the rind into the creamed mixture. Beat the eggs in a bowl, then gradually beat into the mixture with a wooden spoon.

3 Sift the flour, a pinch of salt and the spices over the mixture. Add the sultanas, currants and chopped peel and mix well, adding the juice from the orange to give a fairly soft consistency. Spread half the mixture into the tin.

4 To make the almond paste, sift the icing sugar into a bowl and stir in the caster sugar and the almonds. Beat in the eggs and lemon juice and mix to a stiff paste.

5 Roll out one-third of the paste on a surface dredged with icing sugar to an 8 inch (20cm) diameter circle. Place on top of the cake mixture, cover with the remaining cake mixture and smooth the top.

6 Bake in the centre of the oven for 2½ hours, covering lightly with foil after 1 hour, till a skewer inserted in the centre comes out clean. Remove from the tin and leave to cool on a wire rack.

7 Meanwhile, roll out half the remaining almond paste to an 8 inch (20cm) circle and reserve. Divide the remaining paste into 12 pieces and roll each into a ball.

8 Preheat the grill. Warm the jam in a saucepan and brush over the top of the cooled cake. Place the almond paste circle on top and arrange the balls or "apostles" around the edge of the cake, flattening them slightly with a fork.

9 Beat the egg white till slightly frothy and brush over the almond paste. Grill for 5–10 minutes till golden brown. Leave to cool completely before serving.

Sultana loaf cake

A tea-time standby, this sultana loaf cake is sure to be popular

TEA-TIME Cuts into 16

Overall timing 1½ hours

Equipment 2lb (900g) loaf tin, bowl

Freezing Foil-wrap, seal, label and freeze. Freezer life: 6 months. To use: thaw in wrappings at room temperature for 3–4 hours

INGREDIENTS

8oz	Self-raising flour	225g
	Salt	
1 teasp	Ground ginger	5ml
4oz	Butter or margarine	125g
2oz	Caster sugar	50g
6oz	Sultanas	175g
2 tbsp	Runny honey	2×15ml
1	Egg	1
7 tbsp	Milk	7×15ml

METHOD

1 Preheat the oven to 350F (180C) Gas 4. Grease and base-line the loaf tin.

2 Sift the flour, a pinch of salt and the ginger into a large bowl. Rub in the fat till the mixture resembles fine breadcrumbs. Stir in the sugar and sultanas, then make a well in the centre.

3 Add the honey, egg and half the milk and mix with a wooden spoon, gradually drawing the dry ingredients into the liquid. Add the remaining milk if necessary to give a soft dropping consistency.

4 Spread the mixture into the loaf tin and smooth the surface. Bake in the centre of the oven for 45 minutes. Cover the top lightly with foil and bake for a further 30 minutes till the loaf is springy when lightly pressed.

5 Run a knife round the sides of the tin and turn the cake on to a wire rack. Leave to cool completely before serving.

Below: Sultana loaf cake – packed with goodies such as ginger, honey and sultanas, this is the perfect cut-and-come-again cake

Madeleines with cinnamon

Dainty, pastry-based cakes that originated in the town of Commercy in France. If you don't have shell-shaped madeleine sheets, use round bun trays instead

TEA-TIME Makes 16

Overall timing 50 minutes plus chilling

Equipment 3 bowls, 2 madeleine sheets

Freezing Open freeze at end of Step 6. Remove from trays, foil-wrap, pack in rigid container, cover and label. Freezer life: 1 month. To use: replace in trays then thaw at room temperature for 2 hours. Complete Steps 7 and 8

INGREDIENTS

	Pastry	
6oz	Plain flour	175g
3oz	Butter or margarine	75g
1 tbsp	Caster sugar	15ml
1	Egg yolk	1
	Water to mix	
	Filling	
4oz	Butter or margarine	125g
4oz	Caster sugar	125g
2	Eggs	2
2oz	Ground almonds	50g
¼ teasp	Almond essence	1.25ml
4oz	Self-raising flour	125g
1 teasp	Ground cinnamon	5ml
	Milk to mix	
	Apricot jam	
1 tbsp	Icing sugar	15ml

Below: Madeleines with cinnamon – dredged with a mixture of caster and icing sugar

METHOD

1 To make the pastry, sift the flour into a bowl and rub in the fat till the mixture resembles fine breadcrumbs.

2 Stir in the sugar and egg yolk and enough water to mix to a soft but not sticky dough. Knead lightly till smooth, then roll out on a floured surface to ¼ inch (6mm) thickness. Use to line the madeleine sheets. Trim the edges, cover the sheets and chill for 30 minutes.

3 Preheat the oven to 375F (190C) Gas 5.

4 To make the filling, cream the fat and all but 1 tbsp (15ml) of the caster sugar till pale and fluffy.

5 Lightly beat the eggs with a fork and add, a little at a time, to the creamed mixture, beating well between each addition. Add the almonds and almond essence, and sift in the flour and cinnamon. Fold in with a metal spoon, adding enough milk to give a soft dropping consistency.

6 Remove pastry shells from fridge. Put ½ teasp (2.5ml) of jam into each one, then spoon cake mixture into each case.

7 Bake in the centre of the oven for 15–20 minutes till the filling is golden and springs back when lightly pressed. Remove from the oven and allow to cool slightly. Remove from the tins and cool on a wire rack.

8 Mix the icing sugar and the remaining caster sugar together and sift over the tartlets before serving.

Chestnut cake

Two layers of rich chestnut sponge sandwiched with sweetened cream make up this delectable cake. Sugar sifted over a chocolate coloured coating gives the finishing touch

TEA-TIME Cuts into 12

Overall timing 2½ hours plus cooling

Equipment 10 inch (25cm) loose-bottom cake tin, 2 bowls, saucepan

Freezing Complete to end of Step 5. Wrap uncut cake in foil, seal, label and freeze. Freezer life: 3 months. To use: thaw at room temperature, then complete Steps 6–8. The finished cake can also be frozen in a rigid container, but this reduces freezer life to 1 month

INGREDIENTS

6	Medium-size eggs	6
9oz	Caster sugar	250g
8oz	Can of unsweetened chestnut purée	227g
3oz	Ground almonds	75g
	Grated rind of 1 lemon	
½ teasp	Ground cinnamon	2.5ml
	Filling	
¼ pint	Carton of whipping cream	150ml
2 tbsp	Icing sugar	2×15ml
	Icing	
1 tbsp	Cocoa	15ml
8oz	Icing sugar	225g
2 tbsp	Rum	2×15ml
	Warm water to mix	

METHOD

1 Preheat the oven to 350F (180C) Gas 4. Grease and base-line the tin.

2 Separate the eggs. Whisk yolks and sugar in a bowl till pale and thick. Put bowl over a pan of simmering water and add the chestnut purée a little at a time, whisking well between each addition. Remove from the heat and gently fold in the almonds, lemon rind and cinnamon with a metal spoon.

3 Whisk the egg whites till stiff and fold into the mixture with a metal spoon.

4 Spoon the mixture into the tin and smooth the surface. Bake in the centre of the oven for about 55 minutes, till centre springs back when lightly pressed.

5 Remove from the oven and allow to cool slightly. Remove from the tin and leave to cool on a wire rack.

6 To make the filling, whip the cream with the sifted icing sugar till stiff peaks form. Cut the cooled cake into 2 layers and spread the bottom half with cream. Top with the second cake layer, taking care that the cream does not ooze out.
7 To make the icing, sift the cocoa with all but 2 tbsp (2×15ml) of the icing sugar into a bowl and mix with the rum and enough warm water to give a smooth coating consistency. Spread icing over the top and sides of the cake with a palette knife. Leave to set.
8 Cut five 1 inch (2.5cm) wide strips of greaseproof paper and place in a row on top of the cake. Sift the remaining icing sugar over, then carefully remove the strips of paper to leave a brown and white striped top.

Cherry and lemon loaf

Made by the rubbing in method, this loaf has the typical crunchy, melt-in-the-mouth texture – at its best eaten on the day of making

TEA-TIME

Overall timing $1\frac{1}{2}$ hours

Equipment Mixing bowl, 2lb (900g) loaf tin

Freezing Wrap in polythene or foil. Seal, label and freeze. Freezer life: 6 months. To use: thaw, unwrapped, at room temperature (3–4 hours)

INGREDIENTS

8oz	Self-raising flour	225g
	Pinch of salt	
4oz	Butter	125g
4oz	Caster sugar	125g
4oz	Glacé cherries	125g
	Grated rind of 1 lemon	
1	Egg	1
4fl oz	Milk	120ml

Below: *Cherry and lemon loaf – complementary flavourings, crumby texture*

Mix the butter and flour with the fingers to achieve a breadcrumb-like texture

Wash the syrupy coating from the glacé cherries, dry well, then halve into bowl

The consistency should be soft, but mix should only drop from spoon if flicked

METHOD

1 Preheat oven to 350F (180C) Gas 4. Grease loaf tin, line base. Sift all but 1 tbsp (15ml) of flour into bowl, add salt.
2 Rub in butter until mixture resembles fine breadcrumbs. Stir in sugar. Wash and dry cherries, roll in reserved flour. Halve into crumb mixture.
3 Add lemon rind. Make a well in centre and break in egg. Gradually mix dry ingredients into centre, adding enough milk to give a soft consistency that won't drop unless flicked from the spoon.
4 Put mixture into tin, smooth surface. Bake in centre of oven for 45 minutes. Cover with greaseproof, bake for further 30 minutes. Cool on a wire rack.

Praline-topped lemon cake

A layered cake filled with rich lemon butter cream and topped with a crunchy caramel and nut mixture

TEA-TIME Cuts into 8

Overall timing 1½ hours

Equipment 3 bowls, sieve, 8 inch (20cm) cake tin, heavy-based saucepan, rolling-pin

Freezing Open freeze. When firm place in a rigid container, cover and label. Freezer life: 6 months. To use: unwrap and thaw at room temperature for 4 hours

INGREDIENTS

4oz	Butter	125g
5oz	Caster sugar	150g
4	Eggs	4
5oz	Plain flour	150g
3oz	Cornflour	75g
2 teasp	Baking powder	2×5ml
2 tbsp	Grated lemon rind	2×15ml
2oz	Chopped almonds	50g
	Butter cream	
5oz	Butter	150g
5oz	Icing sugar	150g
1	Egg yolk	1
2 tbsp	Lemon juice	2×15ml

METHOD

1 Preheat the oven to 350F (180C) Gas 4. Grease and base-line cake tin.
2 Cream the butter and 4oz (125g) of the sugar until light and fluffy.
3 Separate the eggs and beat egg yolks into butter mixture. In a bowl, whisk egg whites until stiff.
4 Sift flour, cornflour and baking powder together and fold into creamed mixture with lemon rind. Carefully fold in the egg whites.
5 Pour cake mixture into prepared tin and smooth surface. Bake on centre shelf of oven for 50–60 minutes until top springs back when lightly pressed. Turn out on to a wire rack and leave to cool.
6 Stir remaining sugar and 1 teasp (5ml) water in a heavy-based saucepan over a low heat until dissolved. Stop stirring and boil until caramelized to a pale golden colour. Add almonds and mix well. Remove from heat and spread on to a greased marble slab or baking tray. Allow to cool and set hard, then break into tiny pieces with a rolling-pin.
7 To make the butter cream filling and topping, cream the butter and sifted icing sugar till soft, then add egg yolk and lemon juice. Mix well until smooth.
8 Cut cake into 3 layers. Spread the top of each layer with butter cream and sandwich together. Sprinkle the broken caramel over the top pressing it into the butter cream.

VARIATIONS

Crunchy nut topping

Replace the praline with a mixture of 2oz finely chopped toasted hazelnuts, 1oz (25g) finely chopped glacé cherries and 2 tbsp (2×15ml) demerara sugar.

Biscuit crumb topping

Roughly crush 3oz (75g) ginger or chocolate wholewheat biscuits. Mix with 1 tbsp (15ml) demerara sugar and 1 tbsp (15ml) finely chopped crystallized ginger and use to replace praline.

Below: Praline-topped lemon cake – soft and creamy inside, crunchy on top

Above: Lemon and cardamom cake – to taste it at its best, serve while it's still warm

Lemon and cardamom cake

A light tea-time treat that's a little different – spiced with cardamom and cinnamon and sprinkled with split almonds on top

TEA-TIME Cuts into 8

Overall timing $1\frac{1}{4}$–$1\frac{1}{2}$ hours

Equipment 7 inch (18cm) round cake tin, mixing bowl

Freezing Wrap in polythene or foil, seal, label and freeze. Freezer life: 6 months. To use: thaw, unwrapped, at room temperature for 3–4 hours

INGREDIENTS

8oz	Self-raising flour	225g
1 teasp	Ground cardamom	5ml
4oz	Butter	125g
4oz	Caster sugar	125g
1	Lemon	1
1	Egg	1
2 tbsp	Milk	2×15ml
1oz	Split almonds	25g
$\frac{1}{2}$ teasp	Ground cinnamon	2.5ml

METHOD

1 Preheat oven to 350F (180C) Gas 4. Grease and base-line tin.

2 Sift flour and cardamom into a large bowl. Rub in the butter until mixture resembles fine breadcrumbs. Stir in all but 1 teasp (5ml) of the sugar.

3 Grate the lemon rind and squeeze out the juice. Add both to bowl. Mix well. Make a well in the centre and break in the egg. Gradually mix ingredients into centre, adding enough milk to give a soft consistency that won't drop unless flicked from the spoon.

4 Put mixture into prepared tin and smooth the surface. Cut the almonds into slivers. Mix together the almonds, cinnamon and reserved sugar and sprinkle over cake.

5 Bake on centre shelf of oven for 1–$1\frac{1}{4}$ hours or until cake comes away from the sides. Allow to cool in tin for a few minutes, then turn out on to a wire rack and cool completely.

VARIATION

This simple cake can be adapted to make a delicious autumn pudding for 6.

Peel, core and thickly slice $1\frac{1}{2}$lb (700g) cooking apples. Sprinkle with lemon juice to prevent discoloration. Wash and pick over 8oz (225g) blackberries and add to the apples together with 2–4oz (50–125g) demerara sugar and 1 tbsp (15ml) plain flour. Spread evenly over the base of a greased 3 pint (1.7 litre) ovenproof dish. Make the cake mixture as Steps 2 and 3 and then spread the mixture over the fruit. Bake at 350F (180C) Gas 4 for $1\frac{1}{2}$ hours and serve hot with custard or cream.

Above: Double-iced cherry ring cake with sugar-coated cherries

Fresh cherry cake

Fresh sour cherries come into season in late summer and they are the perfect fruit for this cake – dessert cherries are too bland

TEA-TIME Cuts into 8 slices

Overall timing 1½ hours

Equipment 2 bowls, 10 inch (25cm) cake tin

Freezing Cool, wrap in foil, then overwrap in polythene. Seal, label and freeze. Freezer life: 6 months. To use: thaw at room temperature

INGREDIENTS

1 teasp	Oil	5ml
6	Digestive biscuits	6
1¾lb	Fresh cherries	750g
3oz	Ground almonds	75g
9oz	Caster sugar	250g
½ teasp	Ground cinnamon	2.5ml
5	Eggs	5
2 tbsp	Kirsch	2×15ml
1	Lemon	1
4oz	Plain flour	125g

Double-iced cherry ring cake

A well-textured cake made with cherries and given a double covering of icing for good measure. The cake is decorated with sugar-dipped cherries

TEA-TIME Cuts into 12 slices

Overall timing 1¾ hours

Equipment Mixing bowl, small bowl, 9½ inch (24cm) ring tin 3 inches (7.5cm) deep

Freezing Ice the cake but do not add sugared cherries. Open freeze, then wrap and label. Freezer life: 4 months. To use: unwrap, thaw at room temperature, then decorate

INGREDIENTS

7oz	Butter	200g
7oz	Caster sugar	200g
3	Eggs	3
1 teasp	Vanilla essence	5ml
	Pinch of salt	
12oz	Plain flour	350g
2 teasp	Baking powder	2×5ml
5 tbsp	Milk	5×15ml
2 tbsp	Rum	2×15ml
10½oz	Canned cherries	297g
	Icing	
11oz	Icing sugar	300g
1 tbsp	Rum	15ml
	Decoration	
12	Fresh cherries	12
1oz	Caster sugar	25g

METHOD

1 Preheat the oven to 350F (180C) Gas 4.
2 Cream together butter and sugar in a mixing bowl. Separate the eggs. Add yolks to creamed mixture with the vanilla essence and salt.
3 Mix in the flour and baking powder, then milk and rum alternately. Beat two egg whites till stiff; fold into mixture.
4 Drain cherries saving some of the cherry juice. Add cherries to mixture then pour into greased ring tin. Bake in centre of oven for 1–1¼ hours.
5 Remove from tin; cool on a cake wire.
6 To make the icing, mix 5oz (150g) of the icing sugar with 2 tbsp (2×15ml) of the juice from the cherries and pour over the top of the cake, leaving it to drip down the sides. Mix the rum and 1 tbsp (15ml) water with rest of icing sugar and pour over the first icing.
7 Wash and dry cherries. Dip first into remaining egg white, then caster sugar. Arrange on top of cake and leave to set.

METHOD

1 Preheat the oven to 350F (180C) Gas 4.
2 Oil the cake tin. Crush the biscuits and sprinkle over inside of tin.
3 Wash and dry the cherries. Remove stones. Arrange over the base of the coated cake tin.
4 Mix together the almonds, 2oz (50g) of the sugar and the cinnamon.
5 In another bowl, beat together the egg yolks, remaining sugar, Kirsch, grated rind and juice of the lemon. Stir in the almond, sugar and cinnamon mixture, then fold in flour lightly using a spatula.
6 Beat the egg whites until fairly stiff. Fold into the cake mixture using a metal spoon. Spread over the cherries. Put in the middle of the oven and cook for 1 hour 10 minutes.
7 Turn out and cool on a cake wire. To serve, dredge with icing sugar.

Below: Fresh cherry cake – dredge with icing sugar, then slice for tea

Gingerbread

The melting method used here gives the classic moist gingerbread texture

TEA-TIME Cuts into 9 squares

Overall timing $1\frac{1}{4}$ hours

Equipment Bowl, saucepan, 7 inch (18cm) square tin *or* 8 inch (20cm) round tin

Freezing When cold, wrap, label and freeze. Freezer life: 6 months. To use: thaw in wrapping for about 2 hours

INGREDIENTS

8oz	Plain flour	225g
1 teasp	Bicarbonate of soda	5ml
$1\frac{1}{2}$ teasp	Ground ginger	$1\frac{1}{2}\times$5ml
2oz	Black treacle	50g
4oz	Golden syrup	125g
3oz	Margarine	75g
2oz	Soft brown sugar	50g
2	Eggs	2
2 tbsp	Milk	$2\times$15ml

METHOD

1 Preheat the oven to 325F (170C) Gas 3. Sift flour, soda and ginger into bowl.
2 Place treacle and golden syrup in saucepan with margarine and brown sugar. Heat till melted.
3 Beat eggs and milk. Pour melted ingredients, then beaten eggs into dry ingredients. Mix to thick batter, pour into greased tin base-lined with greaseproof. Bake in centre of oven for 1 hour.

The trick with treacle and syrup is to put tin on scales and measure required amount

The melted ingredients are mixed into dry ingredients before eggs are beaten in

Mixture should be of thick batter consistency. Cook in greased and base-lined tin. Below: Gingerbread – moist and rich cake

Walnut and orange cake

This is made by the creaming method. Use either standard margarine or the soft, luxury type; the latter makes creaming easier. The texture is fine and close – the method is also used to make madeira cakes, small fairy cakes and victoria sponge sandwich

TEA-TIME

Overall timing 1 hour 50 minutes

Equipment 7 inch (18cm) round cake tin, mixing bowl

Freezing When cold, wrap, label and freeze without icing in a rigid container. Freezer life: 6 months. To use: thaw in wrapping for 3 hours

INGREDIENTS

6oz	Margarine	175g
6oz	Caster sugar	175g
3	Eggs	3
2oz	Walnut pieces	50g
	Grated rind of ½ an orange	
6oz	Plain flour	175g
1½ teasp	Baking powder	7.5ml
	Pinch of salt	
2 tbsp	Orange juice	2×15ml

METHOD

1 Preheat the oven to 325F (170C) Gas 3. Grease the tin well. Line the base with greaseproof paper and grease again.

2 Beat the margarine in a bowl till light. Gradually add the sugar and continue beating till pale and fluffy.

3 Add the beaten egg, a little at a time, beating well after each addition. Add walnuts and grated orange rind. Sift and fold in the flour, baking powder and salt, alternating with the orange juice. When the mixture is smooth and will drop easily from a spoon put into the tin and smooth top with a spatula. Bake for 1¼–1½ hours, or until a skewer inserted in the cake comes out clean.

Below: Walnut and orange cake – madeira-type cake with fruit and nut flavourings

Margarine and sugar are beaten till pale and fluffy, then beaten eggs are added

Sifted flour, orange juice and walnuts are folded in carefully with a metal spoon

Spoon the creamy mixture into a deep tin that's been well greased and base lined

Smooth the top with a spatula before baking so the cake will cook evenly on top

Orange layer biscuits

Short-textured, orange-flavoured biscuits joined together with a little marmalade and topped with icing and candied peel. You can make individual biscuits if you prefer, but you'll need extra icing

TEA-TIME Makes about 16

Overall timing 50 minutes

Equipment Baking trays, 3 bowls, 2 inch (5cm) fluted biscuit cutter

Freezing Prepare to end of Step 2. Shape dough into a sausage, foil-wrap, seal, label and freeze. Freezer life: 6 months. To use: half thaw in fridge, cut dough into slices, arrange on trays and bake, completing Steps 3–6

INGREDIENTS

1	Orange	1
4oz	Butter or margarine	125g
4oz	Caster sugar	125g
1	Egg	1
8oz	Plain flour	225g
1oz	Candied orange peel	25g
6oz	Icing sugar	175g
3 tbsp	Marmalade jelly	3×15ml

METHOD

1 Preheat the oven to 350F (180C) Gas 4. Grease the baking trays. Wash the orange and finely grate the rind. Squeeze out the juice and reserve.

2 Cream the fat and caster sugar in a large bowl till pale and fluffy. Beat the egg and add to bowl a little at a time, beating well between each addition. Add the grated rind and the sifted flour and mix to a firm paste. Knead lightly.

3 Roll out on a floured surface to $\frac{1}{8}$ inch (3mm) thickness. Cut out circles with the biscuit cutter, rerolling the dough as necessary, and arrange on the baking trays. Bake just above the centre of the oven for 15–20 minutes till firm and pale golden.

4 Allow to cool on the trays for 2–3 minutes, then transfer to a wire rack to crisp and cool.

5 Meanwhile, finely chop the candied peel. Sift the icing sugar into a bowl and mix with enough orange juice to give a thick coating consistency.

6 Warm the marmalade and brush over half the biscuits. Place plain biscuit on top of each, spoon the icing over and sprinkle with candied peel immediately. Serve when icing sets.

Above: Orange and almond sponge and, in the bowl, Orange layer biscuits – tea-time treats which use both orange rind and juice

Orange and almond sponge

Though fatless, this sponge keeps moist because of the ground almonds

TEA-TIME Cuts into 10

Overall timing 1 hour plus cooling

Equipment 9 inch (23cm) cake tin, 3 large bowls

Freezing Make as Steps 1–3. Wrap, seal, label and freeze. Freezer life: 4 months. To use: thaw for 4 hours at room temperature. Complete Steps 4 and 5

INGREDIENTS

1	Large orange	1
5	Eggs	5
5oz	Caster sugar	150g
$3\frac{1}{2}$oz	Self-raising flour	100g
	Pinch of salt	
$\frac{1}{4}$ teasp	Ground ginger	1.25ml
$\frac{1}{2}$ teasp	Ground cinnamon	2.5ml
5oz	Ground almonds	150g
	Almond essence	
5oz	Icing sugar	150g
1 tbsp	Curaçao	15ml

METHOD

1 Preheat the oven to 400F (200C) Gas 6. Grease and base-line the tin. Wash the orange. Grate the rind and squeeze out the juice. Separate the eggs and put the egg yolks into a bowl with the sugar. Whisk till the mixture is pale and thick.

2 Sift the flour, salt and spices over the mixture and add the ground almonds, 3 drops of essence, grated rind and 3 tbsp (3×15ml) of the orange juice. Fold in gently with a metal spoon.

3 Whisk the egg whites till stiff but not dry and fold into the mixture with a metal spoon. Carefully pour mixture into the tin and smooth the surface. Bake in the centre of the oven for about 35 minutes till springy to the touch. Remove from the tin and cool on a wire rack.

4 Sift the icing sugar into a bowl and add the Curaçao and 1 tbsp (15ml) of the remaining orange juice to make an icing that will coat the back of the spoon.

5 Pour the icing on to the top of the cake. Lift the wire rack and tap it several times on the working surface so that the icing flows over the cakes and trickles down the sides. Leave to set.

Chocolate kisses

In France these delectable confections are called *baisers*, which literally translates as "kisses"

DESSERT or TEA-TIME Makes about 20

Overall timing 1¾ hours

Equipment 2 baking trays, greaseproof paper, 2 bowls, piping bag with star nozzle

Freezing Do not join meringues together. Pack in shallow rigid containers, cover, label and freeze. Freezer life: 3 months. To use: thaw at room temperature for about 1 hour, then sandwich with cream

Storage Place in airtight container with screw-top. Store in cool place for up to 2 months

INGREDIENTS

4	Egg whites	4
2 teasp	White wine vinegar	2×5ml
1 teasp	Vanilla essence	5ml
	Pinch of salt	
8oz	Caster sugar	225g
1 tbsp	Cocoa	15ml
½ pint	Carton of double cream	284ml
1oz	Grated chocolate	25g

METHOD

1 Cut 2 pieces of greaseproof paper to fit trays. Run one side of each under the tap and place, wet side down, on trays. Preheat oven to 300F (150C) Gas 2.

2 Put whites, vinegar, essence and salt in mixing bowl and beat with an electric or rotary mixer till stiff peaks form. Gradually add 6oz (175g) of the sugar, beating continuously till mixture is glossy and hard to beat. Using metal spoon, gently fold in sifted cocoa and remaining sugar mixed together.

3 Spoon into piping bag and pipe 1¼ inch (3cm) diameter swirls on to the trays, leaving ½ inch (12.5mm) space all round. The mixture should make 40–44. Bake for 1½ hours until they are dry.

4 Remove from oven and place meringues on wire rack to cool, or turn them upside down on the trays.

5 Just before serving whip cream and fold in chocolate till stiff. Spoon into piping bag. Pipe on to half the meringues, and place the remainder on top to "kiss" the cream.

Ginger cookies

Rolled oats and desiccated coconut give a lovely nutty texture to these little biscuits flavoured with mixed spices and ginger. They're good with mid-morning coffee, too

TEA-TIME Makes 30

Overall timing 40 minutes

Equipment Bowl, saucepan, 2 large baking trays

Freezing When cold, pack in rigid container, cover, label and freeze. Freezer life: 6 months. To use: thaw at room temperature for 1 hour

Storage Airtight container

INGREDIENTS

3oz	Rolled oats	75g
2oz	Desiccated coconut	50g
5oz	Plain flour	150g
1 teasp	Mixed spice	5ml
1 teasp	Ground ginger	5ml
6oz	Caster sugar	175g
1½ teasp	Bicarbonate of soda	7.5ml
2 tbsp	Boiling water	2×15ml
4oz	Margarine or butter	125g
1 tbsp	Golden syrup	15ml

METHOD

1 Mix oats, coconut, flour, spice, ginger and sugar together in a bowl. In a cup mix soda with boiling water.

2 In small saucepan, melt margarine or butter with golden syrup. Remove from heat and mix in soda/water. Pour into dry ingredients and mix well.

3 Preheat oven to 325F (170C) Gas 3. Grease baking trays and place heaped spoonfuls of mixture at well-spaced intervals, leaving enough room all round as the mixture will spread.

4 Place trays in oven towards the top – in two batches if necessary – and cook biscuits for 20 minutes. Lift cookies immediately off tray with a spatula and place on a cake wire to cool.

time savers

Ovens will never again need major cleaning if, after cooking, you wipe over all the warm surfaces with a damp cloth sprinkled with bicarbonate of soda. Greasy marks disappear and you'll leave a good protection for the next cook-up.

Honey galettes

From Brittany as well as other parts of France, galettes are flat, round pastries which are sometimes built up in layers to form a cake, or served as biscuits. For a more sophisticated taste, try using 2 tbsp (2×15ml) rum instead of the lemon juice

TEA-TIME Makes 8

Overall timing 40 minutes plus chilling

Equipment Mixing bowl, 2 baking trays

Freezing Cool, pack into rigid container, cover, label and freeze. Freezer life: 6 months. To use: spread on baking trays and refresh in oven at 375F (190C) Gas 5 for 5 minutes until crisp

INGREDIENTS

6oz	Self-raising flour	175g
3½oz	Softened butter	100g
2oz	Thick honey	50g
1 tbsp	Caster sugar	15ml
1	Lemon	1
1	Egg	1
	Granulated sugar	

METHOD

1 Preheat the oven to 375F (190C) Gas 5. Sift the flour into a mixing bowl. Make a well in the centre and add the softened butter, honey and caster sugar.

2 Grate the rind from the lemon and add to the bowl with 1 tbsp (15ml) of the juice. Separate the egg and add the yolk to the bowl. Mix well together with a wooden spoon until the mixture forms a ball and leaves the sides of the bowl clean. Cover and chill for 30 minutes.

3 Divide mixture into 8 and roll out each piece on a lightly floured surface to a circle about ½ inch (12.5mm) thick. Place on baking trays.

4 Whisk egg white lightly and brush over biscuits. Sprinkle each biscuit with 1–2 tbsp (1–2×15ml) granulated sugar. Bake for about 15 minutes, then remove from trays and cool on wire rack.

Right: Honey galettes – golden brown biscuits flavoured with lemon and honey and topped with a crisp sugar coating for a tea-time treat

Cooked cheesecakes

Cooked cheesecakes for dessert or a special tea-time. They take between 1 and 2 hours to make but you must add cooling and chilling times. All are baked in 8 inch (20cm) springform tins or loose-bottomed cake tins. As all are quite suitable for freezing they can be made in advance and stored till needed.
To freeze: cool, then open freeze. Remove from tin. Wrap in foil, then overwrap in polythene. Seal and label. Freezer life: 1 month. To use: thaw at room temperature for 4–6 hours, or overnight in fridge

Granny's

INGREDIENTS

8oz	Plain chocolate digestive biscuits	225g
4oz	Butter	125g
8oz	Cream cheese	225g
8oz	Curd cheese	225g
2	Eggs	2
6oz	Caster sugar	175g
1 teasp	Vanilla essence	5ml
$\frac{1}{2}$ pint	Carton of soured cream	284ml
1	Lemon	1

METHOD

1 Preheat the oven to 375F (190C) Gas 5. Grease and base-line tin.
2 Crush biscuits with a rolling-pin. Reserve 2 tbsp (2×15ml) of the crumbs. Melt butter in a saucepan, remove from heat and stir in the crumbs. Spread crumb mixture evenly over tin base.
3 Place both cheeses in a large bowl and beat until well blended.
4 Place the eggs and 4oz (125g) of the sugar in a bowl and whisk until beaters leave a trail. Add essence.
5 Gradually add the egg mixture to the cheeses, whisking all the time to give a smooth, creamy consistency. Pour on to the crumb base and bake in the centre of the oven for 35–40 minutes until firm (gently shake tin: if centre doesn't wobble, cake is cooked).
6 Grate the rind of the lemon, then squeeze the juice. Place rind in bowl with soured cream and remaining sugar. Beat well. Add 2 tbsp (2×15ml) of lemon juice and mix well. Pour the mixture over the top of the cooked cake, return tin to the oven for a further 10 minutes.
7 Remove from oven and sprinkle with remaining crumbs. Allow to cool, then chill, preferably overnight.

Raspberry

INGREDIENTS

4oz	Plain flour	125g
2	Egg yolks	2
2oz	Caster sugar	50g
$\frac{1}{4}$ teasp	Vanilla essence	1.25ml
	Pinch of salt	
2oz	Softened butter	50g
1lb	Curd cheese	450g
1 tbsp	Gelatine	15ml
4 tbsp	Hot milk	4×15ml
4 tbsp	Sugar	4×15ml
2 tbsp	Raspberry liqueur	2×15ml
$\frac{1}{2}$ pint	Carton of double or whipping cream	284ml
1lb	Fresh raspberries	450g

METHOD

1 Preheat the oven to 400F (200C) Gas 6. Put flour on to a work surface. Make a well in centre and add the egg yolks, sugar, vanilla and salt. Add the butter in pieces and quickly knead mixture together to make a dough. Wrap and chill for 30 minutes.
2 Roll out the dough and use to line the base of the springform tin. Prick with a fork then bake blind in centre of the oven for 20 minutes. Cool in tin.
3 Push curd cheese through a sieve into a bowl. In another bowl, soak the gelatine in a little cold water and, when firm, stir in the hot milk. Add to cheese, together with the sugar and raspberry liqueur. Stir till thick.
4 Whip the cream in a bowl till stiff. Mix cream with cheese and pour on to cooled base. Chill until firm.
5 Arrange raspberries on the top of the cheese, and chill again before serving.

Rum and raisin

INGREDIENTS

	Base	
4oz	Plain flour	125g
2	Egg yolks	2
2oz	Caster sugar	50g
$\frac{1}{4}$ teasp	Vanilla essence	1.25ml
	Pinch of salt	
2oz	Softened butter	50g
	Filling	
3oz	Large stoned raisins	75g
4fl oz	Rum	120ml
1lb	Curd cheese	450g
4oz	Softened butter	125g
4oz	Caster sugar	125g
	Grated rind of 1 lemon	
4	Eggs	4

METHOD

1 Make and bake base as Raspberry cheesecake, but ease dough up sides of tin as well. While base is cooking, proceed with Steps 2 and 3.
2 Wash raisins and place in saucepan with the rum. Bring to boiling point, remove from heat, cover and leave.
3 Push curd cheese through sieve into bowl. Add softened butter, sugar and lemon rind and beat till well combined. Add eggs and beat till creamy, then stir in cooled raisin and rum mixture.
4 Remove base from oven. Reduce temperature to 350F (180C) Gas 4.
5 Pour cheese mixture into tin, smooth top and bake in the centre of oven for 1 hour 10 minutes. Cool in the tin. Run lightly oiled knife round edges before releasing the spring.

Creamy

INGREDIENTS

	Base	
4oz	Digestive biscuits	125g
1oz	Brown sugar	25g
2oz	Butter	50g
	Filling	
12oz	Cream cheese	350g
4	Eggs	4
3oz	Caster sugar	75g
	Grated rind of 1 lemon	
2 tbsp	Lemon juice	2×15ml
$\frac{1}{4}$ pint	Carton of soured cream	150ml

METHOD

1 Preheat the oven to 375F (170C) Gas 3. Crush biscuits in a bowl. Mix in sugar and melted butter. Grease tin and line with biscuit crumbs. Press down lightly with back of a spoon.
2 Beat cheese till smooth in a bowl. Separate the eggs. Mix yolks into cheese with sugar, lemon rind, lemon juice and soured cream.
3 In another bowl, beat the egg whites with salt till very stiff. Fold into the cheese mixture.
4 Put mixture on to the base and smooth top. Bake in centre of oven for $1\frac{1}{4}$ hours.
5 Remove cake from oven and allow to cool for 10 minutes. Then, release spring on tin and leave cake to cool. Place on serving plate and chill.

Right: Cooked cheesecakes — and each serves 8–10. They are (from the top): Granny's, Raspberry, Rum and raisin, and Creamy

No-cook cheesecakes

These cheesecakes don't have to be cooked, but some need chilling overnight. For all, use 8 inch (20cm) springform or loose-bottomed cake tins, base-lined with greaseproof. To freeze: do not decorate, open freeze, wrap and label. Storecupboard cheesecake is the exception – freeze filling in tin without Crispie base. Freezer life: 2 months. To use, thaw overnight in fridge, then decorate. Allow Storecupboard cheesecake to thaw for 4–6 hours at room temperature, make Crispie base and spread over top when set, invert on to serving plate. Decorate and chill

Storecupboard

INGREDIENTS

2oz	Plain chocolate	50g
1oz	Rice Crispies	25g
1	Tangerine jelly tablet	1
8oz	Cream cheese	225g
2	Egg whites	2
11oz	Can of mandarin oranges	312g

METHOD
1 Break the chocolate into bowl over pan of simmering water and stir gently till melted. Do not overheat or allow water to get into chocolate. When melted, remove bowl and stir in Crispies so they are evenly coated.
2 Line base of tin with greaseproof. Cover evenly and smoothly with the chocolate mixture. Chill.
3 Break up jelly tablet and place in saucepan. Drain syrup from mandarin oranges and make up to ¼ pint (150ml) with water. Add 2 tbsp (2×15ml) of the syrup to jelly, and cook over a very low heat till jelly melts – be careful not to let it boil.
4 Remove from heat and add rest of syrup. Chill until just beginning to set.
5 Beat cream cheese in bowl till smooth, then gradually beat in syrupy jelly. In a bowl, whisk whites to soft peak stage, then fold gently into cheese and jelly mix.* Pour on to crumb base and chill for 3 hours until set. Arrange drained mandarin oranges on top and chill again before serving.

*See special freezing instructions above.

Chestnut

INGREDIENTS

8oz	Digestive biscuits	225g
4oz	Butter	125g
	Filling	
15oz	Can of unsweetened chestnut purée	425g
8oz	Cream cheese	225g
4 tbsp	Condensed milk	4×15ml
2 tbsp	Lemon juice	2×15ml
½ pint	Carton of double cream	284ml
2 tbsp	Rum	2×15ml
4oz	Unsalted butter	125g
4oz	Caster sugar	125g
6oz	Plain chocolate	175g
2 tbsp	Boiling water	2×15ml
	Plain chocolate or chocolate crisps	

METHOD
1 Make base as Surprise cheesecake, but take crumbs 1 inch (2.5cm) up sides.
2 Divide chestnut purée and place one half in bowl with cream cheese. Beat well. Mix in condensed milk and lemon juice. Whip half the cream. Fold into chestnut mixture with half rum.
3 Spread mixture over crumb base. Smooth top. Chill for 15 minutes.
4 Cream butter and sugar until light and fluffy, beat in other chestnut purée. Melt chocolate in bowl over pan of simmering water. Stir in water. Remove from heat. Cool slightly.
5 Beat chocolate into butter mixture. Stir in rest of rum. Spread mixture over cake. Chill for 15 minutes.
6 Whip rest of cream and decorate top of cheesecake with it and grated chocolate or crisps. Chill till ready to serve.

Surprise

INGREDIENTS

	Base	
8oz	Nice biscuits	225g
4oz	Butter	125g
	Filling	
8oz	Cream cheese	225g
8oz	Curd cheese	225g
11oz	Condensed milk	350g
1	Large orange	1
4 teasp	Gelatine	4×5ml
12oz	Fresh strawberries	350g
1 teasp	Icing sugar	5ml
1 teasp	Caster sugar	5ml
¼ pint	Carton of double or whipping cream	150ml

METHOD
1 Grease tin well, then base-line. Crush biscuits finely. Melt butter and stir in. Press half on to base of tin. Chill.
2 Meanwhile, place cream cheese in a bowl and gradually beat in curd cheese till well mixed. Beat in condensed milk. Grate the rind of the orange and add. Squeeze the orange and place juice in a cup with the gelatine. When mixture is firm, place cup in hot water over gentle heat; stir until gelatine has dissolved. Remove cup, cool slightly.
3 Trickle the gelatine into cheese, beating well till evenly blended. Pour half the mixture over crumb base.
4 Wash and dry 8oz (225g) of the strawberries, then slice and arrange over the cheese. Cover with rest of cheese, crumbs. Smooth surface. Chill overnight.
5 Turn cheesecake out upside down on to a flat plate. Sift both sugars over the top. Whip cream and pipe rosettes around edge. Top with strawberries.

Florentine

INGREDIENTS

1	8 inch (20cm) sponge cake	1
4 teasp	Gelatine	4×5ml
2	Eggs	2
4oz	Caster sugar	125g
1lb	Curd cheese	450g
2	Lemons	2
¼ pint	Carton of double cream	150ml
1 tbsp	Icing sugar	15ml

METHOD
1 Split sponge in 2 layers.
2 Mix the gelatine with 3 tbsp (3×15ml) water in a small bowl. When firm, place bowl over simmering water, stir till gelatine dissolves. Separate eggs.
3 Add the yolks and caster sugar to the bowl and stir over the heat until the mixture coats the back of the spoon. Remove from heat, cool slightly.
4 Beat cheese in mixing bowl with grated rind and juice of 2 lemons till smooth, then fold in gelatine mixture.
5 Whisk the cream until it just begins to thicken, then fold into the cheese. Whisk the egg whites to soft peaks and fold in gently till even and smooth.
6 Put the bottom half of the sponge into 8 inch (20cm) springform tin. Pour cheese mixture over and cover with other layer of sponge. Chill, preferably overnight. Dredge with icing sugar.

Right: No-cook cheesecakes (from top) Storecupboard, Chestnut, Surprise and Florentine

Almond gâteau

It is said that no one can make this magnificent cake as they do in France. They'd be surprised to know their secrets have been revealed! Serve soon after baking

TEA-TIME Serves 6–8

Overall timing 2¼ hours

Equipment Bowl, 8 inch (20cm) and 9 inch (23cm) saucepan lids, pizza pan or baking tray

Freezing Open freeze unbaked and unglazed pie; or bake, leave to cool, then wrap, label and freeze. Freezer life: 3 months. To use: thaw unbaked pie in fridge for 8 hours, glaze and bake. Refresh baked pie from frozen in oven at 350F (180C) Gas 4 for 30 minutes; cover with foil if over browning

INGREDIENTS

13oz	Packet of frozen puff pastry	375g
3oz	Softened butter	75g
3oz	Caster sugar	75g
2	Eggs	2
4oz	Ground almonds	125g
2 tbsp	Amaretto di Saronno or rum	2×15ml
1 tbsp	Icing sugar	15ml

METHOD

1 Thaw the pastry if using frozen. To make filling, cream the butter and sugar till light and fluffy. Beat in 1 whole egg and 1 egg yolk, reserving white. Fold in the ground almonds and Amaretto or rum. Cover and leave in the fridge for 40 minutes.

2 Roll out the pastry to ¼ inch (6mm) thickness. Using the saucepan lids as a guide, cut out two circles. Place the smaller one on a wetted pizza pan or baking tray.

3 Place the almond filling in a ball in the centre of the pastry, leaving at least a 2 inch (5cm) border all round. Brush pastry edges with water.

4 Place second pastry circle on top, pressing edges together to seal. Using a knife, trim, then knock up edges and crimp. Chill for 15 minutes.

5 Preheat the oven to 450F (230C) Gas 8.

6 Remove pie from fridge and brush with reserved beaten egg white. Leave for 1 minute, then brush again.

7 Using the tip of a sharp knife, score the top of the pastry to make a swirl pattern. Cook for 20 minutes, then reduce temperature to 400F (200C) Gas 6 and cook for a further 25 minutes, or until well risen and golden brown.

8 Remove from oven and increase heat to 475F (240C) Gas 9. Sift icing sugar over pie and return to oven for 4–5 minutes to glaze. Remove from baking tray or pizza pan with palette knife and place on serving plate.

Below: Almond gâteau – light and tender puff pastry cake from France. The almond filling must be well chilled before baking

Eccles cakes

English pastries with a "sugar and spice and all things nice" filling

TEA-TIME Makes 12

Overall timing 30 minutes

Equipment Bowl, pastry cutter, 2 baking trays

Freezing Wrap cakes in foil, seal, label and freeze. Freezer life: 6 months. To use: refresh foil wrapped pastries in oven at 400F (200C) Gas 6 for 5 minutes

INGREDIENTS

9oz	Packet of frozen puff pastry	250g
6oz	Currants	175g
2oz	Candied peel	50g
1oz	Demerara sugar	25g
1oz	Butter	25g
½ teasp	Ground mixed spice	2.5ml
1	Egg white	1
	Caster sugar	

METHOD

1 Thaw the pastry and roll out on a lightly floured board to a large rectangle and cut out twelve 4 inch (10cm) circles with a cutter. Preheat oven to 425F (220C) Gas 7. Lightly brush baking trays with water.

2 In a bowl, mix together the currants, peel, sugar, butter and spice. Place a little of the mixture in the centre of each pastry circle.

3 Moisten pastry edges, pull together into centre to cover filling and seal firmly. Place, join side down, on wetted baking trays. Flatten slightly, then make 2 or 3 cuts on top with a sharp knife.
4 Brush with lightly beaten egg white and dredge with caster sugar. Bake for 10–12 minutes till well risen and golden, then cool on wire rack and serve.

Mince pies

This most traditional of Christmastide treats can be made in advance of the festivities. Take out just as many as you need from the freezer and cook or reheat as necessary

DESSERT Makes 15–20

Overall timing 30 minutes

Equipment Bun trays, rolling-pin, 2½ inch (6.5cm) and 2 inch (5cm) pastry cutters, bowl

Freezing If using bought frozen pastry, the pies should be cooked, then cooled before freezing. Open freeze uncooked mince pies in bun trays. Pack cooked or uncooked pies in rigid containers, cover and label. Freezer life: 3 months. To use: wrap cooked pies in foil and heat through at 350F (180C) Gas 4 for 20 minutes. Return uncooked mince pies to bun trays and bake at 425F (220C) Gas 7 for 20–30 minutes till golden

INGREDIENTS

8oz	Shortcrust pastry	225g
8oz	Mincemeat	225g
3 tbsp	Brandy	3×15ml
6 tbsp	Milk	6×15ml
2 tbsp	Caster sugar	2×15ml

METHOD

1 Preheat oven to 400F (200C) Gas 6. Grease the bun trays.
2 Roll out the pastry on a floured surface. Stamp out 20 rounds with the larger cutter, then 20 rounds with the smaller cutter, re-rolling the pastry as necessary. Press the larger rounds into the bun trays.
3 Mix the mincemeat and brandy in a small bowl and divide between the tarts.
4 Dip the remaining pastry rounds in the milk, then place one on to each tart. Using a fork, press the edges of the pastry together firmly to seal. Sprinkle the caster sugar over the mince pies.
5 Bake towards the top of the oven for about 20 minutes till golden. Serve hot or cold.

Eclairs

Perhaps the most irresistible of all pastries, éclairs are as easy to make as they are to eat. The paste should be firm, the oven hot so they rise in a flash – just like lightning

TEA-TIME Makes 16

Overall timing 1½ hours

Equipment Saucepan, 2 baking trays, piping bag and ½ inch (12.5mm) plain nozzle, 2 bowls

Freezing See Chocolate profiteroles, page 143

INGREDIENTS

4oz	Plain flour	125g
8fl oz	Water	220ml
3oz	Unsalted butter	75g
¼ teasp	Salt	1.25ml
3	Eggs	3
	Filling	
½ pint	Whipping cream	300ml
2 tbsp	Caster sugar	2×15ml
	Topping	
4oz	Icing sugar, sifted	125g
2 teasp	Drinking-chocolate	2×5ml
1–2 tbsp	Hot water	1–2×15ml

Below: Eclairs – topped with a selection of different flavoured glacé icings

METHOD

1 Prepare choux paste as for Chocolate profiteroles, page 143. Preheat the oven to 425F (220C) Gas 7.
2 Spoon paste into the piping bag and pipe fingers of paste, about 3 inches (7.5cm) long on greased baking trays. Cut the paste off with a wet knife, pressing blade against edge of nozzle after piping each length. Leave plenty of space between fingers so they have room to expand during baking.
3 Bake éclairs for about 30 minutes till golden and crisp. Remove from oven and transfer to a wire rack. Make a slit down the side of each éclair to allow the steam to escape and leave them to cool completely.
4 In a bowl beat the cream with the sugar until just thick and holding soft peaks. Spoon cream into cooled éclairs and place on wire racks over sheets of greaseproof paper (this will catch any drips of icing).
5 In another bowl blend the icing sugar with the drinking chocolate dissolved in the hot water. The glacé icing should be thick enough to coat the back of a spoon. If too thick, add a little more water; if too runny, add more icing sugar.
6 Dip top of one éclair at a time into chocolate glacé icing. Place on wire rack until icing is set. If icing starts to set, place over a pan of hot water for a minute or two until it is soft enough to work with again, but don't let it get too hot.
7 Arrange éclairs on serving plate and eat the same day.

Above: *Danish pastries – different shapes to make from one of several batches*

1 Butter is enclosed in dough, then rolling and folding process begins

2 Dough is turned, rolled and chilled 3 times before shapes are cut and filled

Danish pastries

True Danish pastry is light, made with yeast, and slightly flaky. The amount in this recipe makes 15 cockscombs, envelopes or windmills, or 8 crescent shapes

TEA-TIME

Overall timing 2 hours including chilling time

Equipment Small bowl, large bowl, 2 baking trays

Freezing Cool, pack in foil containers, cover, label and freeze. Freezer life: 1 month. To use: thaw, wrapped, for 1–2 hours or in hot oven for 5 minutes

INGREDIENTS

3fl oz	Milk	90ml
1 teasp	Caster sugar	5ml
1 teasp	Dried yeast	5ml
9oz	Plain flour	250g
½ teasp	Salt	2.5ml
6oz	Butter	175g
1oz	Caster sugar	25g
1	Egg	1
4oz	Icing sugar	125g
2 tbsp	Water	2×15ml
1–2oz	Split almonds	25–50g
	Glacé cherries	

METHOD

1 Warm milk till hand hot. Place half of it in bowl and sprinkle on 1 teasp (5ml) of the sugar and the yeast. Leave in a warm place for 10 minutes until slightly frothy. Add rest of milk.

2 Sift together flour and salt, rub in ½oz (15g) of the butter. Mix in yeast mixture, rest of sugar to make dough. Cover, chill for 10 minutes. Shape remaining butter into an oblong.

3 Roll out chilled dough into an oblong twice the size of the butter. Place butter in centre and enclose it, overlapping edges across the middle. Seal sides by pressing lightly with rolling-pin.

4 Turn dough so folds are at sides. Roll into an oblong three times longer than it is wide. Fold bottom third up, top third down. Cover, chill for 10 minutes.

5 Repeat turning, rolling and chilling twice more. Roll out pastry into oblong 15×9 inches (38×23cm). Shape as desired (see instructions, right) and fill with almond paste or confectioner's custard.

6 Preheat oven to 425F (220C) Gas 7. Arrange shapes on baking trays and prove in a warm place for 20 minutes. Brush with beaten egg and bake for about 18 minutes. Toast almonds.

To make icing Stir icing sugar and water over gentle heat till glossy. Trickle icing over hot pastries and decorate.

To make the shapes shown above, cut the 15×9 inch (38×23cm) oblong of dough in these ways before cooking:

Cockscombs *Cut oblong into 15 squares – about 3 inches (7.5cm) each. Spread a "sausage" of almond paste in centre of each and fold in half, sealing with beaten egg. Make cuts in folded edge, almost to cut edges, spread out in a fan shape.*

Envelopes *Cut oblong into 15 squares – about 3 inches (7.5cm) each. Place a blob of almond paste in middle of each and fold opposite corners (2 or 4) to centre, securing tips with beaten egg.*

Windmills *Cut oblong into 15 squares – about 3 inches (7.5cm) each. Make diagonal cuts from each corner almost to centre. Place a touch of almond paste or confectioner's custard in centre and fold one corner of each triangle to it. Press down firmly to secure.*

Crescents *Cut oblong into two, each 7½×9 inches (19×23cm). Turn each oblong so long side is facing. With a sharp knife, mark out a large W taking all lines to top and bottom of dough, with the centre peak coming half-way along the top edge. You will then have 3 equal triangles, and a fourth can be made by overlapping the two long edges of the 2 smaller triangles, and firmly pressing together before rolling.*

Aberdeen butteries

Scottish favourites that are a cross between Danish pastries and French croissants. As it's hard to re-roll this sort of dough without losing layers, cut into simple shapes with a sharp knife

BREAKFAST OR TEA-TIME Makes 20

Overall timing 2½ hours

Equipment Large bowl, polythene, baking tray

Freezing Cool, pack in foil containers, cover, label and freeze. Freezer life: 6 months. To use: thaw for 1–2 hours or reheat in hot oven for 5 minutes

INGREDIENTS

½oz	Fresh yeast *or*	15g
2 teasp	Dried yeast	2×5ml
7fl oz	Warm water	200ml
12oz	Strong plain flour	350g
2 teasp	Salt	2×5ml
6oz	Butter	175g

METHOD

1 Cream the yeast and water until smooth. Sift the flour and salt into a large bowl and make a well in the centre. Stir in the yeast liquid, adding more warm water if necessary, to give a soft but not sticky dough.

2 Knead for 5 minutes, then cover with oiled polythene and leave in a warm place till doubled in size.

3 Knock back dough and roll out on a floured surface to a rectangle 10×8 inches (25×20cm). Cut the butter into small cubes. Dot half the butter over the middle third of the dough, then fold in the top and bottom thirds.

4 Give dough a half turn so side seam is to the left. Roll out to the rectangle once more. Fold in top and bottom thirds and chill in fridge for 15 minutes.

5 With side seam facing you, roll out chilled dough to rectangle. Dot with remaining butter and repeat folding, rolling and folding process. Chill for a further 15 minutes.

6 Roll out dough to rectangle and cut into 20 squares, slices or diamonds with a sharp knife. Arrange, upside down, on floured baking tray. Cover with oiled polythene and leave to prove till doubled in size.

7 Preheat the oven to 425F (220C) Gas 7. Bake dough pieces in centre of the oven for about 20 minutes, or until well risen and pale golden. Serve hot with butter and marmalade or jam.

Almond crescents

These are very like the Austrian *Kipfeln* which are eaten at breakfast with coffee but they're sweet enough for tea-time or after dinner

TEA-TIME, PETIT FOURS Makes 20

Overall timing 30 minutes plus cooling time

Equipment Baking tray, mixing bowl, palette knife or egg slice, wire rack

Freezing Make dough, shape crescents, open freeze, then pack and wrap. Freezer life: 6 months. To use: unwrap and proceed as Steps 6 and 7 right, but lengthen cooking time by 10 minutes

Storage Airtight tin

INGREDIENTS

5oz	Nibbed almonds	150g
2oz	Caster sugar	50g
	A few drops of vanilla essence	
1	Egg white	1
1oz	Plain flour	25g
1	Egg	1
1oz	Flaked almonds	25g
2 tbsp	Milk sweetened with icing sugar	2×15ml

METHOD

1 Preheat the oven to 400F (200C) Gas 6. Grease baking tray.

2 In a bowl, mix nibbed almonds with caster sugar and vanilla essence. Moisten with egg white until evenly combined.

3 Add flour and gather mixture together with fingertips.

4 Divide into "nut-sized" pieces. With lightly floured hands, roll into small cigar shapes with pointed ends.

5 Brush each one with beaten egg and then sprinkle with flaked almonds. Bend into a crescent shape.

6 Place on baking tray, brush lightly with any remaining egg. Bake towards the top of the oven for about 10–15 minutes until evenly coloured.

7 Remove from oven and brush immediately with sweetened milk. Using a palette knife or egg slice, carefully loosen crescents and transfer to wire rack to cool.

Below: Almond crescents for tea-time

White bread

Use this recipe to make bread to any shape (plaits, loaves, rounds). You can also add 1oz (25g) wheatgerm to the mixture with the flour or brush top with salted water and sprinkle it on before baking

BREAD Makes 2 small loaves

Overall timing 3 hours minimum

Equipment 2 bowls, polythene bags, loaf tins

INGREDIENTS

1¼lb	Strong plain flour	600g
2 teasp	Salt	2×5ml
½oz	Lard	15g
½oz	Fresh yeast *or*	15g
2 teasp	Dried yeast *and*	2×5ml
1 teasp	Sugar	5ml
¾ pint	Warm water	400ml

METHOD

1 In a bowl, mix the flour and salt then rub in the lard.

2 In another bowl, blend the fresh yeast with the warm water. If using dried yeast, dissolve the sugar in the warm water and sprinkle dried yeast on top. Leave till frothy, about 10 minutes.

3 Add the yeast liquid to the dry mix and work to a firm dough that leaves the bowl clean, adding a little extra flour if needed.

4 Turn the dough on to a lightly floured surface and knead by folding the dough towards you, then pushing down and away from you with the palm of your hand. Give the dough a quarter turn and repeat the kneading process. The dough should be kneaded till it feels firm and elastic, not sticky. It will take about 10 minutes.

5 Make dough into a ball and place in a lightly oiled polythene bag.

6 Leave the dough to rise till it doubles in size and springs back when lightly pressed with a floured finger.

7 Turn the dough on to a lightly floured board, divide into two, then flatten each piece firmly with the knuckles to knock out the bubbles. Knead to make a firm dough.

8 Shape the loaves then place each dough piece in greased 1lb (20×10×6cm) loaf tins. Place inside a lightly oiled polythene bag and put aside till the dough rises just above the tops of the tins – 1–1½ hours at room temperature. Preheat the oven during this time to 450F (230C) Gas 8.

9 Bake the loaves in the centre of the oven for 30–40 minutes or until the loaves shrink slightly from the sides of the tins and the crust is deep golden brown. For a crustier loaf, turn the loaves out on to a baking tray and bake for a further 5–10 minutes.

Quick white bread

Adding 25mg of vitamin C (ascorbic acid) to the yeast makes it work faster and cuts down the making time. The tablets can be bought at chemists and health food stores

BREAD Makes 1 loaf

Overall timing 1½ hours

Equipment Bowl, mixing bowl, baking tray or loaf tin

INGREDIENTS

1oz	Fresh yeast	25g
12fl oz	Warm water	350ml
1 tablet	Vitamin C	25mg
½oz	Lard	15g
1¼lb	Strong white flour	600g
2 teasp	Salt	2×5ml
1 teasp	Sugar	5ml

METHOD

1 Blend the fresh yeast in the warm water. Crush vitamin tablet and add to the yeast liquid.

2 Rub the lard into the flour, salt and sugar. Add the yeast liquid and mix to a dough that leaves the bowl clean.

3 Turn the dough on to a lightly floured board or work surface and knead till smooth and elastic.

4 To shape dough into a cottage loaf, divide it into two pieces with one about a third bigger than the other. Shape both into rounds, place smaller one on top. Press handle of wooden spoon through centre of both pieces. If preferred, shape dough into rolls.

5 Place on baking tray and cover with oiled polythene. Leave loaves 40–50 minutes, rolls 25–30 minutes.

6 Brush top with beaten egg or dust with flour. Bake in a hot oven 450F (230C) Gas 8. Loaves bake for 30–35 minutes, rolls for 15–20 minutes.

Soda bread

Quick to make as no rising time is needed. Use either strong white flour or half strong white, half wholemeal. If you use buttermilk, reduce the cream of tartar by half

BREAD Makes 1 loaf

Overall timing 1 hour

Equipment Bowl, baking tray

INGREDIENTS

1lb	Strong white or white and wholemeal flour	450g
1 teasp	Salt	5ml
2 teasp	Bicarbonate of soda	2×5ml
4 teasp	Cream of tartar	4×5ml
1oz	Fat	25g
9fl oz	Milk or buttermilk	250ml

METHOD

1 Sift the flour, salt, soda and cream of tartar into a bowl.

2 Rub in the fat and add enough milk to make a soft dough. Turn the mixture on to a floured board or work surface and knead lightly for a minute.

3 Shape into a ball and place on a greased baking tray. Mark with a cross, cutting almost to the base of the dough.

4 Bake at 425F (220C) Gas 7 for 40–50 minutes till well risen, lightly browned and firm underneath.

Below: Use basic bread recipes to make a variety of different loaf and roll shapes. Some of the traditional shapes are shown here

Wholemeal bread

A delicious bread which can be made into many shapes. To add crunch, crack 2oz (50g) whole wheat grain in liquidizer for 1 minute, and add with the flour. Save some to sprinkle on top after brushing with salted water (Step 6)

BREAD Makes 2–4 loaves

Overall timing 3 hours minimum

Equipment 2 bowls, polythene bags, loaf tins

INGREDIENTS

3lb	Wholemeal flour	1.4kg
2 tbsp	Salt	15ml
2 tbsp	Brown sugar	15ml
1oz	Lard	25g
2oz	Fresh yeast*	50g
$1\frac{1}{2}$ pints	Warm water	850ml

* or 1oz (25g) dried yeast – see Step 2 of method

METHOD

1 To make the dough with fresh yeast, mix the flour, salt and sugar together in a bowl. Rub in the lard. In another bowl, blend the yeast with the water. Add to flour and mix to scone-like dough that leaves the bowl clean.

2 To make the dough with dried yeast, dissolve 1 teasp (5ml) of the sugar in 9fl oz (250ml) of warm water in a bowl. Now sprinkle the dried yeast on top. Leave till frothy, about 10 minutes. In a mixing bowl, mix flour, salt and the remaining sugar. Rub in the lard, then add the yeast liquid and the rest of the water. Mix to scone-like dough.

3 Knead the dough thoroughly till it feels firm and elastic and no longer sticky. This should take 5–10 minutes.

4 Shape the dough into a ball and place in an oiled polythene bag. Leave the dough to rise till it doubles in size.

5 When risen, turn the dough on to a board and knead again till firm. Divide into 2 or 4, flatten each piece firmly with the knuckles to knock out air. Shape and place in loaf tins.

6 Brush the tops with a little salted water and put each tin into an oiled polythene bag. Leave to rise till the dough comes to just over the top of the tin and springs back when pressed with a floured finger – about 1 hour at room temperature. Preheat the oven during this time to 450F (230C) Gas 8.

7 Bake the loaves on the middle shelf of the oven for 30–40 minutes. Turn out and cool on a wire rack.

Milk rolls

Continental rolls with a lovely butter flavour, soft inside and crisp outside

BREAD Makes about 15 rolls

Overall timing About 3 hours

Equipment Large bowl, baking tray

INGREDIENTS

$\frac{1}{2}$oz	Fresh yeast *or*	15g
2 teasp	Dried yeast	2×5ml
$\frac{1}{4}$ pint	Lukewarm milk	150ml
9oz	Plain flour	250g
$\frac{1}{2}$ teasp	Salt	2.5ml
1 tbsp	Caster sugar	15ml
$3\frac{1}{2}$oz	Soft butter	100g
2 tbsp	Milk	2×15ml
1 teasp	Caster sugar	5ml

METHOD

1 Blend yeast with lukewarm milk in a bowl. Sprinkle on 2oz (50g) of flour, mix to a batter. Set aside till frothy – 10 to 20 minutes in a warm place.

2 Mix rest of flour with salt and sugar, then add to batter. Mix by hand to soft dough that leaves bowl clean. Add a little more milk if necessary.

3 Turn dough on to lightly floured surface, knead till smooth and no longer sticky. Place dough in oiled polythene bag and leave for 1 hour in warm place.

4 Place dough in large bowl. Cut butter into small pieces. Make a hollow in dough and drop in 2–3 pieces of butter. Knead or squeeze into dough. Continue in this way till all butter is used (a rather messy operation but the dough will gradually become silky and smooth).

5 Turn on to floured surface. Divide into egg-size pieces and shape into rolls. Place on greased baking tray. Lightly make a cross on each with the back of a knife. Cover tray with oiled polythene bag and leave in warm place till rolls double in size – about 30 minutes. Preheat oven to 375F (190C) Gas 5 during this time.

6 Heat milk and sugar to just warm, brush over rolls. Bake just above centre for 30 minutes till golden brown. Cool on cake wire.

Rolls with cumin

Satisfyingly crisp rolls with the flavourful taste of cumin seed

BREAD Makes 12–14 rolls

Overall timing 2 hours minimum

Equipment 2 bowls, baking tray

INGREDIENTS

$\frac{1}{2}$oz	Fresh yeast *or*	15g
2 teasp	Dried yeast	2×5ml
8fl oz	Lukewarm milk	220ml
1 teasp	Caster sugar	5ml
11oz	Strong flour	400g
$\frac{1}{2}$ teasp	Salt	2.5ml
2 tbsp	Cumin seeds	2×15ml
1oz	Butter	25g
1	Lemon	1
1	Whole egg	1
1	Egg yolk	1
1 tbsp	Milk	15ml

METHOD

1 If using fresh yeast, dissolve it in lukewarm milk in a bowl. If using dried yeast dissolve caster sugar in $\frac{1}{4}$ pint (150ml) of the milk. Sprinkle on dried yeast and leave till frothy.

2 Mix flour and salt in another bowl. Make a well in the centre and pour in yeast liquid. Mix well. Cover and leave to rise for 15 minutes in a warm place.

3 Meanwhile crush 1 tbsp (15ml) of the cumin seeds in a mortar with a pestle. Place in a bowl and mix with half the butter and the grated rind of a lemon.

4 Mix this into the dough, together with the whole egg. Knead the mixture till the dough is glossy and no longer sticky. Place in oiled polythene bag and leave for 45 minutes to rise.

5 Preheat oven to 425F (220C) Gas 7. Knock back dough and knead lightly. Make rolls about $1\frac{1}{2}$in (4cm) in diameter and place on greased baking tray, leaving space all round for expansion. Cover with oiled polythene, leave 10 minutes till doubled in size.

6 Beat the egg yolk with 1 tbsp (15ml) milk and a little salt and brush it over the rolls. Sprinkle the rest of the cumin seeds on top and bake in the centre of the oven for 25 minutes.

Freezing Wrap freshly baked bread in polythene bags or foil. Freezer life: white and brown breads, 1 month; enriched breads, 2 months. If freezing unbaked dough, increase yeast by 50 per cent when making. Freeze before or after proving and place in bags large enough for second proving. Freezer life: unproved white and brown, 1 month; unproved and proved enriched, 6 weeks. To use: thaw for 6 hours, knock back, leave to rise, bake. Rolls can be half-baked, cooled and frozen. Cook from frozen.

Currant buns

One of the simplest ways of using the sunshine goodness of currants

TEA-TIME Makes 12

Overall timing 2¼ hours

Equipment 2 bowls, saucepan, 2 baking trays, wire rack

Freezing Cool, pack in polythene bag, seal, label and freeze. Freezer life: 1 month. To use: thaw for 1 hour

INGREDIENTS

1lb	Strong plain flour	450g
1 teasp	Sugar	5ml
1oz	Fresh yeast *or*	25g
1 tbsp	Dried yeast	15ml
½ pint	Milk	300ml
2oz	Butter	50g
½ teasp	Salt	2.5ml
1 teasp	Ground mixed spice	5ml
4oz	Currants	125g
2oz	Caster sugar	50g
1	Egg	1
2 teasp	Caster sugar	2×5ml
2 tbsp	Milk	2×15ml

METHOD

1 Put 2oz (50g) of the flour in a small bowl. Make a well in the centre and add the 1 teasp (5ml) sugar and yeast. Warm the milk and pour half of it into the well. Blend until smooth, drawing the flour in from the sides of the bowl as for a batter. Leave in a warm place until mixture becomes frothy. Melt butter and leave to cool.

2 Sift remaining flour, salt and spice into a mixing bowl. Stir in the currants and sugar. Make a well in the centre. Pour in the yeast mixture and add the cooled butter and the egg. Stir, then add remaining milk as required to form a soft but not sticky dough.

3 Knead dough on a floured surface until smooth and elastic. Cover with oiled polythene and leave in a warm place until doubled in size.

4 Turn out dough on to a floured surface and knead to break up any large pockets of air. Cut into 12, knead each piece into a smooth bun. Place on baking trays leaving space for buns to spread, cover with oiled polythene and leave to prove till doubled in size.

5 Preheat the oven to 375F (190C) Gas 5.

6 To make the glaze, dissolve the caster sugar in the milk and brush lightly over the buns. Bake in the centre of the oven for 15–20 minutes. While still hot, brush with the remaining glaze.

Swiss fruit bread

Preserved fruit is frequently used in bread making and here sultanas and candied peel are kneaded into the dough towards the end of the method. Serve this very light, airy bread at tea-time or at breakfast. It's also good lightly toasted

TEA-TIME Makes 3 small loaves

Overall timing 40 minutes plus rising

Equipment Sieve, large mixing bowl, 3×5–6 inch (13–15cm) round cake tins or soufflé dishes

Freezing Place cooled loaves in separate polythene bags or wrap in foil, then seal, label and freeze. Freezer life: 3 months. To use: thaw in wrapping at room temperature for 2–3 hours

INGREDIENTS

1lb	Strong white flour	450g
1oz	Fresh yeast *or*	25g
4 teasp	Dried yeast	4×5ml
1 teasp	Sugar	5ml
½ pint	Milk	300ml
2oz	Melted butter	50g
1	Egg	1
2oz	Caster sugar	50g
4oz	Sultanas	125g
3oz	Candied peel	75g
	Grated rind of 1 lemon	
½ teasp	Salt	2.5ml
1	Egg white	1

METHOD

1 Grease the cake tins or soufflé dishes. Sift 4oz (115g) of the flour into a large mixing bowl. Make a well in the centre and add the yeast and sugar. Warm the milk until hand-hot and pour on to the yeast and sugar.

2 Stir well with a wooden spoon, as for a batter, gradually drawing in the flour from the sides and ensuring there are no lumps. Leave in a warm place for 15–20 minutes until frothy.

3 Stir the melted butter and beaten egg into the yeast mixture. Add the sultanas, peel and lemon rind and sift in the remaining flour and salt. Mix to a soft dough.

4 Knead on a lightly floured surface until smooth and elastic. Cover with oiled polythene and leave in a warm place to rise till doubled in size.

5 Tip dough on to a floured surface and knead again till smooth. Divide dough into 3 pieces and knead each into a smooth ball.

6 Place in tins or dishes, cover with oiled polythene and leave to rise again till doubled in size.

7 Preheat the oven to 400F (200C) Gas 6. Lightly beat the egg white and brush over the loaves. Bake in the centre of the oven for about 35 minutes, changing shelf position after 20 minutes to prevent uneven cooking. Test the loaves to see if they are ready by tapping lightly on the base. If they give a hollow sound, the loaves are cooked.

8 Remove loaves from oven and cool in the tins for a few minutes. Turn on to a wire rack to cool, then slice and serve with butter if liked.

Below: Swiss fruit bread – an airy, sweetish bread with sultanas and candied peel

INDEX

FREEZER NOTES